Our Tribe

Our Tribe

*Queer Folks,
God, Jesus,
and the Bible*

REV. NANCY WILSON

 HarperSanFrancisco
An Imprint of HarperCollins*Publishers*

HarperCollins®, 📖®, and HarperSanFrancisco™
are trademarks of HarperCollins Publishers Inc.

FIRST EDITION

Library of Congress Cataloging-in-Publication Data
Wilson, Nancy L.,
    Our tribe : queer folks, god, jesus, and the bible
/ Nancy Wilson. — 1st ed.
    Includes bibliographical references.
    ISBN 0-06-069396-7 (pbk.)
    1. Homosexuality—Religious aspects—
Christianity. 2. Homosexuality—Biblical teaching.
3. Bible—Criticism, interpretation, etc. 4. Gay
men—United States—Religious life.
5. Lesbians—United States—Religious life.
6. Metropolitan Community Church. 7. Wilson,
Nancy L. I. Title.
BR115.H6W55   1995
261.8'35766—dc20   95-12266

95 96 97 98 99 ❖ HAD 10 9 8 7 6 5 4 3 2 1

*To Paula, for a wonderful life of love and surprises,
and for listening to all my stories. . .*

> *Set me as a seal upon your heart,*
> *as a seal upon your arm;*
> *for love is strong as death,*
> *passion as fierce as the grave.*
> *Its flashes are flashes of fire,*
> *a raging flame.*
> *Many waters cannot quench love,*
> *neither can floods drown it.*
> *If one offered for love*
> *all the wealth of her house,*
> *it would be utterly scorned.*

SONG OF SOLOMON 8:6 AND 7

Contents

Acknowledgments

In some ways, writing a book is a very solitary thing. In many other ways, though, if you are the pastor of a church, it is not! This book originated in the context of pastoring MCC Los Angeles. About eight years ago, Rev. Evelyn Kinser worked with me on the idea of moving from the "defense" to the "offense" in treating the subject of homosexuality in the Bible, which evolved, in the changing political vocabulary of our community, to "Outing the Bible." Evelyn was a constant source of encouragement and challenge to me.

Through moving many times, earthquakes, mortgage woes, and untold grief and loss, I have learned from the members, friends, staff, and board of MCC Los Angeles the truth of Psalm 46:

> God is our refuge and strength,
> a very present help in trouble.
> Therefore we will not fear, though
> the earth should change,
> though the mountains shake in the
> heart of the sea.

Thanks to the Core Staff for your dedication and love, and all you have taught me: Dr. Lori Dick for wisdom and vision and quiet presence; Rev. Ken Kerr, for your passion for all who are marginalized and vulnerable, especially the young and the old; Rev. Jose Gonzalez, for your passion for justice and for loving so many who are ill and dying with AIDS. Thanks also to Dr. Teri Tompkins; Cathy Spiess; Richard Davis; Alejandro Escoto, Rev. Barbara Haynes, and Jane Syftestad, whose energy and musical gifts have both sustained us and propelled us into a new era.

Thanks to the Board for giving me the time to complete this book and for your vision and steadfastness in hard times. Thanks to: Jan Stone, a rock of strength, single-minded in her determination for MCC Los Angeles and me to be all we were meant to be; Gil Gerald; the relentless Ivy Bottini; Judy Hosner; Nathan Meckley (for giving me hope in those early days and for your excellence in so many things); Don Lamb; Pam Cassidy; Tom Anderson; and Mario Perez.

Thanks to the many other MCC Los Angeles members and friends who have taught me so much: Sharon Parker, fellow writer and mischief-maker; Carol "Woody" Wood, for sitting on my shoulder, and for all your notes and prayers and encouragement over the years; Marsha Stevens and Suzanne McKeag; Glen Payne and Jose Curiel; Linda, Kath, and Jamaal. Thanks to Viva Kinser, Tom Carlisle, Wallace Rice, Griff Guenther, and all the rest of you who taught me how to be a pastor.

Special thanks to those who assisted in the making of this book: Bless you, Sandy Williams for trips to the library, and Jakely of Forman Graphics. Norm, what can I say? Working and doing MCC Los Angeles with you is an amazing adventure. Your gifts are one of our great treasures.

For a kind editor with a sense of humor and a lot of patience, no one can compare with Kevin Bentley.

This book would not have happened without Fr. Malcolm Boyd. When we were doing a "gig" together in San Francisco, Malcolm told me I had to write this book. You are my fairy godfather!

Thank you, Rev. Troy Perry, for starting MCC; for seeing my potential in those early days; for being an incredibly openhearted, open-minded leader; for being willing to be the prophet of God. Thanks to my sister/brother Elders in MCC: Rev. Don Eastman, Larry Rodriguez, Rev. Darlene Garner, Rev. Wilhelmina Hein, and Rev. Hong Tan. For your encouragement, thanks to Rev. Freda Smith and Rev. Jean White. Thanks to: my friend Rev. Sandi Robinson; Colette Jackson, for making plays out of my sermons; Rev. Kit Cherry, for advice about writing a book; fellow activist and writer Dr. Mel White—bless you for coming out and into MCC and for challenging us all the time! Thanks to: Dr. Dusty Pruitt, who offered friendship and support when I so much needed it years ago;

and colleagues Rabbi Denise Eger and Rev. Dan Smith for your support and encouragement. Thank you Jean Gralley, artist and friend, especially for my first love letters!

Thanks to my very diverse family: Ravi Verma, my spiritual brother, friend, ally; Terri, Dyan and Hannah Ullman-Levine, for safety and home and friendship, and for understanding all the times I had to be gone because of my work; Sherri and Davine; Jackie, Donna, Taylor, and Colin, who put up with me writing during our vacation time in Morro Bay. Thanks to: our extended Longman family—Judi and Jennie—for sharing your children with Paula and me, especially Rechal, Jody, Matt, and Nicholas on occasion; Judy, Jordan, and Andy; my mother, Barbara Wilson, for your encouragement and love; David (and family) and Mark, biological brothers, and friends; the Chase clan; my other Mom, Marian Schoenwether; and Paula, to whom this book is dedicated.

Thanks to Lois (you know what for), and to N.T. for taking me on.

I want to remember some of my heavenly friends, in addition to the ones who come up in the stories that follow: Vicki Goldish, I still miss you; Rev. Sandy Taylor; Rev. Jim Harris; Dr. Gary McClelland; Edith Perry; and hundreds of others. Dr. John Boswell, whose brilliance can never be replaced—what a model of courageous gay scholarship! Thank you Rev. Danny Mahoney, assistant pastor extraordinaire, who on your deathbed told me to finish the book. You were so proud of me, and I miss you every day. Thanks to Patrick, who stuck around only long enough to take care of Danny. Thank you God, finally, for my dear father Ralph, whose laughter, love, and playfulness are such a blessed memory.

Introduction

Tribal Tales

Theologically speaking, I'm trying on the label *queer millennialist*. No one knows what that is, and we're all bored by and sick of most theological labels and categories. Many of these labels are breaking down anyway, as enormous cultural changes take place. Also, "queer millennialist" sounds both playful and radical.

I'll start by telling a sweet queer story. In addition to being the pastor of the oldest publicly queer church in America (and perhaps the world), I have been for about fifteen years Metropolitan Community Church's (MCC's) official lesbian ecu-terrorist. (Actual title: "chief ecumenical officer.") It has been my job to coordinate the strategies and policies of our Ecumenical Witness and Ministry Department. I work with and train MCC clergy and laity to interact with (that is, *terrorize*) ecumenical (inter-religious) organizations.[1] This is, of course, nonviolent terrorism. I realize that "terrorism" is a loaded word these days. We queer folk have literally been terrorized by a homophobic world, seem to emotionally terrorize ecumenical organizations just by showing up.

When the World Council of Churches came to Los Angeles after the uprising of April 29, 1992, I was called upon to participate with others in "sharing our perspectives" about life in L.A. vis-à-vis the various police departments, conditions for our community, and other issues.

The council decided to host listening posts in the African-American, Korean-American, Hispanic-American, and other communities; the gay and lesbian community was a last-minute add-on. Seeing the lineup of speakers, I knew it was my job to get more representation from gay and lesbian people of color in particular. But I knew something *else* was also missing. We ecu-terrorists tend to be rather "churchy" folks, able to speak fluently the language of the church. What would it be like for the World Council of Churches to hear just raw, queer rage, unecumenized, uncensored?

Plus, as a meddling pastor type, I knew that people like Rob needed to be heard by just such a group. A few months before, after a community meeting, Rob and I went to a popular new gay coffee shop in West Hollywood. We had been working on a project together: the third monument in the world to honor gay and lesbian protest. It was to memorialize several actions that had taken place on the Crescent Heights Triangle in West Hollywood, the most recent of which was the beginning of two solid weeks of nonviolent protests against Governor Pete Wilson's vetoing of the gay and lesbian rights bill, AB101. Sitting in that coffee shop, Rob had finally popped *the* question: "How can you be a Christian? You seem like a really great person." Rob was a thirtyish, wide-eyed activist still struggling with addiction recovery issues and in love with queer politics (most of the time). He was a very tall, handsome, fair-haired, beach-boy type who still had traces of adolescent gangliness.

I tried to account for myself. I tried not to be defensive about the church's wretched record of sexism, racism, and homophobia. To say a few good words about Jesus. And then without having said too much, to turn the tables (I have always liked *this* part of following Jesus.). So I said, "Did you grow up in church?"

Rob flushed. Then he grinned, "Yeah, I grew up going to Lutheran parochial school."

"So," I said, "when did it happen? When did they break your heart?"

Bingo. He had that "How did you know?" look on his face. I find that for many gay and lesbian people, *it* happened long before they knew they were queer. "Oh, yeah," Rob said, "there was the Jack Benny thing."

The Jack Benny thing. At six, Rob had taken piano lessons from a Lutheran church schoolteacher. While on his way to his piano lesson one day, he heard the news that Jack Benny had just died. Rob loved Jack Benny. I immediately understood. As a child, I had loved the comics and impersonators the best. There was Jack Benny, effeminate violin player, making fun of himself for our enjoyment. People admired and loved Jack Benny, and as queer as it may sound, he made Rob feel safer in the world. I know he made me feel safer, too. Full of grief and questions, Rob asked his piano teacher, "Will Jack Benny go to heaven?"

"No," came the clear-cut answer. No. No. He was not Christian, or Lutheran, or *something*. So Rob learned that God didn't love Jack Benny.

Or at least that Lutherans didn't believe that God loved Jack Benny. Rob's heart asked, How can I love someone or something that God doesn't love enough to take into heaven? Or that God even hates? Everything shattered in Rob's very tender and new life of faith. And it never got put back together again, at least not in the church.

Incomprehensible cruelty: heaven without Jack Benny. Without comedy or effeminate men. Who wants to go there? An exclusive, hard-nosed God—the God who made Jack Benny, who could with his eyes, the flick of a wrist, the perfect timing, make the world laugh—that same God wouldn't take Jack in? *What's wrong with this picture?* Just telling the story was painful for Rob. At first he thought it was silly. But then it became clear. *The Jack Benny thing* was Rob's first clue that the church that had raised him taught of a God who might not really love him after all. If God didn't want Jack Benny, what chance would Rob have? And how could he appeal this decision? So Rob left the Lutherans to their Jack Benny–less heaven.

I told Rob that it was just possible that what he had really rejected was not God and maybe not even Christianity but a very tragic interpretation of both. I saw the spark of hope in Rob's eyes. It was that spark, the hope that survives shame and rage, that I wanted the World Council folks to see. And they did. Just months after our coffeehouse encounter, Rob testified before members of the Central Committee of the World Council of Churches about gay and lesbian oppression and about his struggle with this "God thing." So the conversation had appropriately shifted from Jack Benny to God. Rob addressed the Central Committee as a *queer national* and was eloquent and passionate.

Rob ducked in and out of church at MCC for the next two years, full of queer ambivalence. Before he died of AIDS, he called me from his hospital bed with a great sermon idea for me about somebody he remembered from his Lutheran Sunday school days. Some guy named Job. "I think Job was refusing to be a victim! Like me—why don't you preach about that?"

MILLENNIAL MUSINGS

On the eve of the third millennium, we are closing the books on what politicians, sociologists, historians, theologians, and others are calling the most violent century in the recorded history of the world. (By the way, it was reported after the Jeffrey Dahmer tragedy that a disproportionate number of mass murderers are *Lutherans.* This may be little comfort to most of us, but Rob frankly felt a little validated by that troubling statistic.) Perhaps living in Los Angeles recently has made me view the state of the world with special intensity. In Los Angeles, the First and Third Worlds are meeting more and more. Los Angeles is a city teeming with languages and cultures in a shifting human landscape. Neighborhoods change as fast as do the stores in minimalls.

It is also a city located in a desert. This means that the land itself is really only created to handle a sparse density of life, especially human life. The millions who inhabit this region do so unnaturally, as a result of human manipulation, technology, and intervention. When the very natural (for the most part) phenomena of earthquake, fire, and floods occur, the toll of life and property is *astronomically* exaggerated by the population explosion of the last half of this century.

In the first years of the last decade of the millennium, in Los Angeles, we have had frightening, apocalyptic experiences: devastating fires, prolonged recession, political uprisings, the worst flooding in five hundred years in the region, and a devastating earthquake. Is Los Angeles a symbol of the last dying cry of this violent century, or a peek into what is to come?

I don't know if anyone has managed to capture the effect this has had on the people who continue to live here. Somehow all the sunny promise of California as the land of prosperity and fun and Hollywood glitz (the American version of the Promised Land) has literally crashed and burned. We can't quite count on it like we did. Human need and human greed have collided here in a pre-millennial drama.

My use of the word *millennial* is both serious and playful. Millennialist thought in Judaism and Christianity is a particular form of eschatology (that is, thinking about the *end times*—how the world will end, how God will *wrap it all up).* The actual word *millennium* comes from the root *mil,* which means thousand, as in "thousand years." In Jewish and Christian writings there is the promise of an *interregnum*—an in-between time that may last literally for one thousand years or for some symbolic amount of time. Rabbis, church fathers, church reformers, and nineteenth- and twentieth-century American religious sectarian leaders have debated for over two millennia about the details. There are those who believe it will happen before Christ returns or the Messiah comes; others believe it will happen after Christ returns.

Sometimes this imagined time period is called the "eighth day of creation." It will be characterized by any number of things: the destruction of evil, the creation of a new heaven and earth, and the enjoyment on earth of eternal bliss. Some prophets predict the return of the *ten lost tribes*, while others describe it as the gathering together of *people and tribes*. Millennial fantasies have included predictions of unprecedented earthly fertility, peace, and harmony not only among humans but among animals and between animals and humans. Some have imagined endless sumptuous dining and even uninterrupted enjoyment of *nuptial bliss!* Millennial thought has often been overtly material and sensuous. But there is also a downside to the millennial vision: a prediction of Armageddon, the world rule of the anti-Christ, suffering, wars and *rumors* of wars. And, of course, there are debates about whether such suffering will follow or precede an idyllic millennium.

Narrow, literal views of the millennium have characterized some of the more bizarre cults and some particularly negative, exclusionary Protestant sects. Is fascination with millennialism always tied to the more neurotic, escapist forms of faith? On the other hand, a lot of the proliferating New Age philosophies and theologies also abound with quasi-millennialist visions.

When I use the word millennialist, I am not choosing among several traditional, fixed views of the "end times." I simply want to understand the human longing for "heaven on earth"; the persistence of the vision of the "peaceable kingdom" in the midst of contemporary planetary crisis; and a little bit of what Jesus meant by this *kingdom that is in our midst and yet to come.*

According to some of us, the world's calendar is getting ready to turn the page on one millennium and open the page to another. On the eve of that millennial shift, the gay and lesbian movement has *appeared.* Judy Grahn offers a wonderful metaphor for this gay and lesbian millennial surge:

> Purple book jackets appeared on books and dictionaries produced by gay poets and writers of both sexes, and purple T-shirts announced gay slogans of affirmation from diverse groups of people from all over the country. As though some mysterious hand had planted bulbs all over the land, we lavender folk sprang up spontaneously flowering in the color we had learned as an identifying mark of our culture when it was subterranean and a secret.[2]

Leaders of the 1993 Gay/Lesbian/Bisexual March on Washington called for a new *gay* or *queer nineties.* But why should we settle for only a decade? Black history month in the United States is February, the shortest month of the year, and gays and lesbians get only the last decade of a whole millennium. It figures.

What about the possibility of a queer millennium? Does that sound too greedy? A queer interregnum, a truly in-between time. A *time-out* for the planet! After all, we queer folks are the quintessential *in-between* folks. Judy Grahn, Mark Thompson, and many others have been documenting the "in-between" gay and lesbian culture and sensibility for decades.

So just what in the world is going on? I think we are having a violent reaction of rage and helplessness because of the destabilization of nations and economies, overpopulation and the resulting poverty and hunger, and the sweeping technological changes that do *not* seem to *solve* these problems but only simultaneously to worsen them and to make us more acutely aware of them on a daily basis. There is much debate about whether or not we are simply polluting and poisoning ourselves to death. Some say the environmentalists are a bunch of fanatics who don't appreciate the resiliency of nature. But the truth seems to be that there is a planetary immunological crisis going on, born of the increasing toxicity of the environment—a universal AIDS.

In such a toxic environment, the poor, the minorities, and the politically vulnerable populations will be the first to exhibit signs and symptoms of the deteriorating immunological picture. It is the canary-in-the-mines syndrome. When miners wanted to know if a particular mine shaft was safe from poison gases, they sent in a canary first. If the canary returned, the miners felt safe to go in. On our planet today, poor people, people of color, women and children, and gays and lesbians are the canaries (or sitting ducks, if you prefer). Those who have any kind of privilege (gender, race, class, sexuality, age) are better able, for a time, to buffer and insulate themselves from the toxic environment—from AIDS, cancer, and other diseases. But not forever.

There is also an increasing moral and religious toxicity in reaction to so much social upheaval, change, and worldwide political challenges. This phenomenon is called in many religions *fundamentalism*. In a century of increasing relativity of values, morality, and religion, fundamentalism provides absolutes and identifies the enemies. It is a kind of collective mental illness that includes obsessive thinking, tunnel vision, and functions much like other addictions. The growing threat of the religious right is being unmasked in our time—that is, in what has popularly been called the *age of rage*.

WHO *Are* GAY AND LESBIAN PEOPLE?

What does it mean to be a gay or lesbian or bisexual person in this age of rage? It was the poet Judy Grahn who first spoke powerfully to me about an anthropology or sociology of what she calls *transpeople* (a broad category including gay men, lesbians, transvestites, and transsexuals). For a long time I have believed that *theological anthropology* (in the old days, this was called the *"doctrine of man"*) was the church's major problem in acceptance of gays and lesbians. Are gay men and lesbians a *lobby* for a certain kind of behavior that we want the church to legitimize, or are we a *kind of people?*

And if we are a kind of people, just what kind are we? Michael Cartwright[3] has traced the way nineteenth- and twentieth-century African-American writers, historians, sociologists, and theologians have struggled with questions about black identity. They had to overcome the *poisonous pedagogy* of the white Christian slaveholders who exegeted Genesis 9:20–27 and 10:6–11, the story of Ham, in a racist way. Blacks also had to ask the question, "For what reason did God create us? Why did God deliver us from slavery?" Underneath was the question, "And why didn't God do it sooner?" or "Why did God let slavery happen at all?" As a pastor of a multicultural church in Los Angeles, I recall the painful voice on the other end of the phone of a black gay man telling me that his lover, HIV-positive and addicted to drugs, had spent the better part of the morning crying out, "Why does God hate us?" He meant African-Americans, that particular *us*. Does our racial or sexual identity have purpose . . . meaning? Does our collective suffering or redemption mean anything?

It is relatively for new gays and lesbians for this question to be above ground. The *"love that dare not speak its name"* did not dare to theologize much about itself—or even to philosophize much—until recent decades. We are new at asking such questions even semipublicly. The *problem* with religions that personalize God (like Christianity) is that it then seems illogical not to personalize disaster or triumph. In theological circles, this problem is called *theodicy*: understanding how evil and oppression can exist in a world created by a good god. As a lesbian pastor in the gay and lesbian community, I have had hundreds of conversations with people agonizing about whether God truly created *us* as we are. And if so, could God love us; and if so, why was there so much suffering, pain, and homophobia? The truth is, I'm not sure I ever really stopped long enough in the early frenetic, even dangerous days to ask those questions myself. I do, however, remember asking them one night in a restaurant in Vancouver, British Columbia. ("Why does the Church hate us? Where does homophobia come from?")

The occasion was a "top-secret" meeting between the leaders of the National Council of Churches of Christ (NCC) in the United States and the Universal Fellowship of Metropolitan Community Churches (UFMCC) in the summer of 1983.[4] Tensions within the NCC had been mounting over the issue of UFMCC's application for membership. The Eastern Orthodox churches had issued a statement to the press in the spring, indicating that if UFMCC were ever declared *eligible* for membership by the governing board, they would leave the council. But in fact, the membership committee of the council (which included an Orthodox member) had unanimously voted in March 1982 that we met all five criteria for membership, and a vote by the council to ratify that judgment had already been postponed for a year and a half.

Meanwhile, UFMCC and most of the council were unaware that the president, Bishop James Armstrong, was experiencing a deep emotional crisis that would result in his surprise resignation, surrounded by scandal and rumor, in November 1983. These were the early Reagan years. Ronald Reagan and his administration had no use for the NCC and its liberal reputation. In fact, it was on the heels of the Reagan election that both *Reader's Digest* and *60 Minutes* did very biased and damaging exposés on the political activities of the NCC and the World Council of Churches (WCC). This exposure was a major source of political and financial anxiety for the council. So it was with some dismay that the leadership of the NCC also found itself having to deal with an application for membership from a controversial denomination serving a less-than-acceptable minority: homosexuals!

I had admired James Armstrong since my college antiwar activism days. He had *been there.* He was well known for having negotiated with the American Indian Movement (AIM) in the early seventies during the siege at Wounded Knee. He was a classic liberal-activist churchman. I knew gay people who knew him and had worked for him. When he had treated MCC so very coolly in the early days of our application process, I felt disappointed. He knew better, I thought. Where was the courageous moral leadership that we needed at this time?

So when a leader of a major U.S. denomination called me at my home one late spring morning, proposing a top-level, hush-hush meeting with Rev. Troy Perry and myself, I was open and enthusiastic. At last, a chance to talk face-to-face with Armstrong, Dr. Claire Randall (general secretary of the NCC and an extraordinary churchwoman), and the leaders of four of the most powerful and traditionally more liberal denominations.

Meanwhile, all was not well at our headquarters in Los Angeles. At the time, I worked full time for the Fellowship as Clerk of the Board of Elders. In late May we had learned of the tragic, mysterious death of Reverend Perry's lover, Greg Cutts. Greg was in the process of emigrating from Canada, after a two-year struggle. Life had been very stressful for Troy and Greg as they tried to manage a long-distance relationship. Both of them were very happy about Greg's impending move. But over the Victoria Day weekend, Greg died in his sleep. In the chaotic weeks that followed, I informed the NCC of Greg's death and told them that we would have to postpone our meeting.

As it happened, all of them would be in Vancouver in July 1983 for the WCC General Assembly. Our UFMCC finances at the time were dismal. But NCC leaders managed to arrange funding for airfare for one of us to Vancouver, and Troy and I went to meet them "off campus" in a nearby restaurant.

I was very worried about Troy and wondered whether or not he should even go to this meeting. But Armstrong had initially talked to him about it, and Troy was curious, I think. To make things more complicated, Greg had died in Vancouver. When we attended the meeting in July, it had only been one month since Troy had been there for Greg's funeral.

We were very cordially greeted in the restaurant. After some small talk, one of the denominational leaders, Arie Brower of the Reformed Church in America, said softly to Troy, "We are sorry to hear about your recent loss." The Hallmark-greeting-card phrasing seemed awkward but well intentioned. And I was grateful that someone had been willing to acknowledge publicly that Troy's lover had died.

What happened then was a classic case study of the relationship of Metropolitan Community Churches to the NCC. Troy misunderstood the offer of condolences. What he did not know is that people in the liberal middle-class-dominated world of ecumenical politics and etiquette say things like that to put to *rest* a certain matter, not to open it up. The people in that room, though they had known each other for years, knew little, if anything, about each other's personal lives. That became all too evident when Armstrong later resigned. But Troy mistakenly thought he was in a safe place—in the company of Christian leadership in the U.S.

People who, like him, knew the loneliness and pressures of leading a denomination—people who *loved the Lord*. So when someone reached out with condolences, Troy just opened up. He told them about Greg's death. About how hard it was to meet his spouse's parents for the first time at his funeral. He cried. He spoke very simply and sweetly about his love for Greg and about how he met Greg. All the time I watched their faces. How much they did not want to be hearing this! How unaccustomed they were to this level of intimate, open, vulnerable sharing of love and grief. He pressed every homophobic, sex-phobic, intimacy-phobic button they had. They looked stunned and helpless, shifting in their seats. They impatiently cleared their throats. I, too, felt helpless. I was certain that if one of them said anything to hurt him, I'd simply have to turn some tables over right there in the restaurant. Mercifully, Troy stopped. We took a breath, and Bishop Armstrong switched the subject and got down to it.

What *I* did not know was that not everyone at that table knew what he was about to say. The bishop leaned toward us, looked right at me, and said (I'm paraphrasing, but not too much), "I know you love Jesus Christ and the church of Jesus Christ. If you really do, you will spare us the agony of having to take a divisive vote in the fall that will only cause *you* pain. Please prayerfully consider withdrawing your application for membership." I don't remember if I even looked at Troy, although I swear I could feel his blood run cold. But Armstrong had addressed me. In a flash, I pictured the dear faces of my UFMCC colleagues and friends as I would try to explain to them how withdrawing our application was the right thing to do, what Jesus *really* wanted. Then, thankfully, my crap detector kicked in.

Somehow I managed not to throw up the expensive salmon dinner and to reply. Basically, I said, "No way." And something like "And don't think that by withdrawing our application it will spare us pain. Gay and lesbian people experience pain at the hands of the church of Jesus Christ every day. We are prepared to endure the pain of rejection as our cross to bear at this time in history. One of the reasons MCC is coming to the NCC is to witness visibly to the spiritual awakening in the gay and lesbian community and also to make visible the lethal homophobia of the church. We're sorry, but we think Jesus is with us in this process, and if you do the right thing, God will be with the NCC."

That ended the discussion. Afterward Troy let me know that he would leave the ecu-politics to me; he preferred the cutthroat secular politicians any day. But to the point of the story: sometime during that evening I managed to spend a little time with Claire Randall. I told her about MCC's worldwide ministry, including our predominantly hetero-sexual churches in Nigeria among the "untouchable" people. Suddenly she became interested. I enjoyed her questions, her interest in UFMCC, her insights, and what felt like her genuine respect and support of a kind. And then I asked the question. I had never personally asked this question of anyone. I chose this strange moment to ask my question of this older, close-to-retirement feminist veteran of countless ecumenical skirmishes and adventures. I remember that very private moment when I simply asked her, "Why do you think there is so much fear and resistance toward UFMCC?" (Really: *Why do they hate us so?*) She sighed, looked nowhere in particular, and said, "Well, I guess when you talk about sex and the Bible in the same breath, they just go nuts."

Not an explanation but an excellent description: "They just go nuts."

A few months into my co-pastorate at MCC Boston in 1973, I was consecrating communion. It was a warm summer evening. Suddenly, from the second pew, a man none of us had seen before got up, ran to the front of the sanctuary, knocked over the communion elements, punched me in the face, and ran out of the church before anyone could stop him.

They just go nuts.

So, Who Are We?

Who are gay men and lesbians? Sometimes, in my deepest self, I feel like we are some ancient tribal remnant that has survived and that now appears to be dispersed among every other earthly tribe—a transtribal tribe!

But others see homosexuality as purely a social construct, with no visible, demonstrable core or essence. A kind of behavior(s) so despised that those who practice it seek to take refuge in the concept of homosex-uality as an *identity*.

Then there's all the hypothalamus hype: genetics, brain compo-nents. Next they'll be feeling the bumps on our skulls. Still others see homosexuality as a matrix of factors, causes, constructions.

The truth is, I don't know what to think. Nor do many lesbians and gay men. Some of us do believe that we chose our orientation. Most, in my experience, speak of it more in terms of a discovery—a gift given before we were aware of receiving it.

Over the years I have had several experiences of what I feel is something akin to lesbian and gay tribal memory. I say this with a sense of caution and humility. For me, being a lesbian was not a choice. The only choice was how I would or would not accept who I was. And it was not *only* a discovery. For me—and this is admittedly romantic—it has also felt like my *destiny*. Martin Buber said, "We must believe in Destiny, and that it stands in need of us."[5]

In June of 1972 I marched down Fifth Avenue with my lesbian friend Jean in one of New York's earliest Gay Pride parades. I'd only been out of the closet for three months. And there I was walking down Fifth Avenue next to Jill Johnston, author of *Lesbian Nation*, and the original "queer national", and author Isabel Miller. I don't think I ever closed my mouth for four hours. The most queers I'd ever seen in one place together before that had been maybe five or six. We were at least fifty thousand people: drag queens, leather queens, lesbian separatists—a raucous, irreverent, heart-pounding throng. We marched breathing fire and freedom. I learned a new word that day: *dyke*. It made me smile when I said it, though I couldn't tell you why. As we moved up Fifth Avenue, I fell in love with this movement. Whatever part of me was still doubting, still wondering if I was not just in love with this *one* particular woman—just a phase, a fluke—evaporated in the steamy June New York Sunday afternoon heat. Everyone smiled at everyone, we delighted in one another, no strangers among us: my tribal initiation.

I first attended an NCC governing board meeting in May 1982, ten years later. Adam DeBaugh, a lay leader in UFMCC, and I arrived in Nashville, each of us with some prior ecumenical experience but not with the NCC Governing Board. Almost three hundred people met, including the press and visitors, at a large Methodist church in Nashville. We walked in just as the opening service began. All eyes discreetly turned in our direction in a silent, dread-filled chorus of "They're here!" No one officially greeted us, and we hadn't a clue about what to do or whom to talk to.

Later that day a kindly Methodist asked me in hushed tones, "Well, what is your strategy?" I remember feeling totally naked ("Strategy! Oh, no! I forgot to wear my strategy!"), like one of those nightmares where you show up to teach or preach without your sermon notes . . . or clothing . . . or something essential. We had a kind of *ecumenical innocence*. We had applied for membership and assumed we'd just go through their process. Why did we need a *strategy*? So, strategically naked, after the opening worship service, we positioned ourselves quite awkwardly, as if we were ushers or greeters, and shook hands and handed out pamphlets (like church bulletins) to Governing Board members who were leaving for a cigarette or bathroom break. Right away we were accused of being pushy. Ecumenical etiquette crashing. Some strategy. Who knew?

But back to that opening worship service. Suddenly, sitting in the last aisle in that huge church, I realized some things. The NCC and I were (are) the same age. I thought of all it had taken to bring us together at this moment in history. Suddenly, I sensed *them* in the room: gay men and lesbians through the ages. In the churches, burned by the churches, persecuted by the churches, serving the churches, loving and hurting. *They* were there. They knew I was there. I had this overwhelming sense of a mystical communion of gay and lesbian saints, some of whom had served this council in its better days. I wept for them and for us, for their longing, pain, and shame, for their need even now for vindication and for a voice. And I felt so small, and young, and inadequate. But also so loved and watched over by them. From that moment until this, they have never left me. And many thousands have been added to their numbers.

Then everyone stood together and sang a song I had loved a long time, the text written by an angry, questioning son of the church:

> *Once to every [soul] and nation*
> *Comes the moment to decide,*
> *In the strife of truth with falsehood,*
> *For the good or evil side. . . .*
> *Then it is the brave [one] chooses,*
> *While the coward stands aside,*
> *Till the multitude make virtue*
> *Of the faith they had denied.*
>
> *By the light of burning martyrs,*[6]
> *Christ, Thy bleeding feet we track,*
> *Toiling up new Calvaries ever*
> *With the cross that turns not back;*
> *New occasions teach new duties,*
> *Time makes ancient good uncouth;*
> *They must upward still, and onward, who would*
> *Keep abreast of truth.*
>
> JAMES RUSSELL LOWELL

The NCC were singing our song! But did they know it yet? And, oh, *they* were also singing right along with us. The presence of my heavenly tribe sustained me that day and in every NCC governing board since.

Later on in the NCC adventure, we held three "consultations." One of these was on "Biblical Issues and Homosexuality." One of the presenters was Dr. Robin Scroggs, a New Testament Pauline scholar. He is a heterosexual scholar who has been willing to take another look at the traditional passages in Paul that have been used to condemn homosexuality and homosexuals. One of Dr. Scroggs's theses is that the New Testament simply doesn't address the situation of contemporary gay and lesbian people because in his opinion, male homosexual relationships were in New Testament times all pederastic. In the midst of that meeting, it suddenly occurred to me that he might be suggesting that there were no ancient gay men and lesbians who had mutually consenting adult relationships. When I asked him if that was what he meant, he paused, then said, "Yes."

"How do you know that?" I asked.

His argument was one of silence. I felt this horror and rage in me that could not shut up. How could he just say that there were no people like me, like us, of our tribe, in those times? How dare he say that! And how unfortunate to argue from silence.

But more than that, I had to ask myself, "How do I know we *were* there?" Judy Grahn has certainly documented us (and not as pederasts, either) in ancient history, folklore, mythology, and literature. But how did I know that day? I realized that I knew it in my guts. In my heart, in my body, and blood, and spirit, and wherever else it is that we just know things. The heavenly tribe was there, some of whom preceded New Testament times. They knew. And they now had a way of getting my attention. Dr. Scroggs's remark, his theories, *seemed* harmless enough on the surface. But to me they were something akin to genocide. I felt all this terrible grief at the suggestion that *they* (we) had not been there all along. Closeted, for sure—quiet, oppressed, silent—but *there*.

Israel, too, had a complex process of identity formation. Who are the Jews? Are they a race or a tribe, a religion or a nation, a culture or a set of traditions? They are a people with a vague prehistory. They were shaped by the historical crucibles of the Exodus and Exile; by courageous leaders; common oppression; covenant values; by storytellers and events. They were forged from an amalgam of tribes and peoples.

What name would we—did we—call those who would want to dissect a Jewish hypothalamus? *Nazi*, I think. So how come our collective hypothalami are so dissectable? So terribly interesting? For those of us who long for sexual orientation to be not our fault (something like dia-betes), the *hypothalamus thing* must seem like an enormous relief. But I am skeptical, to say the least. What creates community? What creates tribe? Why do some tribes last, some don't, some disappear into the mists of time?

There is a certain critical tension about this *tribal identity thing*. I remember reading death-of-God theologian Richard Rubenstein's book *After Auschwitz* when I was in college. I recall his searching questions about the implications of the Jewish concept of chosenness, its permuta-tions in Christian thought, and the terribly twisted notions of chosenness that characterized the Nazi doctrine of Aryan supremacy. He asked if the concept of chosenness, no matter how humble or benign, might lead inevitably to doctrines of exclusiveness and superiority. To many, of course, Rubenstein's critique sounded all too much like *blaming the victim*. How-ever, his critique of what I call "tribal ontology" is perhaps more relevant than ever in these days of global ethnic conflicts and growing fundamen-talism. The dilemma of tribal theology and tribal biblical hermeneutics is discussed at length in the book *Out of Every Tribe and Nation* by Justo Gonzales.[7] On the one hand, "there is always the likelihood that any the-ology that claims to be *universal* is no more than theology from the partic-ular perspective of those who are in power."[8] In other words, the dominant tribes set the agenda, and get to "universalize" *their* tribal theology. On the other hand there is the danger of what he calls the romanticization of cul-ture in which groups may "idealize [their] culture as if it were perfect and did not stand in need of correction from the gospel."[9] No culture is free from human problems and divisions. There has to be a delicate balance between the search for the universal and the context of tribal particularism. We must acknowledge that we live in a world of shifting hierarchies—and for some of us, they don't shift fast enough!

So, do gay and lesbian people identify more with our tribe(s) or more with our humanness? Does our tribal identification give us the courage and strength to claim our humanness? Or does it urge us to com-pare ourselves, to judge ourselves as worse or better than others? Those in whatever dominant group or culture always want all the rest of us to focus on our generic humanness, on how alike we are, not on our differences. Is the notion of generic humanness essentially classist, racist, sexist?[10]

Only twenty-five years ago, Rev. Troy Perry had to write, in an open letter to the church (from *The Lord Is My Shepherd and He* [sic] *Knows*

I'm Gay), "I am not a creature from the other darkness, I am a man of flesh and blood."[11] In many places in the world, it is our humanness as gays and lesbians that is still the issue.

I met Kiron (not his real name), a gay East Indian man, the way I meet many people these days. His lover, Jerry, was dying of AIDS. Jerry's parents stayed in Kiron and Jerry's home in Los Angeles during Jerry's final days. Jerry's mother, in fact, lived there for months. Kiron cared for Jerry until he had to go to the hospital. Jerry's parents were never openly rude to Kiron, but he knew they had never approved of Jerry's lifestyle. Nevertheless, Kiron showed them every kindness, gave them a key to his home, was very hospitable. The day after Jerry died, Kiron went to work in his law office as usual. He was not out to his colleagues or clerical staff and felt he could not risk being absent from work, *even the day after his lover of six years had died.*

When he returned home that night, the apartment felt strange. Then he realized that Jerry's parents had left. And they had taken many things. All of Jerry's possessions but not *only* that: they had stolen things that had belonged to both of them. Precious photographs, personal effects. Kiron collapsed in grief and rage. In order for these good, churchgoing folks to do such a thing, they had to be willing to see Kiron as less than human, not deserving of ordinary human courtesy and respect, much less gratitude. They had to be willing to negate all the evidence of the love and commitment between their son and this gentle, good man. Kiron never saw Jerry's parents or any of his things again.[12]

This tension between our tribal and our human identity is a difficult issue for gay men, lesbians, and bisexuals.

I met Chris Cowap in 1974 at the first meeting of the NCC's Commission on Women in Ministry. It was an incredible gathering of about 120 or so powerful women church leaders and feminists. My invitation was a last-minute one, thanks to Roy Birchard, pastor of Metropolitan Community Church of New York who doubled as a secretary for the Presbyterians at the "God Box" (a term of affection for the Inter-Church Center, 475 Riverside Drive in Manhattan). I got a *gay underground* invitation, which meant that I would never know precisely how I got invited.

I was twenty-three at the time and still at MCC Boston, and I was the only *out* lesbian at this meeting. Just by showing up, I evidently caused quite a stir, and people went out of their way to either greet me or avoid me. By the end of the weekend, after dozens of midnight tearful conversations and hallway comings-out, I'd guess that nearly one-third of those women were dykes or well on their way. It was an exhilarating and exhausting introduction to the world of ecu-feminism of the seventies.

But of all of them, Chris probably affected me the most. An intense, politically savvy lay Episcopalian, career social-justice ecumenist, Chris was already an instant hero to me. When she wanted to speak to me, I was flattered and curious. She just looked at me, shook her head, and said tearfully, "I'm just never going to be able to do it."

"Do what?" I asked. (Duh.)

"Come out, like you." Chris was a dyke! Well, of course. She just kept shaking her head. She told me about her activism in the civil rights movement, her feminist identification, her commitment to progressive environmental causes and to human rights. But, she said, "I can't do this last thing. I can't do this last thing that is really for and about me. And I'm ashamed. When I look at you, I'm ashamed. I'm ashamed I can't do it for myself and that I can't be more supportive of you." I remember just holding her a while and thanking her for coming out to me. I tried to reassure her that I *did* feel supported, just by her *human* example.

From time to time after that, whenever I was in New York, I would try to find Chris while minimizing the danger of exposing her. She moved around in the God Box quite a bit, first to the WCC and then later back to the NCC. I remember sneaking up to her office with Rev. Karen Ziegler, trying to be invisible on the way! ("Nah, I didn't just see two dykes sneaking by into Chris's office, did you?") Chris always looked glad to see me, and the feeling was mutual. Plus she possessed a wealth of knowledge about everything ecumenical. She was my inside track.

Through the ecumenical feminist grapevine I eventually heard about her lung cancer. When we applied for membership in the NCC in 1981, Chris had just gone into remission and was just coming back to work. Seeing her at those meetings was wonderful. She provided great support to us in those days. And eventually around the AIDS issue.

In early November 1983, on the way to the Hartford meeting of the NCC during which they would be voting on our eligibility for membership, Chris tracked me down at my brother's home in Indianapolis. I had stopped by Indianapolis for three reasons. Most importantly, to do my youngest brother's wedding at a large Methodist church. My parents and family would be there. Also, I wanted to have one last chance at a conversation with Bishop Armstrong, whose office happened to be in Indianapolis.

Third, I had had a troubling dream about a former student clergy of mine who had been pastoring MCC in Louisville, Kentucky. I had not seen Sandy in two years, and I missed her and was worried about her. I asked her to come to Indianapolis while I was there.

My conversation with Bishop Armstrong was extremely discouraging. He seemed scattered and hostile, as well he might have been only one week away from his surprise resignation as president of the NCC. And I did get to see my friend Sandy. For a few precious hours a few of us gathered in a little bar on the outskirts of Indianapolis. It would be the last time I would ever see her. She died three weeks later, probably from suicide. We will never know for sure.

But Chris managed to track me down. I liked that. I had always attributed a certain omniscience to her, and this only reinforced it. She opened with "I'm gonna do it!"

"Do what?" (Duh, again.)

"Come out." She said she figured there had to be a reason for all this cancer remission stuff. And this must be it. (Chris always skipped formalities in conversations with me. She talked as if we had spoken just yesterday and not six months ago.) She told me that if the NCC turned MCC down for eligibility or membership, she would publicly come out at the meeting in Hartford. All I could think of was our first meeting and how Chris thought she could never do it. She had been a person for all people but not quite a person for herself. And perhaps now that was about to change. No longer a generic person, Chris could claim her lesbian self.

The Hartford NCC meeting was a zoo. The *Inclusive Language Lectionary* was being introduced. Virginia Mollenkott, a member of the committee, infuriated some of her colleagues by coming out at that meeting in support of MCC. The Lectionary Committee had excited so much attention from the press and religious conservatives that our issue seemed overshadowed at times. The committee had, in fact, been subjected to harassing phone calls and even death threats that had necessitated calling in the FBI. The NCC received much more negative mail about the lectionary than it *ever* received about us in eleven years. But they still published the lectionary, which many of us in UFMCC use.

After days of ecu-political machinations, the die was cast. A poorly written "compromise" motion was adopted that would *postpone indefinitely* their vote on our eligibility for membership.

They couldn't say yes, but they couldn't say no either. (This would become something of a dysfunctional pattern in the UFMCC/NCC relationship, the "come here/go away" version of ecu-teasing.) "We can't bear to think of ourselves as rejecting you, so we'll just call it something else and keep everyone guessing." Except the cynics, of course, who knew all along.

When the vote happened, I was immediately called out into the hallway in front of fifty or sixty reporters, TV cameras, microphones, and so on to read our prepared statement, putting a cautiously optimistic spin on it all. We queers were good sports in those days.

Meanwhile, Chris sat in her seat, a little numb and confused. She had a prearranged signal with Dr. Jane Carey Peck, professor of ethics at Andover Newton School of Theology and on the United Methodist delegation to the governing board of the NCC. If the vote was negative, Chris would stand, and Jane Carey would look for her and yield the floor to her. (As a member of the staff, Chris did not automatically have a voice at the governing board meeting.) The only problem was that when the vote happened, Chris was not sure just *how* negative it was, and she sat there, trying to decide. Then as she told Virginia Mollenkott and me later that evening, she suddenly felt two hands on her shoulders lifting her out of her seat. When she turned around to see who had done it, no one was there.

Jane Carey got the signal and yielded the floor to Chris. The room was utterly still. Someone came running out into the hallway to get me, saying, "Chris is at the mike!" I got into the meeting room in time to hear this:

> DR. JANE CAREY PECK: Jane Carey Peck, United Methodist. I ask for a point of personal privilege in order to yield the floor to a staff member of the Division of Church and Society, one of the valued and leading contributors to our common work, Chris Cowap.

> CHRIS COWAP: I don't want to be here. And I don't have any choice. Dr. Lois Wilson said this morning that "to be a person is to be relational; that's what defines us." I want to define myself in her terms.
>
> I am a daughter; I am a sister; I am an aunt; I'm a friend; I'm a colleague; for almost ten years now I've been a servant in this community of the council; and I'm a woman who loves another woman. And I'm sure with every fiber of my being that I am a child of God and an inheritor of the kingdom of heaven.

When I have felt God's judgment on me—and I have, too many times—it has never been because of the nature of those relationships. It's been because I have allowed them or caused them to be broken, to be not-love.

I said I don't want to be here—right here—and yet I feel compelled right now by the Holy Spirit to be here, saying this. I hear this: not a heavenly choir but a single voice, singing "Hodie! This is the day, Chris, when you must, in love, assert in this community in which you have been called to serve, to these brothers and sisters in Christ with whom you have been in community, you must affirm God's affirmation of you. You can't do anything else." This has not simply been an institutional matter, and you know that I am not speaking as one lone individual. I'm not speaking as a spokesperson; I wasn't chosen as a spokesperson. But you know that there are other people in this room—in the choir lofts, in the sacristies, in the pews, in the seminaries, in your national staffs—for whom I am speaking. I believe that you honestly intend, some of you, to continue in the dialogue and to wrestle with prayer and continued pain with the questions of what it means to be human and what it means to be truly members of one another. And you need to know that there are some of us who feel called by God to be here and to stay here to be in that kind of dialogue with you.[13]

Chris Cowap died four and a half years later of lung cancer. In the years between 1983 and 1988, I had the privilege of rooming with Chris several times at NCC meetings. We never talked about it (she was always curt and businesslike), so I don't know which of us got the bigger kick out of watching people trying *not* to wonder just what was "going on." Mostly what was going on was that Chris would regale me (and sometimes Sandi Robinson, president of MCC's Samaritan College) with wonderful feminist ecumenical folklore. She especially loved to tell Claire Randall stories. While drinking her white wine, Chris (who was mostly bald from chemotherapy) would take off her wig and NCC drag, don her dykish white T-shirt, and talk, and talk, and talk.

And sometimes we touched. Like the time she was in such excruciating pain (from the progressing cancer) that I had her lie on her side while I laid hands on her chest and back, doing light massage and heavy prayer.

Chris eventually succumbed. But not before she had resolved in herself that terrible tension between her commitment to all people and all the earth and her commitment to her own special and lovely tribe. When *they* put their hands on her that afternoon in Hartford, lifting her out of her seat, they helped her to do what had seemed so remote and utterly impossible only nine years before.

I must also thank God for dear Jane Carey, who died of ovarian cancer in 1990. I always wondered if she saw just who it was that stood behind Chris that day in Hartford.

In many ways, the ecumenical movement is the only other "church" I've ever felt completely at home in besides MCC. It has been a source of some of my most powerful spiritual experiences and deepest friendships.

In 1991, I had the privilege of serving as MCC's delegate observer to the World Council of Churches General Assembly in Canberra, Australia. The first Sunday we were there we shared the very first celebration of the Lima Liturgy[14] at a WCC assembly. This was the first chance for this world ecumenical assembly to celebrate communion with the carefully crafted and negotiated words. Even the Eastern Orthodox agreed on the *wording* of the liturgy. The only barrier was that they, and some others, could still not agree on who was legitimately able to preside over communion. So it was still far from perfect, and incomplete as an ecumenical Eucharist. Nevertheless, the celebration went forward that day, with five thousand or so in attendance under that big, open tent under the big, open Australian summer sky. Outside, conservative Eastern Orthodox people protested the celebration, criticizing Orthodox ecumenists with huge, vilifying signs. I think some fundamentalist critics were there, too.

The liturgy was breathtakingly gorgeous. Aboriginal participation hallowed the ground and space; the processional was grand. A young, tall, adorable lesbian with a buzz haircut towered above the other processors. I noticed her right away. Steve Pieters, Kit Cherry, and I poked each other with the "We are everywhere!" poke.

Then came the invitation to communion, and people began to do just as we do in UFMCC, to stream forward down the aisle, mostly single file, to receive the holy elements. Other than Kit and Steve, I knew no one else in our section of the tent. I probably knew only about two hundred of the five thousand people there that day. Suddenly, I was overwhelmed. I saw the faces of hundreds and hundreds of strangers streaming down the aisles, hungry and thirsty, hardly a dry eye. We were all aware of the beauty and pain and historicity of this moment. And then it seemed to me that I actually *knew* all of these strangers. They looked just like people I served communion to *every* Sunday at MCC Los Angeles. Well, not *just* like, but very close. All races, nations, sizes, shapes, sexualities, ages. I am always amazed at what happens to tired, older, dry, craggy adult faces when they come to communion. How faces soften, open, even glow. How older people start to look younger. Wide-eyed, open, trusting, needy. Unashamed. It was as if I knew every person who streamed forward. Suddenly it was as if I could have told you, if you had asked me, not only every name but every story, their fears, dreams, how they "got over" (a Mahalia Jackson song), how they got there. I began to cry, something I did very infrequently in those days. I remembered Søren Kierkegaard's words to the effect that if we *knew everything* about a person—their pain, fears, losses, loves—we could not help but love them to death. Suddenly, proud to be representing my tribe, I was transported to a posttribal reality. It no longer mattered, everything was dissolving. Especially me. Never in all my life had I experienced the sense of overpowering connectedness to the earth and all her people. And then it shifted just a little bit more. I was a child in a huge family gathering. Somehow along the way I had lost contact with my parents, which was very frightening. But there was this deep consolation, because all the folks around me had this vague *family resemblance* that made me feel safe, at home. Just like the ways my Aunt Betty and Aunt Jo looked enough like my mom so that just seeing them always made me feel secure, like it would all be OK somehow. If I lost my parents, my family, my tribal connections of whatever type, I was still safe in the arms of this extended tribal network. Now my tears were of belonging and relief.

I'm not sure how long that experience lasted. Eventually I got up and made my way forward to the most ecumenical Eucharist the world had experienced to date. Me and my gay and lesbian tribe partook with the rest. One Body. One Blood.

1

Healing Our Tribal Wounds

The religious right in the United States (now often called the "religious wrong" by some) is fond of going on and on about the *gay agenda*. Oh, that we were as well organized as they fantasize! I believe that we must *have* a tribal agenda. Two urgent components of that agenda are *healing our tribal wounds* and *boldly exercising our tribal gifts*.

Lifting the ban on gays and lesbians in the military was not really at the top of the charts in terms of the agenda for the gay or lesbian organizations I have been familiar with until very recently. Reasons for this are probably complicated. A lot of the gay and lesbian establishment are baby boomers, some of whom were antiwar activists in the sixties and seventies, and they were not willing to portray gay and lesbians as promilitary or patriotic. Yet history and circumstances pushed this issue to the top when Bill Clinton was elected president. The idea that many gay and lesbian people have a deep, unfulfilled desire to join the military is patently ridiculous. Yet there are a huge number of gay and lesbian veterans and of gays and lesbians currently serving with honor. Something about the psychology and sociology of minority group legitimacy in the American mind is related to military status. (I could go *on* about that—others have!) It seems to be the test of "true citizenship," which in political currency is the *same thing* as "humanness."

This came home to me recently at the funeral of an older African-American gay clergyman who had been on the staff of MCC Los Angeles for several years. Thomas Walker was a gentle, beloved man who had devoted his ministry to helping alcoholics like himself. I do not remember knowing before his death that Thomas was also a navy veteran.

I presided over his funeral, which was attended by many of his family, by the pastor of their congregation (Progress Baptist Church, Compton, California), and by many MCC people and members of Alcoholics Anonymous. Thomas, in his death, had assembled a very eclectic group. As we bid him farewell at the end of the funeral and after the last "Amen," the director of the funeral home, as is customary at the funerals of veterans, gave an American flag to the family. We were gathered in the lower level of the mausoleum in which Thomas was being buried. I had forgotten about this final bit of funeral procedure. As the funeral director took the flag to present it to Thomas's brother, he said something like "On behalf of the president of the United States, a grateful nation presents this flag to you." Grief cracked open like a huge egg, at least for the UFMCC folks. I thought about how many times I had been at the funerals of veterans. The words had always seemed like an afterthought, even an intrusion. But context is everything. This time the context was history itself. Only a few months before, a new president of the United States had actually uttered aloud the words "gay and lesbian" for the very first time and had, at great political cost to himself, declared his belief that we were citizens, human beings, worthy of military status (in other words, human dignity and rights). If he never did another thing, the fact that he did that for us was an incredible, costly gift. So when this funeral director said those words at the funeral of a black gay veteran, it all just came together. We just wept as he said, "On behalf of the president"—the president, Bill Clinton, someone who can at least say the words "gay and lesbian"—"a grateful nation." Imagine. The United States expressing its gratitude for *our* Thomas.

Comparisons of oppression are at times very odious to me. But the *feeling* in that room reminded me of the feelings I saw in another room just weeks later, at the conclusion of the federal trial of the four officers accused of violating the civil rights of Rodney King. The picture of the sanctuary of First AME Church in Los Angeles comes to mind, and the tears of relief and joy. And Jesse Jackson wiping away his own tears, saying, "It's just so hard to have to go through all this drama to get simple justice." Nothing in that whole day touched me more than that comment. The joy and bitterness commingled. One battle was more or less resolved, but all the problems remain. The war goes on.

All this drama for some simple justice. Just to be considered human, worthy of citizenship, worthy of heaven.

When I say I'm a queer millennialist, it has to do with the *justice in heaven and on earth* stuff. In times of slavery and its aftermath, the question about black people's souls, about that dimension of their humanness, was a *de*humanizing topic of discussion. But eventually it almost seemed as if heaven, for blacks, and in fact for all poor people, was often viewed as a consolation prize for having no justice on earth.

For gays and lesbians, it's a little different. Being able to be closeted means that gays and lesbians have been able to pass and use race, gender, or class privilege, where possible, to get the goodies here on earth. In fact, there is a growing stereotype, very much encouraged by the gay and lesbian political establishment, that gays and lesbians are a white, wealthy minority who can push our agenda. Well, I know a lot of poor, working-class, and nonwhite gays and lesbians. Lesbians are disproportionately represented in every women's prison I've ever visited, and these were not lesbians who were only lesbian during their prison sentence.

But the issue of heaven has been really touchy for gays and lesbians. It's the "Jack Benny thing." So I make it my practice to talk about heaven casually, freely, and frequently, as if, with Emily Dickinson, "the chart was given," like I am familiar with "the spot," and of course we're all going to get there.[1] *And I won't go without you.*

Once, while debating Jerry Falwell on Ron Reagan Jr.'s television show, I got to deliver one of my favorite "gays goin' to heaven" sound bytes. I said, "Jerry, the only reason I would want to die before you is that I want to be on heaven's welcome wagon and see the look on your face when you get there." He actually chuckled, turned to me at the break, and said, "That was very good!"

When the National Council of Churches of Christ voted in the fall of 1992 to *take no action* on our request for observer status (as if that in itself were not an action!), I managed to be able to say how grateful I was for UFMCC because it was there that I learned that, thank God, "it was easier to get into heaven than into the National Council of Churches of Christ in the U.S.A.!" That little *sound byte* made it to newspapers in Holland, Hong Kong, and around the world. I liked saying it because it assumes that gay and lesbian people are eligible for heaven. That assumption is contained in the grammar of the sentence. And when I speak about

God or heaven, I always want gay men and lesbians to hear the assumption of our eligibility (for heaven, if not for the NCC).

THE WOUNDS OF FALSE WITNESS

What are the wounds of our people—the gay, lesbian, bisexual, transgender communities and tribes?

Clearly, rejection and abandonment are at the top of the list. Rejection and abandonment by our families, churches, synagogues, governments. But also high on the list for me is the damage caused by *slander.* There is no explicit condemnation of homosexuality among the Ten Commandments in the *Bible,* but there *is* a commandment against *bearing false witness against your neighbor.* Virginia Mollenkott and Letha Scanzoni wrote a book with the wonderful title *Is the Homosexual My Neighbor?* If the answer to that rhetorical question is yes, then the assumption must be that gay and lesbian people are human, are our neighbors, and that it displeases God if we tell lies about them! The Bible doesn't seem to say whether it's worse if the lies are told out of malice or ignorance. False witness is false witness.

The fact is that the *radical* or *religious* right breaks the Ninth Commandment every day, using ignorance and fear of homosexuality and homosexuals to raise millions and millions of dollars. But they are not alone. The whole church and other religious bodies have borne false witness about gays and lesbians for at least a millennium.

One of the most painful false negative stereotypes about gay and lesbian people is that we are child molesters. For many, many years, police statistics have demonstrated that the vast majority (over 90 percent) of child molesters are heterosexual men. There is no factual basis whatsoever for the belief that gay men or lesbians are any more likely than heterosexuals to seduce or molest children or adolescents. Yet this fear and false witness are kept alive in the popular mind. It is one of the underlying discomforts many people have about gays in the military: parents whose children in their late teens or early twenties are joining the military fear that they will be corrupted by predatory homosexuals.

This false witness has increased the stigmatizing of homosexuality and is one of several factors that brings homophobia to the irrational, fevered pitch we experience. But most important, gays and lesbians have our own internalized response to this stigma. One of our responses has been to be afraid of children and of interacting with them to avoid any possible cause for the accusation of child molestation. This has come out as a thinly veiled hostility toward children. I remember particularly in the seventies when we called straight people *hets* or *breeders* and the children were *rug rats* or *curtain climbers*. There was the occasional lesbian mother who still had custody of her children, and a very rare father or two. But children did not often get a warm reception at gay and lesbian gatherings in those days, and in some places today, they still do not. Over time, many gays and lesbians had less contact with their own children, their nieces and nephews or with children in general. In a kind of defensive maneuver, gay men and some lesbians insulated themselves from children and from this potential slander.

Underneath that defensive posture always lurked the deep-seated fear, "What if *they* are right?" Are children really safe with us? When I became the Pastor of MCC Detroit in 1975, the church had a *policy* that no one under the age of eighteen could attend MCC without being accompanied by a parent or guardian. I was stunned that a church would feel it was too risky to welcome unaccompanied minors. This was both a fear of the false accusations that could be made *and* a deep-seated uneasiness that maybe children weren't really safe with us. And that was simply internalized homophobia. I told them I would not pastor a church where children were not safe or welcome. And in any case, we couldn't keep them away. The children managed to find us on their own.

Roger was thirteen when he came to MCC Detroit. He knew he was gay, and he was very *mature*-appearing for his age, as well as sexually precocious. He often managed to get into gay bars and was constantly harassed at school. He was working "the block" (every city has a gay cruising area where closeted gay or bisexual men pick up hustlers or street kids for quick sex). A very closeted member of my church picked Roger up, then realized how old he was. The member called me in a panic. He brought Roger to me at the church office and dropped him off. I called his mother. She couldn't handle him, and I, in fact, got written permission from her for him to attend the church. Two adult men in the church took Roger under their wing. These were two men who did not exploit him sexually but gave him support and sometimes even shelter. They did this at great risk to themselves. We managed to help get Roger safely through junior high, and he eventually moved to San Francisco to complete high school.

Metropolitan Community Church of Los Angeles tells the story of a young boy (not older than twelve), a runaway, who appeared on the steps of the church on a Sunday in the early seventies. He wanted to go home. So the assistant pastor took him to the police. It is hard for anyone who is not gay or lesbian and over thirty-five to understand what an enormous act of courage this was on the part of the pastor. The pastor explained what had happened, and the police spent time interrogating the boy, trying to find out, among other things, if these homosexuals had molested him in any way. Finally, one of the officers said, "Son, do you know what kind of church this is?," and the boy thought for a minute and replied, "I don't know, I guess it's just a church for everybody." That story has been told a lot at MCC L.A. It contains a lot of healing messages.

UFMCC says we are a church for everybody—even children. In the 1980s, two things happened, it almost seems simultaneously: the AIDS epidemic (which began devastating the gay male community especially) and the lesbian (and to a lesser extent, gay male) baby boom. More lesbians and gay men were fighting for the right to have full or partial custody of their children from heterosexual marriages or relationships. And lesbians were seeking other ways to have children, especially through artificial insemination and adoption. Some gay men also donated sperm or sought to adopt.

Many MCC churches now have child care or children's programs. But there is still resistance to this in the gay and lesbian community—remnants of the negative power of false witness.

I have come to believe that our capacity to welcome children into our gay and lesbian families, organizations, churches, and so on is one measure of how much healing we have experienced. Our resistance to children is our resistance to our own healing. The safer children are with us, the safer we are with ourselves and each other.

This is also related to the relatively new "inner-child" psychology. As we welcome real live children, we also have to face our own wounded inner child. More often than not, our gay or lesbian inner child was rejected, abandoned, or abused. I believe that oftentimes our families knew before we did that we were gay or lesbian. At least that we were *different*—they may not have known why. But we were different, some of us "passing" for straight better than others. And that difference was *not* perceived as a good thing. It caused us to be punished, humiliated, targeted for abuse.

It has not been easy for gay men and lesbians to admit these child-hood wounds, partly because of another false witness. That one said that we *became* gay or lesbian because of an "absent father" and an "overbear-ing mother"; or because we were molested by an older homosexual (and then wanted to grow up and be one?); or molested heterosexually (and we hated it and wanted *not* to be one of them?) One old gay expression used to be that one "turned" gay like milk that was "turning" sour! In any case, to admit to having been targeted for emotional or physical abuse seemed to be contributing to a negative stereotype! So many of us were anxious—in fact, overanxious—to prove that we came from "normal" homes and parents, which most of us did. Except that today, in the 1990s, we know that "normal homes and parents" in America are often very vio-lent and abusive—something we did not know as well in the sixties, sev-enties, and early eighties.

If you read Troy Perry's two books, separated by nearly two decades, you can see the difference. In the *Lord Is My Shepherd and He Knows I'm Gay*, Troy presents a mostly happy childhood picture, glossing over some crucial issues. In *Don't Be Afraid Anymore*, he tells some terrible stories about violence in his family and childhood. It became safer and more acceptable for Troy to tell those stories in the late 1980s.

And telling those stories is what we must do if we are to heal and if we are really to be a safe haven for the children we want to welcome into our lives.

I met Rechal in October 1985. She was three years old, and I met her in prison.

She and her mother were in prison together in a special facility oper-ated by the California Correctional System. This program and several oth-ers like it probably had good theory and intentions. It was a locked facility for women who had infants or toddlers. The theory was that these women and their children would benefit from not losing contact with one another during the crucial formative years. Also, the women could be given assis-tance in learning parenting skills.

Instead, this program, in my opinion, amounted to women in prison providing the care for these children for free, so that the state would not have to pay for their support while the mothers were in prison—a budget-cutting reform. I observed no classes or other assistance in parenting skills. And because these women were locked up twenty-four hours a day, they had twenty-four-hour sole care of the children, no breaks provided.

Jessie was an attractive thirty-eight-year old career criminal and the mother of Rechal (by artificial insemination). Jessie had been introduced to the Mexican equivalent of the Mafia at an early age by her family. She laundered money, did robberies. She was openly proud of the fact that she had refused to engage in prostitution and had always lived her lesbian identity. She had been party to a killing, something she could never bring herself to talk about with me.

As happens with organized crime, Jessie had ended up owing someone a lot of money (she was a heroin addict). Rechal was a late-in-life baby that she desperately wanted to have, and she finally really wanted to get off drugs and out of the organized crime scene. So she agreed to assist in *one last* diamond heist to pay off her debt. She was arrested, and Rechal was taken from her.

While in prison, Jessie heard of UFMCC. When she got released to this special facility, she contacted me at UFMCC's headquarters. She had called other gay and lesbian organizations looking for support or help—to no avail. MCC Los Angeles had just begun an outreach program at California Institute for Women, and Jessie's lover, Carol, gave her our phone number.

Jessie was shocked when someone actually called her back. She was looking for legal assistance for her twelve-year-old retarded daughter who was being held in the Juvenile Hall. I got a referral for her and then asked her if she wanted me to come visit her. She was cautious but said yes. A few days later I showed up, wearing my clerical collar, at the facility (which was temporarily housed in one wing of a rehab center in South Central Los Angeles).

After I cleared security, they let me in the locked ward. Jessie and Rechal greeted me.

I picked up three-year-old Rechal and fell in love at first sight. She sat on my lap, pointed to my collar, and said, "Jesus?" Then she asked me if I was a boy or a girl (Rechal had only been to Catholic churches at this point in her life). After we established my true name and gender, I got to know them both—over several months.

Jessie asked me to baptize Rechal and to become her godmother. It was clear that Jessie had few friends and resources that she could count on, and her family was simply not an option. Jessie began testing me. Was I reliable? In retrospect, I know she was trying to determine if her child would be safe with me.

After many long months, after taking care of Rechal for three weeks while Jessie recovered from surgery in the institution, I helped find a housing situation for Jessie and Rechal with the plan that they would receive support and help from the MCC community.

It seemed ideal. My friend Judi had an adopted son and a large home. We worked on the finances, the roommate arrangement, and I began talking with Jessie about what she really wanted in her life. She was a jazz pianist, and she was going to play in church sometime soon. She had been off drugs since before Rechal was born. It seemed very hopeful to me.

One week after their release from prison, Jessie died of a heroin overdose in the bathroom of my friend's home. Rechal was with her for four hours, curled up beside her, before Judi and her son came home and found them.

The next week was a nightmare of waiting to find out about Rechal's whereabouts. The police had taken her into protective custody and would not let me take her home with me. Judi and I spent days talking about what was best for Rechal. Judi had a lot of experience with children who had been traumatized. We came to the conclusion that if Judi could adopt her, I could continue to be in Rechal's life as an "extra mommy"—that is, godmother.

Miraculously, in March of 1986, an L.A. court agreed. When Rechal's grandmother decided to try to get involved, an independent, court-appointed guardian investigated. It was Rechal's grandmother who had gotten Jessie involved in organized crime and probably with drugs. The court believed us, and Rechal now has a home and a wonderful, large family that includes other abandoned, endangered children.

Rechal is an incredible blessing in my life. She is one of thousands and thousands of children who have been lucky enough to find safe, loving, gay and lesbian homes to live in. Gay men and lesbians were among the first people to offer foster care and adoption to children with HIV and AIDS. When others were afraid or turned off, gay men and lesbians, who already had had lots of contact with people with AIDS, were not afraid to touch or love these children. Lesbians founded most of the agencies that service children with HIV and AIDS. The wounds from the false witness of church and society against us will take a long time to heal, especially the insinuation that we are gay or lesbian because of a poor upbringing, and that we are all consequently child molesters. Only telling the stories of the healing of our own families of origin from this false witness, and the creation of our own families of choice (which often include children), will begin to heal these wounds completely.

THE WOUNDS FROM PROJECTION AND REPRESSION

I think the other way in which gay and lesbian people and other sexual minorities experience oppression is that we have endured the massive projection of society's sexual fears and fantasies.

Most minorities experience sexual projection as part of their oppression. African-Americans, male and female, experience sexual projection as part of the package of white racism. African-American men have been stereotyped as sexually obsessed and violent (there is, for example, the "myth of the black rapist"),[2] and African-American women have been stereotyped as promiscuous. Asian-Americans are considered sexually exotic by the white majority, and Latins are supposed to be "hot." And of course, sexism's major features include the projection of male fears and fantasies onto women so that women are not real people but objects available for male sexual pleasure or objects over which men can exercise power and control.

If racial and ethnic minorities are the objects of sexual projection, how much more is this true for sexual minorities where the issue of sexuality is already at the forefront of the debate?

Society's hatred and loathing of homosexuals is really about the collective shame, guilt, fear, and self-hatred in our culture at large, especially as these are related to issues of sexuality.

Presbyterians and Human Sexuality, published by the Special Committee on Human Sexuality of the Presbyterian Church in the United States, said this: "The special committee noticed how the problem of homosexuality is commonly used in our churches to refer indirectly to any and all forms of sexual nonconformity, whether among gay persons or non-gays. Homosexuality is typically invoked in a rhetorical, almost formulaic way to signal that something has gone wrong. However, homosexuality often remains an abstraction, unrelated to—and uninformed by—real people. It functions primarily as a powerful symbolic carrier of people's fears and discomfort about sexuality in general."[3]

I'm tempted to say here, "We knew that!" Gay and lesbian people, however, *do* and *do not* know this. Sometimes it comes out in the kind of campy, teasing, "gotcha" gay-pride rhetoric: "Two, four, six, eight, is your husband really straight?" "We are your worst fears and your best fantasies." "We are the people your mother warned you about." And so on!

At other times we gays and lesbians are ourselves bewildered. In many ways we are symbolic of the current struggle over changing sexual roles that is going on in many cultures. That struggle is occurring in the context of a global women's movement that seeks to expose and bring about the end of patriarchy. No wonder there is lots of fear and projection going on.

If Judy Grahn is correct in her theory that gays, lesbians, and transpeoples function to explore the future for the culture, then it is possible that society will project its fears about the future (especially its fears about gender and sexuality) onto us.

I never feel as queer at home or at MCC Los Angeles as I do when I am in a predominantly heterosexual setting, like at the NCC meetings. Just by showing up, I trigger people's questions, fears, anxieties, and fantasies about homosexuality or sexuality in general. This is exhausting. And yet, it feels like it is part of my job to invite questions, speculations, *even* their projections. But I find myself wanting to retreat to the safety of the gay/lesbian "ghetto."

It is one thing to experience the sometimes amusing/sometimes insulting projections of ordinary everyday garden variety homophobes. It is still another thing to be the projection of the church's or society's fears to the degree that one is labeled evil or demonic. This is another experience that ordinary gay and lesbian people have—some frequently, some from time to time. I know many gays and lesbians who have been forbidden to have any contact with their own or their siblings' children because of the assumed "toxicity" of their presence or influence. Or other gays and lesbians who have been publicly outed, humiliated, vilified, and literally driven out of a church meeting or Bible study, or pastor's office, or confessional. Many gay and lesbian individuals do not have the resources internally to cope with these experiences. Some do not understand that this is a result of homophobia. They really believe they must deserve it, even if they can't figure out why.

The other wound related to projection is that of repression. We become obsessed with what we repress. Our culture has historically been sexually repressive and has *become* sexually obsessive. The gay and lesbian movement is both a consequence of and a contributor to this progression from repression to obsession. If society has repressed homosexuals and homosexuality, then it is also likely to become obsessed with it. Just think of how often gays and lesbians have been the subject of talk shows over the last ten years or so. Talking about homosexuality almost assures a good audience. Televangelists know that by talking about us on television or in their fund-raising mail they will get a lot of attention and response. If both repression and obsession are unhealthy and damaging responses to the gift of human sexuality, than what *should* be happening?

Gift. That's the key, I think. Sexuality is a part of our humanness that needs to be accepted, nurtured, and valued as a gift.

Meanwhile, however, homosexuality does not *feel* like a gift to the dominant culture! It represents all the "bad" things that sex is: dirty, promiscuous, shameful, perverted, weird, unhealthy, predatory, bad for children, nonproductive.

Many heterosexual people imagine that *gay* sexuality *feels* perverted, weird, and slimy, even to us! As gay and lesbian children grow up, we learn, overtly or indirectly, how dirty and awful "it" is. Then comes the conflicting thoughts, feelings, longings, desires. How can I want to touch and be touched in a way that feels "bad" or that God and everyone else will hate?

I remember first knowing that there were gay men when I was in junior high school. The limited information I had was that they all lived in Greenwich Village, New York, or on Fire Island (off of Long Island, where I lived). They were men who wore dresses and acted effeminate, I thought. It was years before I knew that they actually had sex with each other and I learned the words *queer* and *lezzie*.

A "lezzie" was a tomboy who forgot to grow out of it. I was a tomboy who was making a valiant effort to grow out of it. Lezzies wanted to be boys. I may have even known that lezzies wanted to touch other girls the ways boys were supposed to want to touch girls. Actually, I didn't know very much about that either, come to think of it. I knew the essentials about the mechanics of heterosexual intercourse. But my mother told me that you were only supposed to do this when you were married. She blushed when she told me. And she told me it was enjoyable. I remember having serious doubts about that at the time. I knew that my parents hugged and kissed — I saw them do it. And they certainly liked it. *I* liked being hugged and kissed. So they hugged and kissed, and then, at some opportune moment, he stuck his penis into her vagina. I did not even understand this as a *process,* only as an event! I did not understand *lovemaking* as an activity that would take some time. Only gradually, I suppose, as I saw peers "making out" or as movies became a little more graphic did I understand anything about heterosexual sexual arousal. So it was all very strange and mysterious. I was in seminary and twenty-one years old before I ever recall seeing an erect penis. It was an eighty-year-old disabled priest's in the hospital where I worked. (He was on a powerful drug whose side effect was sexual arousal.) Every other penis I'd seen had been flaccid. Only then did I actually understand how the penis *got* into the vagina.

I do remember the night that my friend Jean came over to the house where I was baby-sitting. Jean was moving to Connecticut. I was almost fifteen, she was fourteen. It broke my heart to have to say good-bye. She walked over early one evening, and we knew that her grandfather was going to come get her in half an hour. I had put the babies to bed. We sat on the stairway that led to the den. On an impulse that I think I understood more than I really wanted to, I put my arm around her shoulder. I longed to do that—to do more, although I wasn't exactly sure what. It was my first *homoerotic gesture.* I pulled her to me sideways, just a little, sitting next to her on the stairs. I loved Jean; I hated that she was leaving me. I wanted to touch her. I did.

Twenty-five years later Jean and I would finally talk about that moment and others like it that had shaped our adolescence. Jean told me that she had searched for pictures of the feeling she had when I had held her. The closest thing she had found was a classic picture of Jesus touching someone in a gesture of healing. I cried when she wrote to me about that. (Speaking of repression, Jean told me the fact that she'd made a religious connection to *my* touch was probably why she found UFMCC before she found her clitoris!) Jesus, touch, sexuality. Watch out, Nancy, they're going to go nuts!

The hard part for me as an adolescent was that I could not afford to know that my longing to touch Jean was about my sexuality.

So I repressed my natural, developing lesbian sexual longings or compartmentalized and mislabeled them. Then I waited for the heterosexual desires, lust, to sort of *happen* to me. It never quite did. Not clearly. Not enough. So I kept waiting and waiting and meanwhile became a great student and a musician. I also got into religion. I kept very, very busy.

I remember going to the movies to see D. H. Lawrence's *The Fox* with the woman who would eventually become my first lover. We were probably juniors in college at the time. I had never seen a woman kiss another woman on the mouth. This film contained one scene in which a woman actually kissed another on the mouth in a *prone position*. I cannot describe my mixed feelings of excitement, anticipation, and terror, and I remember covering my face with my hands and peaking through. Then, in an instant, it was over. No one died. I do, however, remember the noises of disgust from the audience. It really didn't look strange or awful to me. And I didn't want to think about that!

Part of healing and coming out for me was the process of "unre-pressing," actually uncovering the truth about sexual feelings, touching, arousal, pleasure. Learning to find out for myself, not to take anyone else's word for it. Not even D. H. Lawrence's. Beginning, day by day, to throw off the projection, the fears. I'm still learning how to do it.

I had to learn that there is nothing particularly exotic or weird about homosexuality. I had to learn to recover from my own sexual and emo-tional isolation. To recognize sexual arousal, erotic impulses, and fantasies in myself. To learn how my own body likes to touch and be touched. I had a lot of remedial work to do. I had starved myself sexually, because I thought this would keep me from being punished and despised.

If sexuality is a part of life, a gift to help us be more fully alive, Jesus must have included sexuality in his promise, "I came that they may have life and have it more abundantly" (John 10:10).

After I came out, and came into UFMCC, I immediately had to deal with sexual projection. On top of being an open lesbian, I came out publicly almost immediately as a lesbian clergy, a pastor in a gay church. In the late fall of 1972, my picture appeared on the front page of the city section of the *Boston Globe*: instant public queer at age twenty-two.

In about 1974, when I was pastoring MCC Worcester, I got a call from someone who wanted to talk to me. We had no church office, except in my kitchen. For reasons of safety, I didn't meet strangers in my home very often, but when I did, I always made sure that my lover or another member of the church was present. For some reason, it was more conve-nient to have this man come talk to me in my kitchen, while Heather waited in the living room.

A mousy-looking older white man appeared at my door, looking a little anxious. He sat in my kitchen, hemmed and hawed, then began telling me about himself. He had asked me early on if I was a lesbian, and I had said yes. He then told me about a visit to a massage parlor in western

Massachusetts, and over a long half hour, he told me that a woman there had given him an enema, which he had found sexually stimulating. It turned out that this was a *new* experience for him (and since I had never heard of such a thing, it was becoming a new experience for me!). The massage parlor had been closed down. He also thought that *this* woman was a lesbian. Sooo, finally he got around to asking me if since I was a lesbian, would I be willing to give him an enema?

Well, no one at Boston University School of Theology had prepared me for this type of pastoral counseling inquiry. I continued to manage my facial expression while clearly and firmly telling him that I would not be willing to give him an enema. Also, that I was afraid that he did not have a very good understanding of what a lesbian was and that I was the pastor of a church. You know, a place where people sat in pews (or in our case, on folding chairs), and sang hymns, listened to a sermon, took communion, and went home. No enemas.

Actually, I was neither sarcastic or unkind. I felt sorry for him because he did not quite know how to get his needs met. On some level of human connection, I certainly understood. I told him to ask for help at a particular notorious bookstore in town that might have "referrals." (I bet the Lutheran pastor in town would not have been able to handle it that way!)

It did shake me up just a bit, though, to think of the many fantastic and unusual ways in which people viewed me (and other UFMCC or gay and lesbian clergy). In some ways, I feel like I am a modest, rather conventional person in my sexual needs and expression. In the seventies, especially, UFMCC clergy were often the only openly gay people in their city or town. This is *still* true in the more rural areas of the United States and in other countries. We had to know more than we might have wanted to know about lots of different sexualities, including (as I found out) information about enemas, sex toys, and bookstores. We spoke at colleges and health classes about our sexuality. We had to learn to speak publicly and comfortably about male and female anatomy and sex practices and how to handle homophobic, ignorant, hostile questions and comments. Over and over and over, we were taught as UFMCC clergy such things as how to put our books about sexuality at eye level in our offices so that parishioners would feel comfortable enough to talk with us about their sexuality. We were to model healthy and open attitudes about sexuality in our words and behavior.

Our parishioners *did* talk to us about sexuality a lot. We helped them come out, helped them talk about relationships, dating, sexual hang-ups, guilt, and fear. It was a kind of on-the-job training: everything you wanted to know and more—much more.

We had to try to help others heal and be comfortable with their sexuality while we were still discovering ours. It's amazing that people survived our early efforts.

I discovered that people are sometimes curious about the sex lives of clergy, including gay clergy. Sometimes people have assumed that I'm celibate (they think I'm a nun). This has been true for heterosexual Christian clergy as well. Troy used to say that when he was in the Church of God of Prophecy, heterosexual male members of his church would boast and hand out cigars when they had fathered a child. When a clergyman fathered a child, however, it was sort of a big secret. The child was a gift from God, as if sex had nothing to do with it.

Sometimes I am surprised by how easy it is for some people to talk about their sex lives and how difficult it is for others. For some people it is a lot harder and even more intimate to talk about their spiritual lives than it is to talk about their sex lives.

People also have incredible psychological *transference* issues with clergy—something I never learned about in seminary. And it's even more complex when you are a clergyperson in a sexual minority community. We are only beginning to know how powerful the role of a clergyperson is in our culture. My experience is that many people project onto me their fears and wishes about God. I think people do this to one degree or another with all clergy. I remember how hard it was for my mother to call the assistant pastor of the church we attended by his first name. He was her age and a kind, committed pastor. But clergy had this aura, this mystique. They weren't quite human in a relaxed sort of way, and maybe we didn't want them to be.

Because clergy are authority figures, they sometimes abuse that authority. Clergy also have a lot of difficulty managing the role. We think we're supposed to be perfect, have perfect families, never have doubts or weaknesses. Then we become hopelessly neurotic and wonder why. Or we become clergy because we're already that way!

People come to my office saying they are afraid of me and don't know why. Usually it's because they were afraid of a clergyperson from early in their life, or more probably, they are afraid of God. Or they fall in love with me, as they are falling in love with God. If they hate God, they sometimes hate me—after all, they can *see* me!

I have had to learn ways to hold up a mirror and help people see what their feelings about me *tell them about themselves.* Mostly, thankfully, the transference really has nothing to do with me! But, if I am needy or vulnerable, I may forget that fact.

I meet women and men all the time who were molested or abused by clergy or church leaders, some of whom were their parents or relatives. It is extremely hard for them to think that they can ever trust a religious authority figure again.

In many ancient cultures, gays and lesbians were *not* the objects of sexual projection, at least not in a negative sense. Native Americans call gays the "two-spirited people," meaning that they have both male and female *spirits.* Gays and lesbians were often seen as specifically blessed, not specifically cursed, as it were, "double" people rather than "half a man" or "half a woman."

So, how are we (modern gay men and lesbians and other sexual minorities) to see ourselves? As broken or as gifted? As both? As wounded healers of our culture's sexual repression-obsession polarity?

Gay men and lesbians are in a sense *forced* to work on our sexual healing just to survive in a homophobic culture. The world needs to know what we have been learning while we have been healing. Because what we have learned together and who we've become as we've learned it are the source of tribal gifts we long to offer to the world.

2

Boldly Exercising
Our Tribal Gifts

It is an audacious thing, on the eve of this millennial shift, to claim purpose and meaning for gay and lesbian people on the planet. How unbelievable to claim that those who were labeled sick, perverted, criminals, and the *foulest* of sinners could have personal, cultural, spiritual, yes, tribal gifts to share!

Part of moving beyond, way beyond apologetics is to assert that we are not an aberration. We are not a deformity, a mistake. We are not a genetic deficiency that needs to be tolerated or eradicated. We are not an annoying group of sex fiends seeking to legitimize perverted sex in the streets or the schoolyards.

We are a necessary part of creation, biologically, sociologically, spiritually. We, *like* others—not more or less than others—contribute to the wholeness, the multidimensionality of creation. *Neither creation nor the church is complete without us.*

Just to prove this point, some of us have had fantasies for years about what it would be like if all gay, lesbian, and transpeople were suddenly visible one day, if we all turned purple at once, and could not hide what a large minority we are. Or if we all just had a massive *walkout* one day. Now, when I claim that we have tribal gifts, it is not accurate or necessary to say that *all* gay and lesbian people have these gifts in equal measure or will necessarily choose to exercise them. But we seem to bear them together.

Gift Number 1
COMING OUT

First we offer the gift of *coming out*. The expression "to come out" is now used generically. It has already been co-opted by the dominant culture. It simply means to tell the truth, to *disclose* the hitherto private, hidden realities of our lives. People come out of the closet about all kinds of things these days, and sexuality is only one of them.

We gay and lesbian people were told we'd better lie to survive. But lying about our sexuality made us sick and afraid. And sometimes it inured us to the act of lying itself. I remember that in the bar culture of my early coming-out days, many people had aliases or nicknames. You just assumed you probably didn't know people's real names or where they really worked or the *real* story of their lives. One had to suspend judgment, not ask too many questions, and not get caught believing too many lies. For some, lying became positively an art form, almost as if in *requiring* us to lie, the world didn't deserve the truth from us. Sometimes, in sad surreal ways, there was more truth in our lying than in the facts that passed for truth. Before the days when sobriety began to heal us, we hardly even held each other accountable for the lying. A lot of it was harmless, anyway, or so we thought. However, we really didn't *like* ourselves when we were liars. So we've stopped lying. And we've paid dearly for the privilege of telling the truth. The truth is costly sometimes. But it is worth it. I'm not sure if I have ever met anyone who has ultimately regretted coming out, no matter what price he or she paid. That excludes, of course, those who died telling the truth about their sexuality.

Gays and lesbians can take courage in Jesus' words, "You shall know the truth, and the truth shall make you free" (John 8:32). Now, I know that he meant the truth about himself and who he was and is. But he said *the truth*. As if all truth *is* connected. Like there aren't different kinds of truth. That every truth is connected to and somehow supports every other truth. To follow Christ is to live in the truth, the whole truth. When the church, or any group or community, tells people that their participation depends on their willingness to lie about who they are, that is degrading and un-Christlike.

I have to confess that I have never understood people who went to seminary, got ordained, and pastored church while lying about their sexuality. I'm not only talking about not mentioning it, or hiding it from view but also blatantly denying it and lying about it. Such people deceive themselves into believing that this is "working for acceptance for gays and lesbians from within." From within what? From within a system of lies, which rewards lying and liars? My bias is that if you're not ready to come out, don't lie to get into seminary, to get ordained, or to get a job in a church. Wait until you can tell the truth and pay the price.

Lying is soul killing. Jesus did not ask us to lie in order to serve him, or God, or the church. Stop lying to yourself. It is the squandering of one of our most treasured tribal gifts: telling the truth, coming out when it is costly and can make a difference.

Why is it so hard to tell the truth in the church? I was present for the NCC general board meeting at which Marie Fortune made a presentation on issues of domestic violence in the context of the church. I watched the audience shut down, as if to say, "No, no, no, don't force us to hear this." The church does not want to hear the truth about its own complicity in violence—toward children, toward women, toward gays and lesbians or anyone else.

M. Scott Peck, in *People of the Lie*[1] did a lot to help me understand the connection between psychology and spirituality in the *diagnosis* of human evil. Peck says that the connection between lying and evil is a complex and profound one. When anyone asks or encourages someone to lie, they expose them to the *tools* of evil. In a sense, the truth is our spiritual equivalent of an immune system. To lie, to encourage lying as a strategy for handling problems, is to compromise our spiritual health. What might the connection be between diseases of the physical immune system and political and psychological oppression, including the rewarding of lying?

Conversely, to tell the truth is to increase our spiritual health. There is a saying in the therapeutic community: "We are only as sick as our secrets." I believe this is why gay and lesbian people need to tell their coming-out stories over and over again. After all the fear, lying, and hiding, telling the truth is positively sacramental. It is a rite of purification. Gay and lesbian people need to bathe and bask in the truth. I think I am most angry about the way in which homophobia at its core has exposed my people to the spiritual dis-ease of lies and lying. We are those who have suffered the oppression not so much perhaps of compulsory heterosexuality but of compulsive lying. The truth is making us free, and becoming truth tellers is a great gift we bring. Any state, church, institution, or individual who *encourages* gays, lesbians, or bisexuals to lie in order to survive (or to "succeed") contributes to the vulnerability of our people to disease and spiritual or psychological sickness.

Gift Number 2
SAME-SEX EROTICISM

Harry Hay calls homosexuality *subject-subject sexuality*[2]—*that is, as opposed to subject-object sexuality.* Now, the truth is that gay and lesbian people are just as capable as anyone of sexually objectifying another. And there are heterosexuals who in spite of patriarchy, manage relationships that are not objectifying. However, it is also true that sex in the Western patriarchal model has *more often than not* been about the eroticization of dominance and dependency. In a culture where men and women are *not* equal politically, most heterosexual sexuality, by definition, lacks the possibility of thoroughgoing mutuality and *informed* consent. That's an astonishing perspective that is at the heart of the feminist critique of culture.

I remember first hearing Freda Smith's poem "Dear Dora/Dangerous Derek Diesel Dyke."[3] She spoke of the special passion of touching and being touched by one whose body is *"as known as your own."* Ours can be a sexuality *not* distorted by the politics of patriarchy *to the degree* that heterosexuality still must be. Even within the very gay and comparatively nonhierarchical MCC church experience, there is—and must be—"church within the church" for lesbians. There has been something absolutely transformative about my relationships with powerful lesbian women who are taking the texts of Christianity, the sacred elements of our tradition, into our own *lesbian hands.* We are daring to uncover the connection of the erotic and the spiritual. The patriarchal, heterosexual model said that friendship was never sexy. But the eroticism of friendship is one of the wonderful tribal gifts we, as gay and lesbian people, bring.[4]

UFMCC holds regular clergy and leadership conferences in the United States to provide continuing education and mutual support. Really, though, these meetings were just an excuse to see our friends—to see the only other people in the world who were trying to make gay and lesbian church with our bare hands, no money, few resources. Except, of course, the resources of our courage and creativity. So we came to Camp Letts (YMCA) in the spring of 1982 in rural Maryland.

Partway through our several days together, someone from the YMCA noticed we were gay. The camp director with whom I had dealt with months before had moved on. The new director claimed to be totally surprised by who we really were. The camp "authorities" tried to make us leave. We had to interrupt our conference, which included the presence of Dr. Jim Nelson (author of *Embodiment,* and a pro-gay heterosexual seminary professor), to strategize about what would happen if they tried to remove us forcibly. They never did. But the whole experience was sometimes referred to as "Camp Letts Not."

That was one of the dramas that characterized the week, but there was another. Tensions between male and female leadership in UFMCC are always present and are more visible at certain times than at others. AIDS was just barely beginning to be understood and experienced at this point.

One of the dynamics that UFMCC leaders, both clergy and lay, always have to deal with is the heterosexism that creeps into our interactions. Because we are mostly gay and lesbian in UFMCC, we somehow imagine that we are *exempt* from the dangers of falling into heterosexist roles and patterns. Well, forget it! Whenever men and women in UFMCC work together, we have to face and identify the inevitable ways in which heterosexual patterns subconsciously emerge. Women assistant pastors in UFMCC will often find themselves playing the role of wife and mommy to men pastors. Or sometimes, just for variety's sake, women and men will switch roles, but the roles are still present.

One of the continuous strains in UFMCC has been the way women often fall into the role of taking care of the men. This can be either overt or subtle. In the age of AIDS, the pressures to take care of men have been incredible for women in our church. These pressures have driven some women away. But they existed prior to AIDS as well. Women were support staff, confidantes, for men. Sometimes we covered up for them. We defended them. We endured sexism from them. We educated them. But by 1982, a lot of the first generation of UFMCC lesbian clergy were already weary and discouraged. We were part of the first wave of women clergy in significant numbers in the history of the church! Many of us who were brilliant, creative, outstanding preachers and teachers felt like *failures* as leaders. We thought of this as a personal issue and not enough as a political, historical, and systemic problem. We blamed ourselves.

All the models of pastoring were male. All the books on how to pastor successfully were by men, for men. Somewhere, inside us, we felt we would never be good enough. And as proud lesbian she-women, we could never admit this to each other! We were tough! We were superwomen! Well, it was a lie. But a miracle happened at Camp Letts. We started talking about it. Like the old consciousness-raising groups of the early women's movement, we began talking about it. Not that we hadn't talked about sexism or inclusive language or all of that for a long time. But now we were talking *to each other*. So the women got together. And it made some of the men nervous. Some of us were thrilled that Dr. Nelson was there. However, we were also furious that when a straight white man said the very same things women had been saying for years, the men believed him! Suddenly, dealing with sexism was an *in* thing to do. So, the women withdrew. The men felt abandoned because, well, we abandoned them! Not forever, but for this time.

It started the first night when a few of us sat around in the dorm and one of the women just started crying about her anger, about a particular man she was having a conflict with, about things she felt hopeless about. We were in a circle, more or less, and I said, "Why don't we pray for you?" A novel idea—clergywomen actually praying for each other. Then I thought (emboldened now), "Why don't we kind of *lay hands on you* while we pray?" Uh-oh. This sounded a little weird. Isn't that the stuff Pentecostals did? But we did it. As we laid lesbian hands on her and began praying, something happened. A sound came from this woman's throat. An explosion of rage and pain, like a huge boil being excised. She sobbed in relief. We were stunned; we held her. It was sort of like we'd landed in the middle of someone else's group therapy session. Then, a little timidly, another lesbian clergywoman said, "Me next." She then told of the pain in her relationship with male colleagues, of her desire to pastor her own church, of her self-doubt. Her fears of her own radical feminism. So, we took turns praying for her. Once again the explosive rage and pain and relief.

I'm not entirely clear about the sequence of things after this point. We skipped dinner, after praying for two or three more women, and then took a break to go to worship services. But we couldn't wait to get back to our newfound experience.

We took over one dorm room, which meant that some women, who felt a little uneasy, decided to move. We tried to negotiate this so that no one would feel pressured to participate or excluded if they did want to participate. I took the lead in suggesting methods of doing the work. Along the way women would interrupt me, correct my mistakes, challenge me, take over from me. Laywomen and clergywomen came to the circle for healing. We eventually split into two circles, the demand was so great. At about three in the morning, my legs got so cramped and sore someone massaged them. But I felt like I had boundless energy and insight. I didn't need to drink or eat or sleep. We continued to pray, cry, laugh, hold each other, push, back off, try again, pray, heal for hours. All night long, in fact. Some attended part of the conference during the next day, some took naps. But then we got right back to it that night. Women came for healing of their careers, for their churches, but mostly for *themselves*. They began to talk about incest and abuse in ways I had never heard in my life. This prefigured all the revelations about childhood trauma that we would continue to hear about for the next ten years.

It was incredible, to say the least. We stopped worrying about the men. We turned the full force, power, and beauty of our spiritual energy and lives toward each other. We glowed with a delicious sense of having *spent* ourselves on each other. We lavished our time and love and touch and listening energy on each other's bodies and spirits. We *loved each other into speech and wholeness,* to amplify Nelle Morton's powerful phrase, "hearing into speech."[5]

There were moments of unbearable pain and stuckness, and women struggled with their fears of telling the whole truth—fears that if they told the truth, no one would believe them. That there would be no one to face it with them. That they would be alone and comfortless before the terror of their past. But we weren't alone. Women who had never laid hands on each other in prayer discovered how gifted we were. We experienced, we failed, we tried again. Some dropped out at different points, needing to rest, needing to grieve quietly, needing to give themselves safe space. No one interfered with the natural rhythms of our comings and goings. We were learning together: we tried to be compassionate. Lucia Chappelle, who participated in this experience, wrote the following new hymn to a familiar Christmas carol:

> *Silent night, raging night,*
> *Women weep at their plight.*
> *Circling nurturers comfort give*
> *Offering new kinds of spiritual gifts.*

Christ's new Body is born,
Christ's new Body is born.

Silent night, raging night,
Ne'er before, such a sight.
Christian lesbians hand in hand
Many theories, one mighty band.
Christ's new Body is born,
Christ's new Body is born.[6]

Many women looked at those days and nights as a turning point. Sometimes, when I think about it, I long for the intensity of that time — that time of a door opening. Some of the learning we did that night survives in the pastoral ministry of dozens of lesbians (and those they've mentored) who have continued to practice the healing arts over the last decade, especially in MCC.

I still think, though, that lesbians, and lesbian clergy in MCC (or the mainline churches) are reluctant to give to each other freely and completely. If we did, would we have to face all the pain of the deprivation we have experienced? Would we have to change the way we do everything? The way we feel about everything? There is something about the power of same-sex eroticism and camaraderie that is essential to the survival of our species in our world. Will the world or the church ever be able to receive that gift?

Gift Number 3
THE HUMOROUS MESSENGER

The "camp meeting" at Camp Letts I described in the previous section included raucous, uninhibited laughter. The healing properties of the physical activity of laughing have been well documented. Also well documented is the place of humor in the gay and lesbian culture.

I can think of no other protest or civil rights movement that has been accompanied by so much self-reflective humor. Mark Thompson writes about this as if it were almost an ethnic or genetic gay and lesbian characteristic in his essay "Children of Paradise: A Brief History of Queens."

The role of the fool, the trickster, the *contrary one* capable of turning a situation inside out, is one of the most enduring of all archetypes. Often cross-dressed, or adorned with both masculine and feminine symbols, these merry pranksters chase through history, holding up a looking glass to human folly.[7]

Holding up a looking glass to human folly. Sometimes humor is a response to the deadly power of tragedy, and its attempts to rob us of whatever joy or hope we possess. I can never forget the chant that would inevitably start at AIDS demonstrations when stone-faced police officers would arrive with their *prophylactic* yellow rubber gloves allegedly to keep themselves from *catching* AIDS while dragging us away to jail:

Your gloves don't match your shoes,
your gloves don't match your shoes!

Nothing about AIDS is funny. Or about the ignorance of the state and those who police it. But these chanters saw something funny in the fanciful, ignorant projections of their persecutors and made fun of them. That humorous way of turning the tables, of laughing in the face of insults, is simultaneously disarming and empowering.

Sacramento, California, is not known for its architectural or aesthetic beauty. So when hundreds of thousands of gay and lesbian protestors took over the capital in October of 1991, a clever chant mocking the stereotype of gay interior decorators was designed for the occasion:

We're here! We're queer! Let's redecorate!

One of the worst slanders directed toward gays and lesbians is that there is something inherently sad, lonely, and pitiful about our lifestyle. Or if there is any humor, it must be self-destructive, à la *Boys in the Band.* I've known thousands of gay and lesbian and bisexual people. The sad and lonely stuff is about oppression, not about sexuality. And the cure for that is coming out. Not that we don't have the same human complaints as everyone else, or our moments or moods, or neurotic friends!

While at the WCC General Assembly in Australia, we were treated to an evening of local Australian entertainment outdoors in a nearby park. Around three thousand people were present. About ten women from the

Christian Lesbian Collective came down from Sydney to support us, as did UFMCC folks from all over Australia and even a few people from New Zealand.

About thirty gays and lesbians sat together that evening on the lawn, amidst the three thousand, thrilled to have found each other in this big crowd on this beautiful continent. Those of us from the U.S. delegation were especially glad to have local gay and lesbian support for our presence at the WCC assembly.

We lounged on the grass together, sharing food, stories, clowning, showing off, introducing ourselves. I sat on the edge of our crowd next to a group of Korean Protestants. The man sitting next to me kept staring at me. We introduced ourselves, just as the program was beginning. He kept asking me questions, and I was a little annoyed at the time. So, probably in hopes of shutting down the conversation, I came out to him about UFMCC. But this only made him want to talk more. He wanted to know how I knew I was a lesbian. How my family felt about it. His questions felt awkward and intrusive. I finally asked him if we could arrange to have a longer conversation when it was easier to talk. He froze up at the suggestion.

And then I saw it, that familiar look of fear on his face, the look of a closeted gay person. I saw the desperate, strained, starved look, utterly humorless. He finally looked at me squarely and said, "Are you happy?"

I was going to answer just for myself, when a familiar sound caught my attention. It was Rev. Steve Pieters (delegate from UFMCC to the WCC) waving his muscled arms above his head in a kind of dance, just screaming with laughter about something, the way Steve can be hunky and nelly in the same moment. Everyone around him was in on the joke. They were laughing, hugging, gesturing wildly. These people who had been strangers just half an hour ago were having the time of their lives. I simply turned to my new friend and said, "Do they look happy?"

He looked over the scene (how could you miss it?) and said with the barest hint of a smile, "Yes."

"All of them are gay," I said.

His mouth just opened, wordless. "I see," he finally said. A little tear was in the corner of his eye. He then felt the need to turn back to his group for the rest of the evening. Though we passed each other many times during the assembly, he never looked at me, and I never spoke to him again.

Gift Number 4
OUR SHAMANISTIC GIFTS OF CREATIVITY, ORIGINALITY, ART, MAGIC, AND THEATER

One of the features in my "pastor's bag of tricks" is my magic act. It's not a real magic act. It's pure spoof, zany and a little bit mad. I started doing it at clergy conferences late at night when I was bored or when I felt my colleagues needed entertaining (sort of like my own version of USO). Then it just took on a life of its own! I occasionally perform it while visiting UFMCC churches or at congregational meetings.

I had loved dressing up and entertaining as a child. But not in the usual ways. Halloween was one of my favorite times. I'd usually dress in some kind of male drag, and then I'd dress up both my brothers and anything else that would stay still long enough. I wrote plays for our neighbor kids and loved to fantasize about being a performer. I didn't feel pretty or feminine, but I knew I could make people laugh. Mostly, I liked making myself laugh.

Once in a while, at serious moments in church, I have a nearly uncontrollable impulse to break into the magic act. Preaching and leading worship and consecrating the elements are all magical, and sometimes they just cry out for a *lighter touch*.

There is this persistent stereotype of "gays and the theater." Gay musical-comedy queens. Lesbian softball as performance art. One of the functions of gay and lesbian people is that we are the *in-between* ones. Judy Grahn says (in *Another Mother Tongue*) that in times of great social transformation and upheaval, we carry messages across gender lines. We are the *berdache* (Native American word for gay male or crossdresser) who patch up broken relationships. We are the *go-betweens* when there are disputes. We are the mediators of conflict and culture. In some ways, we are those who *intercede*, who create the pathway for change, for moving into the next era.

I had a wonderful opportunity to organize gay people to exercise this gift at the WCC General Assembly. One of the contexts of the assembly in Canberra in 1991 was the Gulf War. The WCC decided to hold a vigil to pray for the end of the war.

The U.S. delegation (the largest, with six hundred people) was to lead the closing hour of the vigil at six in the morning. (This was the Sunday morning before the emotional communion with the Lima Liturgy.) In

organizing for the vigil and our participation, Joan Campbell, general secretary of the NCC, had asked for a few volunteers. Well, I knew that at
meetings like this, no one really wants to volunteer for such things. All my
ecu-terrorist training kicked in, and I volunteered. Joan didn't flinch at all,
and I was appointed to the committee, which included some U.S. denominational leaders and WCC delegates.

Our planning committee met briefly outside the worship tent. Rev.
Kit Cherry had made some helpful suggestions. No one else seemed to
have any ideas. The rest of the committee's idea of the good use of an
hour of vigil time was to read more and more boring statements about
how we hate the war. So, to work we went! UFMCC folks (and some
closeted gay members in the group) suggested that we open with a Native
American drum call to worship. Then, after some brief testimony and
prayer, we could invite people forward for anointing with oil.

We decided to use oil because it was a biblical symbol for healing
and for *brotherhood and sisterhood*. We chose Psalms 133:1–2:

> And very good and pleasant it is when brothers and sisters live
> together in unity!

> It is like the precious oil on the head, running down upon the
> beard, on the beard of Aaron.

This would also allow us to use, with a sense of irony, a symbol of
the painful reality that the buying and selling of *oil* was at the heart of this
horrible war.

People seemed to like our suggestion, mostly because they were too
stressed and tired to come up with anything else. Those participating then
told me they didn't exactly know *how* to anoint with oil, so we did a practice session. Actually, I didn't remember anyone ever teaching me how to
do it. It was like I was born knowing how to do this. We suggested using
the conference theme as an anointing blessing, "Come, Holy Spirit,
renew your whole creation," although I explained that the pastors might
want to be free just to pray or bless freestyle, if they felt so moved. Most of
them looked utterly terrified by that suggestion.

Then we began to search for blessed oil. No one seemed to have
any. I had certainly not brought any with me from the United States. No
one on the worship team staff at Canberra had any or knew where to find
some. Finally, one of the staff "gophers" told me he knew where to get oil!
Kit Cherry and I decided to use her empty film cases as makeshift oil vials,

and we got UFMCC people to hold the vials for the blessors during the time of anointing (so that they wouldn't get distracted by the fact that the oil was in film cases!).

I waited forever for this guy to come back with the oil. Finally, he found me: he had the happy look of one who has successfully completed his mission. He handed me a bottle of baby oil. Baby oil! I could just imagine how distracting it would be to be anointing or anointed with the smell of baby oil all around. Can you imagine having this solemn service in the WCC worship tent—and then anointing people who suddenly feel like taking a nap? "They didn't have any olive oil?" I whined. "Olive oil?" he said blankly. Holy oil is not supposed to smell like babies' bottoms! But ever resourceful, our gay spirit rose to the occasion! Steve Pieters just happened to have some frankincense with him. Sure—don't you know people who carry frankincense around with them all the time?!

So I mixed the baby oil and frankincense and put the mixture in the film cases. This did change the smell—well, at least a little. Then we blessed the oil in preparation for the service.

I was comforted by the belief that not very many people would show up at six in the morning for this event. WRO-ONG! Probably over five hundred people were there when it started.

The drumming began, the prayers were said, and then I read the Psalm and talked about how we might transform and restore the image of oil for ourselves that day. How we *needed* to anoint each other and the whole world that morning. And we did. Joan Campbell, Bishop Edmund Browning, myself, and six or seven others began anointing the crowd while an African-American seminarian woman sang, "There is balm in Gilead, to make the wounded whole."

When the bishop of Baghdad (Baghdad, Iraq, that is) came forward that morning to be anointed by Bishop Browning, the room just broke open in solidarity with our pain and our helplessness. Some were too overcome to keep anointing. They collapsed in sobs, on the floor, in their chairs. People wept, prayed, hugged, as the mournful sounds of that spiritual continued. Gay and lesbian delegates to the WCC came forward for anointing, hugged me, and came out to me on the spot. The tent was filled with the power and presence of the God who wanted us to transform not only the WCC but the world, who makes a way where there is no way, who longs to turn swords into plowshares.

Many people spoke to me about how moving and *right on* that liturgy was. I felt a bit mystified. To me, it felt so familiar, so ordinary. Not the context, of course. That was overwhelming and extraordinary. But the liturgy, the anointing. The *sensing of the moment,* inventing liturgy to move and express the fullness of the moment, was what we experience frequently at Metropolitan Community Churches. It made me realize how much I take UFMCC and the gifts of gay and lesbian people for granted. And I loved the *subtext* of the baby oil and frankincense and film case mischief. The humor and joy and the making do with what we have. As Harry Hay says, "turning hand-me-downs into visions of loveliness."[8]

There is also that strange phenomenon we affectionately call our *gaydar*: the radar that across a crowded room often allows gay and lesbian people to identify each other. It is not foolproof, mind you.

At one very tense NCC meeting (in Cleveland, Ohio, 1992), UFMCC and members of the gay and lesbian caucuses pooled our resources and set up a hospitality suite to welcome NCC delegates, create some safe space for ourselves, and have all our literature available. Not many NCC folks showed up. But I began to notice that people were disappearing from our visitors' table and excusing themselves to "person" the suite. Soon the word came back that although the NCC was not availing itself of our hospitality, the gay and lesbian hotel employees were! There was a party going on up there, and as the employees ate up all our food, MCC people shared with them the good news that God does love gay and lesbian people. From that moment on, during the course of the NCC meeting, I could often look across the ballroom and see hotel employees serving coffee to bishops and delegates while rolling their eyes at us!

Harry Hay also reports that "the biologist, Julian Huxley, over half a century ago pointed out that no negative trait [and we know, in biology a negative trait is one that does not reproduce itself] ever appears in a given species millennia after millennia unless it in some way serves the survival of that species. We are a species variant with a particular characteristic adaptation in consciousness whose time has come!"[9]

Gift Number 5
MADE IN THE IMAGE OF GOD

On a recent visit to MCC Minneapolis, I witnessed a new phenomenon: a gay men's softball team. Now, lesbian softball is legendary and an undisputed part of lesbian culture in the United States. But a gay male team? MCC Minneapolis has three teams: two are lesbian, and one is composed of young gay men with shaved, punk haircuts, earrings, and muscled bodies (who want to be lesbians when they grow up?). They have a very cute team name—The Altared Boys—and great T-shirts that say:

> MADE IN THE IMAGE OF GOD—
> not necessarily
> YOUR IMAGE OF GOD!

I believe that gay and lesbian people contribute to a more complete picture of God. If human beings are made in the image of God, then that includes gay men and lesbians. What about us rounds out the image, do you suppose? The God who invented truth, who is always *coming out* (another synonym for revelation?).

I've always felt that God has a sense of humor. Much of the humor in the Bible has long since been lost in the translation, quite literally. But "he [*sic*] who sits in the heavens laughs" (Psalms 2:4). Sometimes I think God plays with me, and we have had some private jokes. For a long time I was afraid to say that out loud. It seemed so grandiose and self-absorbed. I was too sophisticated really to think of God in those affectionate, personal terms.

Sometimes it's just the incredible, illogical synchronicity of things. During one of the worst years of my life (1977), I was driving in the wee hours of the morning from Fort Wayne, Indiana, to Detroit, Michigan, coming home from a preaching engagement. I had recently ended a four-year relationship that had been deteriorating for some time. In addition, there were some nightmarish events and problems that had affected the church. I was exhausted, demoralized, and felt, in the words of Al-Anon literature, "unwanted, unloved, and alone" —and sorry for myself. I turned on the radio and heard a new song: it was Billy Joel's "Just the Way You Are." Later I would learn that Billy was from my home town of Hicksville, New York. Billy's Long Island accent was poignantly familiar and tugged at me on that lonely road—and the words, the saxophone. I changed the station, and the song came on again. That startled me. A new popular tune, I guess! I listened to the words again, full of sweet assurances. I began to have this eerie feeling of not being alone in the car. I could feel the tightness in my chest relax and the sadness and depression lift for a moment. In a little while I turned the dial again—and there it was again. This time it scared me. OK, it's you. You love me. The tears came, I started laughing, "OK, OK, OK. OK, God, you love me. You want to talk to me."

But it didn't stop there. It seemed that every time I walked into a room where a radio was playing, it was on. Other people even noticed it. This went on for months and months. Paula and I were walking through Boston Commons the following summer (we had met just three weeks after my drive from Fort Wayne that night), and a guy was playing that song on a xylophone! Even today, that sweet song appears and interrupts me, especially if I'm feeling a little unwanted, a little unloved, or alone. I don't pretend to understand it; I don't, but I'm trying to accept it. The words and tune just sort of befriended me, as a precious gift from a God who thinks I'm too sophisticated for my own good a lot of the time.

Now, it's one thing to claim that God might actually tolerate or accept gay and lesbian people; it's quite another to claim that people might be able to see God in and through *us* sometimes.

Our church, MCC L.A., had a sort of nervous breakdown about this in the fall of 1989. It was a difficult time. I had been on a thirty-day fast (to pull the church together and call attention to the fact that we might be in danger of losing our church property partly because banks won't give mortgages to churches, much less gay and lesbian churches), followed by gall bladder surgery. I had been out for seven weeks. The church had been worried about me. We were successful in saving the property, able to move into the building and to raise enough funds to keep us going for a while, until we finally got that new loan years later.

But MCC L.A. folks were *weary*. A young, brilliant student clergy was writing the liturgy and preaching for my first Sunday back, All Saints Day. He and a small committee had designed a very innovative gay and lesbian All Saints' liturgy that they knew might be a *little* controversial. Jim thought I had seen it before it "went to press." I had not. Ten minutes before the services began, deacons came roaring into my office telling me I had to *pull* the liturgy. I finally got to see it. In the call to worship it said, "O lesbian God, O gay and gracious God . . . " It was not my style to pull the rug out from under student clergy, even if I think they're being wrong-headed about something. I knew that some of the more conservative and evangelical gay and lesbian MCC Los Angeles folks would be disturbed by these words, but I didn't think it was a matter of life and death. So I got up at the beginning of the service, tried just to acknowledge the conflict and to help us relax and get through it.

Well, it just got worse. I had no idea how frightening and devastating it would be for some people to hear this liturgy. Some folks were oblivious, some loved the liturgy, but many were simply horrified at the phrase "lesbian God."

Part of the problem was that those from evangelical and conservative backgrounds often have difficulty with metaphorical language about God that you cannot document in the Bible. And another part of it was leftover guilt, shame, and doubt about how God feels about us.

I tried to say, "Yes, but you call God the *rock* of your salvation, and you *know* God is not really a rock. . . ." But for them there was a difference between familiar metaphors and this new one. They were partly terrified that someone (some visitor to our church, perhaps) would believe that they were not worshiping the God of the Bible, the God of Jesus, but that somehow this phrase meant they were worshiping their own sexuality. This had been an early stereotype of UFMCC. That we were not really a church, that we were a cover for a gay "social club" or sex club, or that we were just using the veneer of "church" to justify ourselves. All these were (and still are) painful misrepresentations of our church, which we continually battled. Also we struggled not to be so exclusively gay or lesbian—so we were afraid that heterosexual people would not feel welcomed and included by this liturgy. For some people, the articulation of "gay God" seemed like self-worship, like blasphemy, like a betrayal. Too exclusive, too *out there*.

Interestingly enough, however, it was "lesbian God" and not "gay God" that was attacked. At least with the metaphor "gay God," God was still male. That told me a lot.

I tried to communicate, counsel, and teach about metaphorical language about God. For some of the people who had been upset, this helped. For others it didn't. Some wanted me to punish Jim, the student clergy, which I would not do. Some used this event to dump all their fears and angers about the fast on me. Some wanted me to say that the lesbian God thing was a *terrible* mistake. I did believe that not preparing the congregation for that liturgy was a tactical mistake, and I would have done it differently if I'd had the opportunity. But I could *not* say what they wanted to hear: that comparing God to a lesbian or a gay man was a terrible *mistake.*

When I tried to help them hear that God is everything *good* that gay and lesbian people are, just as God is everything good that a rock is, or a lily of the valley, or a shepherd, it just didn't get through.

I tried to say that *we* are not less like God than a rock, or a tree, or a heterosexual person. But when I tried to communicate this, I often hit a brick wall—a brick wall called internalized homophobia. My efforts to name it were met with scoffing, denial, and incredibly painful statements such as "calling God a lesbian is the worst thing you could ever call him [*sic*]." This was spoken by a lesbian.

It broke my heart, and it drove Jim away from the church for perhaps the last time (he'd been Lutheran before he came to UFMCC). It took a long time for us to understand and process that trauma—really to understand how deep the wounds of internalized self-hatred are in our community. When we are very affirming about being gay or lesbian, or about being made in the image of God, we simply scare ourselves to death. Somehow, when we see our sexuality as *part of our connection to the image of God,* we feel we will be accused of making God in our image. (Or we accuse ourselves before anyone else has a chance to!)

OUR SPIRITUAL GIFTS

These, then, are some of our gifts: *truth telling,* most especially in the form of coming out; *same-sex erotic friendship* as a cultural antidote to the eroticization of dominance and dependence; being willing to be the *humorous messenger; creativity and magic;* and *contributing to a fuller image of God.* All of these, in their own way, are spiritual gifts. But are there other more explicitly spiritual gifts that gay men and lesbians might give to the church? What might be some positive elements in gay and lesbian spirituality?

Pro-life Spirituality

I would like to use Mary Daly's method of the "righteous rip-off" for this concept! It seems to me that those who have taken the label "pro-life" are often pro-life only up until birth. (They don't support a nuclear freeze, an end to capital punishment, gun control, or universal day care, for example.) Also, gay and lesbian people have been viewed negatively because we don't reproduce—as if that makes us somehow antifamily, antilife. The fact that we don't reproduce without a great deal of extra effort and inconvenience most of the time means that when we *do* have children, we want them. And we are willing to care for them. Also, many gay and lesbian people raise other people's offspring, as we always have. (How many straight people were raised by "unmarried" aunts or uncles, many of whom were gay or lesbian?)

In addition, gay and lesbian people are wonderful aunts, uncles, and godparents to millions of children. We assist parents, providing backup parenting, adult supervision, and companionship for their children. Also, gay and lesbian people are not just human-centered—we dote on our pets and are historically an *earth-friendly* tribe. We are overrepresented in the helping and caring professions and in environmental and other life-centered movements. The fact that we do not ordinarily reproduce as a result of our sexual activity means that we are helping in the efforts to control population! Overpopulation is never pro-life: it is pro-poverty. We are indeed a people who are *singing for our lives,* who know that silence equals death and that action equals life. Reclaiming our love for life and our life-giving self-image is a great spiritual gift we can give to the world and to the church.

An Irreverent Piety

We are probably in a good position to hold up the mirror of reflection to the church especially. We are, after all, the "in-between" folks. We've been both very much on the inside of the church (as its organists, choir directors, pastors, board members, deacons, bishops) and on the outside, trying to learn how to "embrace the exile," in John Fortunato's famous phrase.

At the same WCC meeting in Canberra, Steve Pieters tells of a conversation with an Australian Anglican. Steve was wearing a lavender clergy shirt and waiting in the lobby for a meeting to begin. An older Australian delegate approached him and said, "In our church, when someone wears that color clergy shirt it means they are a bishop!" To which Steve replied, "In our church, it means we are gay!" (That's not entirely accurate, but

Steve was being playful.) The woman did *not* skip a beat and rejoined, "I guess that's what it means in our church, too!"

Over the years people have sometimes commented on my irreverence. Frankly, I hold back a lot. Not because I think God will be offended but because I don't want to be more misunderstood than I already am. But I see irreverence mostly as *play.* When you really trust someone, you can kid them. You know how far to go. I feel like I have that kind of relationship with God.

My grandfather, part Indian and part reluctant Baptist, had that kind of relationship with God. In one of the few private conversations we ever had, he told me on the way home from church one day that I "should not take this church stuff too seriously." He went on to say that it seemed to him that anyone (namely, Jesus) who would change water into wine must have enjoyed himself now and then. Don't let them take all the joy out of life. "Them," I figured, meant preachers and other religious folks. My grandfather already knew that I was attracted to this "church stuff," and he worried about me because of it! I think he is still a source of my irreverence and my desire for a lighter touch at times.

Church ought to be a place where people are loved, comforted, and uplifted, but also a place where we are shocked, shaken and turned around. Also, a place where we can laugh. I'm not talking about giggling or chuckling but deep, roll-in-the-aisles laughing. Not every Sunday perhaps, but frequently. In the Middle Ages, it was the custom to begin every Easter Sunday morning sermon with a joke. It was the day above all days when we were to laugh in church, to laugh at the devil who had been utterly defeated and outsmarted.

In most UFMCC churches, there will be laughter—in some, a great deal of laughter. Maybe this started because many of us were nervous about being in church and being ourselves all at the same time. Some UFMCC services, even in the sophisticated 1990s, can have just a hint of the barroom rowdiness that is a leftover from the time when noisy, crowded bars were the only places we were more or less permitted to meet. For some people, UFMCC is the only place where they are out of the closet or where they can hold their lover's hand in public. And we have endless arguments about that all the time. What is proper church etiquette in a gay and lesbian church that is open to everyone? Why do people sometimes behave like they are in a bar when they are in a church? Well, it's a cultural thing, I think. And it helped make UFMCC, at least in its first decade or so, a little less *threatening* to people who were frightened of or allergic to too much church.

Part of the theological menu available at UFMCC includes a healthy dose of charismatic theology, worship, and piety, hopefully without the accompanying narrowness and fundamentalism. This is because UFMCC's roots are thoroughly working class, and many of our members are from that background.

Every year MCC Long Beach, California, hosts a charismatic conference. I try never to miss it. There is nothing quite like seeing several hundred gay, lesbian, and bisexual charismatics (or those dabbling in it for the weekend) worshiping, weeping, singing, holding, sweating, and hugging each other, unashamed of their love for God and each other.

One year, the year after the "lesbian God" controversy at MCC Los Angeles—also the year I had just lost thirty pounds (and a gall bladder) in a fast—I attended the Saturday evening service at the charismatic conference. I was having a difficult time. I was recovering from surgery and a church fight. There were many in the church, my family, and the Fellowship who did not understand why I had fasted. I had had a lot of support, but I had also been through a lot of hell that year. The guest speaker was a powerful, heterosexual woman, Erla Duncan, known in charismatic circles for her gifts of knowledge, prophecy, and healing. She is a short woman with a big voice and a rather imposing presence. Erla had taken a lot of heat in her ministry for not condemning gay and lesbian people and for being willing to teach and preach in our churches. I met her for just a few minutes before the service. It was amazing to watch her. She'd call on you (in front of three hundred people!) and just start talking about you to you or prophesying about you. Neither you nor she had any idea of what was going to happen. She'd talk, and people would begin to cry, or shout, or pray. That night she pointed to me. I stood, feeling like a very nervous six-year-old. She prophesied that I would be given opportunities to speak in arenas of national importance, and lots of other things. But then she paused and said, in a booming voice, "But, oh, the devil hates you! In fact, they have weekly meetings about you!" When she said that to me, my face reddened, but the crowd roared. And then I began to laugh. And I couldn't stop laughing. In fact, I laughed all the way home that night. I laughed on the way to church the next day. I laughed about it for weeks, off and on. What a great, sweeping, overwhelming relief!

I did not grow up with theological language that ever talked much about the *devil*, and when I first encountered it in people at UFMCC, it made me nervous. I still haven't sorted out all those issues. But I do know that God has enemies, whatever you choose to call them or it. And if I am God's friend, those forces and folks will also see me as their enemy. I do believe that if you "resist the devil, he [*sic*] will flee from you" (Jas. 4:7); but first, he or she will try to make life miserable for you. Once I was willing to face that *some* of the hell I had been going through was because I had resisted evil, because I had tried to move some terribly stubborn mountains, I was so relieved. Like all folks (including ancient shamans) who do such things, I had to pay a price for it. But ultimately, I was and am safe. Erla Duncan's word to me that night was God's word to me, delivered in the kind of humorous, irreverent way I could recognize. Weekly meetings! Hah!

A *Spirituality That Makes Creative Use of Suffering*

I remember reading Edmund Bergler's book *Homosexuality: Disease or Way of Life?* when I was in college.[10] Bergler's answer to his own question was definitely "disease"! One of the *seven* (deadly?) character defects that he felt were common to all homosexuals was *injustice collecting*. This meant that we stayed up at night obsessing and whining about all the terrible things people had done to us. Of the seven, this is the only one I remember. Perhaps because it stung the most, as if there might be a grain of truth in it for me. Something else to dislike myself for. It touched on all my repressed pain, hurt, and memories of suffering. Did I cherish those memories just a little too much? Was that cherishing a response to never having been able to express them, to air them? They were a part of my *secret life*.

I also did have enough sophistication even then to see that Bergler was playing the blame-the-victim game once again. Homosexuals don't have real suffering, he was saying—it's all either imagined or exaggerated, or they've brought it on themselves and, therefore, it is suffering they deserve.

We deserve to suffer for our "crimes against nature." And because nature herself didn't seem to punish us enough (although, of course, some have wanted to see AIDS this way), the church and state has to do it for her. But was it not a crime against nature to burn millions of women accused of witchcraft in the Middle Ages, or millions of gay men and lesbians in the Holocaust?[11]

I feel very reluctant to assign meaning to human (or other) suffering—like those who say that everything that happens is "God's will." I fully and completely understand the human desire to do that, to explain, justify, *package* suffering—especially to give suffering a purpose. But I think that most suffering is terribly arbitrary and that part of its painfulness is that much of it is unnecessary, preventable, and pointless.

Nevertheless, suffering may have its *uses.* In a way, I view suffering as spiritual compost. It becomes the soil in which many things may grow: bitterness, rage, despair, loneliness, hopelessness; or conversely, compassion, tenderness, openness, kindness, forbearance, patience.

What grows in our compost heaps of accumulated suffering? It is, after all, what grows, not the compost itself, that may have meaning, purpose, even redemptive value. And in saying that, I do not mean to imply anything in the way of an equation. The juice may not always be worth the squeeze. Or more crudely and irreverently, the screwing you're getting may not be worth the screwing you're getting. Not all suffering is good compost. But now and then we get a glimpse of a divine economy that may be large enough to incorporate and heal the suffering of the world. Every now and then.

I met Lew Adams shortly after I became pastor of MCC L.A. He was an "old-timer" in two senses: he was almost seventy years old, and he had been a member of MCC L.A. for at least fifteen years.

Lew came to my office, troubled because he hadn't been baptized and felt he should be. But, he told me, he didn't feel worthy, and he had a hang-up about it. It was a requirement that you be baptized in order to be a member of UFMCC, but somehow that had been overlooked when Lew had become a member.

Lew's best friends frequently "pestered" Lew about this baptism thing, and, well, he thought he probably should do it. But Lew told me he couldn't because it reminded him of his father. Lew's father had been a crazy, abusive, religious fanatic, who starved his children, subjected them to countless beatings, and who had a very bizarre sectarian fundamentalist "Christian" theology. Lew had hated his father. He'd had to eat out of garbage cans as a child. He ran away at age fourteen and went to the Philippines. When he was old enough, he joined the navy. He ended up becoming a victim of the March of Bataan in the Philippines. During his captivity, he personally buried hundreds of soldiers who had died of starvation. Lew was convinced that the only reason he survived was because of his early *childhood training through suffering*. He could eat garbage, he could do whatever it took to survive. Lew volunteered for many things at the church and had a small circle of friends. He was compassionate, serious, and could not bear for anyone to be hungry.

A few years after our conversation, he was diagnosed with AIDS. One day, when he was close to death, he told me that the last few years of his life, with AIDS, had been some of the happiest. He told me he felt fortunate to be one of the few older people with AIDS he had encountered. That unlike so many, he had lived a long life. But what amazed and shocked Lew were all the friends who had rallied to his side during his illness—mostly gay and lesbian friends from MCC L.A. who loved him, prayed with him, kept him company, took care of him. He loved coming to church and felt such a peace and joy there. Finally, just a week or so before his death, he told me he was ready to be baptized. Several friends gathered around, and there was not a dry eye. Lew had a kind of transcendent joy and presence in those last days. There was also the occasional flash of old anger or grief. It took him a whole lifetime to heal from that religious abuse, but he made it. And AIDS became a means of grace for him, as he learned to receive just a portion of the love he had offered to so many all his life. I will never forget his humility and gratitude in the face of horrific suffering. What brilliant flowers grew from this compost of suffering.

Finally, I also believe that gays and lesbians have another gift to give to the church: a new *lens on the Bible*.

3

Texts of Terror

THE POLITICS OF
BIBLICAL INTERPRETATION

My friend Bob Galloway, a rural UFMCC pastor, says
that he thinks Holy Communion should always contain
a warning label, because this sacrament, rightly experienced, has transformative power and can place unforeseen demands on us.

I think the same can be said of the Bible. It is my hope that some
people who read this book will have never read the Bible. At a lecture
recently, one of the participants said to me, "You are so irreverent, you
make me want to read the Bible."

Most gay and lesbian people do not want to read the Bible. And I
don't blame them! They assume, like most people, that the Bible is not
exactly our friend or best supporter! That it is, at best, irrelevant to our
lives or, at worst, our enemy, condemning us to hell.

Robert Goss, in *Jesus Acted Up*,[1] first used the title of Phyllis Trible's
book, *Texts of Terror*,[2] to identify the six Bible passages quoted by fundamentalists and uninformed Christians to condemn homosexuality.[3] These
have become our "texts of terror." Their existence, combined with millennia of misinterpretation, has formed a powerful wedge, keeping lesbians and gay men from any hope of being able to celebrate and
experience the story and poetry of the Bible.

If we dust off an old Bible or actually go out and buy a new one to
read, it *should* come with a warning label. There are rich veins of tradition

and story to be mined in the Bible—and there are also *minefields*. A lot of the "easier-to-read" introductions to the Bible and other helpful reading materials are not accessible, or biblical reference books are written from theological orientations that are sexist or otherwise oppressive; or they are so incredibly technical that you have to have a Ph.D. in theology to read them.

This frustrated me. Because even people who are not sure they believe in God could benefit from knowing something about the Bible. The Bible is still used politically, especially in the United States. Traditional interpretations of the Bible still inform popular notions about God, and these ideas influence politics, personal relationships, values, and attitudes in our culture.

For gay and lesbian people this is especially crucial. I want not only to disarm the Bible bashers but to find a way to *turn their swords (Bible stories and passages) into plowshares*. I even thought of calling this section of the book "Rescuing the Bible from Heterosexual Bigots," following a little bit in John Shelby Spong's footsteps.[4]

One of the most powerful experiences I have as a pastor is the privilege of training UFMCC student clergy and deacons in how to consecrate communion. (Deacons are an order of lay ministry in UFMCC; they may perform many of the rites and sacraments of the church, as well as preach, teach, and provide lay pastoral care for members.) It is positively redemptive to watch gay men and lesbians take the elements of communion representing the Body and Blood of Christ *into their own hands*, quite literally. Their experience of inclusion and empowerment is intoxicating and healing. As they touch the bread and juice, say the ancient words, and preside over this liturgy for the sake of their own people, they become transformed. They will never be the same.

This is also true with the Bible. I hear story after story of gay and lesbian adults walking into church supply and bookstores for the first time, finding it difficult to believe that they are actually there. Asking my advice on what translation to buy. Touching and holding a book that they have always believed was a source of pain and condemnation. Daring to open the book, hoping and hungry. Watching the joy as they begin to appreciate its complexity and as they mine the treasures and negotiate the minefields.

I really appreciate Virginia Mollenkott's chapter on "Building Bridges Between Interpretative Communities" from her book *Sensuous Spirituality*.[5] Among the important things that she says, this is most helpful in trying to develop gay and lesbian biblical interpretative method:

Every human being belongs to an interpretative community. Inevitably, we must communicate from within specific situations. And to be in a specific situation is to be possessed by a *"structure of assumptions, of practices understood to be relevant in relation to purposes and goals that are already in place.".* . . In his groundbreaking 1980 study called "Is There a Text in This Class?: The Authority of Interpretative Communities," Stanley Fish explains that "the self does not exist apart from the communal or conventional categories of thought that enable its operations (of thinking, seeing, reading)." Because *all "conceptions that fill consciousness . . . are culturally derived,"* there is no such thing as a wholly free consciousness. Nobody's interpretive acts are exclusively her own; our interpretations fall to us by virtue of our position "in some socially organized environment."[6]

Mollenkott identifies herself with the "liberation theology" interpretative community and builds bridges with evangelicals, feminists, and others. She further states:

> In each community [of biblical interpretation], there is an (often unwritten and unspoken) agreement about what constitutes evidence and what is irrelevant or beside the point. . . . It is futile for us to fling accusations at each other about creating "a canon within the canon" (that is, emphasizing some Scriptures and jumping over others), because every interpretative community tends to do the same.[7]

When gay and lesbian people first started publicly challenging the traditional reading of the Bible, we were (and still are) vilified for reading and interpreting the Bible for ourselves. As an example, I would like to quote from a letter we received at UFMCC headquarters, not from a fundamentalist but from a member of the Central Committee of the World Council of Churches in 1993:

> I was aghast and appalled at the thinly veiled attempt to twist the Bible and Christian message in what seems to me to be a dishonest, heretical, and even blasphemous manner. I wonder why those of you who believe in homosexuality are straining to give it some semblance of respectability by deliberately misinterpreting the Christian message. I do not have the time to take you up one by one on the heresies and blasphemies contained in the documents you sent. . . . I,

as well as all those who read their Bibles without jaundiced eyes, am firmly convinced that HOMOSEXUALITY is both a SIN and an ABNORMALITY."

So, are we stuck in simply reading the Bible in the context of our interpretative communities? Is there no *objective* way to read the Bible? I think there is not a *neutral* place from which to read and interpret the Bible. However, as Mollenkott states, there is the hope of building bridges across interpretative communities.

Some of our communities are very new at this work of biblical interpretation. We need to be free to experiment, try on new ideas, even make mistakes, change our minds, say the outrageous, without being molested or labeled "heretical" or "blasphemous."

The scare words of *heresy* and *blasphemy* are painfully familiar to women, gays, and lesbians. They are the tools of white heterosexual male domination, especially in the areas of theology and biblical interpretation. They are about control and intellectual terrorism.

I look forward (well, mostly) to the opportunities indeed to take on our critics in "one-by-one" dialogue about our particular claims about the Bible and Christianity that they find heretical and blasphemous.

One of the things I hope to accomplish, however, is to *move away from just defending ourselves* (and our right to engage in biblical texts so that they are not *just* a source of pain for our people) into a more proactive reading of the Bible. Elisabeth Schussler-Fiorenza, in her groundbreaking work *In Memory of Her*, states, "The explorations of this book begin therefore with the hope of moving away from the pervasive apologetic that characterizes most treatments of women in the Bible to a historical-critical reconstruction of women's history and women's contributions to early Christian beginnings."[8]

Moving away from apologetics to "historical-critical reconstructions" is what I hope to *begin*, more than accomplish. For gay and lesbian people, this is more than just a matter of reevaluating our role. We first have to *back up and just begin to document our existence!*

John Boswell has done this quite remarkably in his book *Christianity, Social Tolerance and Homosexuality* and, more recently, in *Same-Sex Unions in Pre-Modern Europe.*[9] John describes his research for the newer book as this amazing process of following a hunch, looking for hints of the existence of actual same-sex couple ceremonies in the Middle Ages. As he followed his hunches, the evidence appeared mysteriously, miraculously. Once he began to believe in the existence of these couples, it was as if they began to appear and to document themselves!

I feel a kinship to John's work in my own work of uncovering our existence in the Bible. One has to break through the barrier of homophobic perception first and *really believe we have always been here.* When we do that, our faith is rewarded. It was pure delight to read the Vatican's (and Eastern Orthodox) mutterings and mumblings and whinings about how Boswell's research couldn't possibly prove what it clearly proves! Gays and lesbians have existed and have been "doing it" (with the church's blessing, apparently) in other less homo-hating times! What has not been done enough, however, is even to document the presence and role of gay, lesbian, and bisexual people in the Bible, and in a positive sense. Mostly, we've been content with trying to prove that the Bible does not unilaterally condemn all homosexual behavior and relations.

There is a certain tension about simply facing the patriarchal context and homophobic possibilities of the Holy Bible. For if it was written in a patriarchal, homophobic context, then it is not only the interpretation of the Bible but also the content itself that contributes to oppressive ideas about us. Is our purpose to refute what the Bible actually says about gays and lesbians? Or to uncover and expose *assumptions* about what is really said? To *redeem* the Bible or to *redeem our community?* Or can both be done? And can one be done without the other?

Fiorenza takes what may be or may appear to be a very radical position in relationship to the Bible when she says:

> A feminist theological hermeneutics [interpretative method] having as its canon the liberation of women from oppressive patriarchal texts, structures, institutions, and values maintains that—if the Bible is not to continue as a tool for the patriarchal oppression of women— only those traditions and texts that critically break through patriarchal culture and "plausibility structures" there the theological authority of revelation. The "advocacy stance" of liberation theologies cannot accord revelatory authority to any oppressive and destructive biblical text or tradition. Nor did they have any such claim at any point in history; such critical measure must be applied to all biblical texts, their historical contexts, and theological interpretations and not just to the texts on women.[10]

In plainer English: a feminist interpretation of scripture will be upfront concerning being selective about which texts will be authoritative *for* women *about* women. Scripture passages that oppress women are not now, nor have they ever been holy or authoritative for women. Since women did not have the resources or power to write or study the Bible, or to vote on the canon of scripture, we have to do that now, after the fact.

This particular political stance in biblical interpretation presses the alarm buttons of those who feel it is blasphemy to distinguish among biblical texts, or to be willing to ignore some. It might also seem to validate the claims of those who accuse feminists, liberation theologians, and gays and lesbians of "picking and choosing" only the parts of the Bible that support our point of view. Of course what Mollenkott and Fiorenza and others say is that we've *all* been doing that *all* along! Only now, at last, it's our turn.

However, I have this incredible picture: every "interpretative community," scissors in hands, cutting out the parts of the Bible that are oppressive. Then we all get together and see what's left. That of course is how some conservatives view this "canon within the canon" idea. However, the truth is, as we begin to discover the powerfully positive things about gays and lesbians in the Bible, aren't conservatives going to want to get out their scissors too? And, Mollenkott says, Protestants, Catholics, fundamentalists—all of us—*already* ignore (use our symbolic scissors on) the parts of the Bible we find troublesome or not supportive of our favorite doctrine or theory. *Most people are just not honest about it.*

It does alarm me just a bit to have someone cut the Bible up too much before I've had my chance really to read it and know it through my lesbian eyes. So let's keep some copies intact. Just in case. Also, although parts of the Bible have *never* been and *never will be* revelatory for me (they are obviously misogynist, or violent, or just obscure or not very interesting) they may serve as very important reminders, as documentation of the history of oppression and the source of our struggles. They, too, are a part of our tribal memory.

For this reason—that *we may never forget*—it is still important for gay and lesbian people to understand how the Bible has been misused to oppress us. It is part of the deshaming and healing of our community.

Is the Bible Our Text?:
A "Tribal Hermeneutic" for Gays and Lesbians

It seems to me that I have always loved the Bible. But I was not always sure that it would love me back.

I remember reading the first Bible I got in Methodist Sunday school. I was determined to read it cover to cover. The print was small. I had no commentary, and weekly Sunday school lessons barely skimmed the surface of biblical stories. I read and read through long, boring, disappointing passages. Often I would come across things that were odd, frightening, or unintelligible. There were lots of endless descriptive details and hard-to-pronounce names and lists. But every now and then I stumbled on a book, chapter, or verse of pure gold, worth all my perseverance. As a lonely twelve-year-old, I had lots of time for this endeavor.

I loved Cranston Clayton's sermons at Hicksville Methodist Church. In his folksy Tennessee drawl, he preached a fervent, antifundamentalist, biblical social Gospel. He preached the Bible story, week after week, from a lectionary of his own creating. Anticipating the biblical illiteracy of a new generation, he retold the Bible for us. He even gave us a *living Bible map:* the parking lot was the Mediterranean Sea, the sanctuary was Israel, the gymnasium was Greece and Europe, and the offices were Egypt! His Bible characters were alive with poignancy and passion. I particularly appreciated that he didn't shy away from the juicier parts.

Clayton didn't care for children very much. He expected that if you were a child sitting through his sermons (which I sometimes did twice on Sundays), you'd better listen like an adult. Oh, the way he *told* the stories of David and Bathsheba, Peter and Paul and Silas, Jesus and Mary Magdalene, made me *want* to preach.

I wanted to make people feel the way he made me feel—like I was right there in those stories, in the thick of the battles, the miracles, smelling the smoke from the burning bush, touching Jesus, feeling Deborah's strength and conviction. I loved the tears, laughter, tales of mercy and cruelty, the scandal, the surprises. He acted, agonized, mused, imagined, painted verbal murals. Also, he seemed to have access to some mysterious repository of *inside information,* important details *missing* from the text itself. I never mistrusted his special source and the way he filled in the gaps.

So at age fourteen I asked my dad to take me to talk to Clayton about becoming a preacher. Clayton just looked at me—the way people squint at people who are somehow barely visible to them. Since I knew he didn't like or notice kids and since I was female, I already knew in my heart that talking to him was a long shot. He spoke to my father mostly. "Aw," he said, "she'll be just like my daughter: go to seminary, marry some preacher, and it will all be wasted on her." My dad, who had a hard enough time just getting to the pastor's office in the first place (it made him nervous), just sat silently. When I pressed Clayton (making him talk to *me*), he finally grunted and gave me the name and address of a woman Methodist minister he knew about in Kansas. End of discussion.

I wrote to her the next day. She eventually wrote back. It turned out that she had been married to a minister. When he died she finally got to go to seminary and got ordained. (She was now in her sixties.) Somehow, I didn't think I could wait that long—or that I should have to. It did occur to me, in a fleeting way, that I could just marry a very old, sick man and kind of get that part out of the way real early. But that seemed grotesque to me. I had also wanted to ask Clayton why he thought God would put ideas about preaching into girls' heads if it was all just going to be a waste. And I had this other feeling that I couldn't explain and already knew not to verbalize: that being married to a man was going to be the least of my problems.

Poor Clayton. He knew the Bible real well. He just didn't know anything about young lesbians who loved the Bible. Mind you, Clayton was not above making homophobic comments. He didn't watch a lot of TV. (How could he? He had to be reading the Bible all the time and figuring out which parts we ought to hear about!) But I remember that in one sermon he talked about two brand-new TV hits. They were "doctor" shows in the early sixties: about *Dr. Ben Casey* and *Dr. Kildare*. Ben Casey was a swarthy, hypermasculine sex symbol. Dr. Kildare was blond and delicate.

Clayton decided to talk about how he didn't care for Dr. Kildare, who was too namby-pamby (read *queer*). He thought Jesus was probably more *rugged* (read *macho*), like hairy old Ben Casey. I remember my strong reaction to Clayton that morning. I took it very personally and wasn't sure why. Partly because I liked Richard Chamberlain (he played Kildare and is an openly gay man today: Clayton's "gaydar" was working). I already knew that I liked boys or men better when they were pretty or a little more like girls. Hairy men kinda scared me. My dad was muscular and strong but had very little body hair (in fact, we always joked about his seven measly chest hairs). He always said it was because his father was part Indian. My dad was soft-spoken and managed, even with his mechanics-scarred hands, to be gentle in his touch and manner. When I got to preach, I thought, I would make Jesus be more like Dr. Kildare. Maybe not so blond, but kind of soft and pretty like Richard Chamberlain. Like my dad, or maybe like one of the women teachers I had a crush on.

Aside from the Ben Casey versus Jim Kildare fiasco, Clayton seemed right about a lot of things to me. For instance, he said that Dr. Martin Luther King, Jr. was a lot like Jesus (and, by the way, not at all like Ben Casey or Jim Kildare!) and that we ought to be a lot nicer to Catholics (in those early Vatican II years).

Somehow, the Bible was in favor of all of this, and if I just kept at it long enough, I would find all that good stuff eventually.

It has taken me nearly thirty years finally to succeed at finding the *really good stuff*. Which is part of the purpose of this book.

In about 1978, Dr. Norman Pittenger came to preach at MCC Detroit. He made the astonishing comment that "actually, the Bible is a greatly overrated book." This still makes me wince and laugh. All those people, over all those millennia, spending their lives poring over, studying, translating a *greatly overrated book*. Working hard to improve its *ratings!* Is that what we do? What I'm doing? Mary Daly once told me she thought that the feminist passages in the Bible would make an interesting *pamphlet*.

So is the Bible an angel I'm wrestling until it blesses me and all gay and lesbian people? Am I just locked in a lifelong "lovers' quarrel" with this book?

I preached my first sermon in seventh grade, in Mrs. Gitlitz's English class. We each had to give a ten-minute speech. Mine was entitled "The Bible and the Science Book: Do They Conflict?" I loved science, especially biology, evolution, and astronomy. It seemed so clear to me that both atheistic views of science and anti-intellectual, antiscientific, fundamentalist views of the Bible were unsatisfactory. I had this passionate desire to communicate this to my peers—most of whom, frankly, couldn't have cared less. Maybe I was passionate because I was one of the only Protestants in my school and neighborhood, and I already knew that others associated the Bible and *all* Protestants with fundamentalism.

My speech did cause a stir among faculty and administration at the school. In that time of challenges about school prayer and the need to create religious tolerance and address the biased perception of Protestant hegemony, it became impossible even to mention religion in the class-room. In my sermon-speech, I had broken the rule. How my heart pounded. How I longed to talk about these issues with someone, anyone. I petitioned the school to have an after-school "club" that could discuss religion. They gave me permission. Steffi, my friend from English class, came—not because she wanted to talk about religion (she was an agnostic) but because she wanted to support me—she thought I was so brave! Four of us met a few times in the library, so it never amounted to much. But I thought a lot about how much pain it must cause God to be misunderstood, misrepresented. And God liked the truth. So why were *people* afraid of the truth?

It never mattered to me whether or not the Bible was accurate as to facts. For some reason, I never equated fact and truth. It never worried me whether the Bible was literally true. Miraculously, I trusted my own heart. My heart leapt equally at the wonders of the cell, the solar system, and the poetry and power of a biblical story. I love the idea of reading what ancient humans of faith felt when they saw the same creation.

Sometime during this time I saw the movie *Inherit the Wind.* I thought that God must have loved the brilliant, free-thinking, doubting, questioning lovers of justice and seekers of truth like Clarence Darrow. God enjoyed them more than the mean-spirited, self-righteous ones who hated under cover of biblical infallibility.

I remember fantasizing about a special place of reconciliation in heaven for God and all the atheists and agnostics who out of love for God's creation and people, rejected perverse human notions of God—especially those supposedly supported by the Bible. There was also a part of me that sometimes fantasized about a special place in hell for religious folks who used the Bible abusively to hurt, alienate, and create an atmosphere of violence toward others. That was difficult because I didn't think there really could be a *hell.* (Although, what *did* God do with Adolf Hitler?) Reluctantly, I made myself imagine their redemption, their healing. It is hard to accept this memory of my own capacity for cruel imaginings. And hard to reconcile my universalism with the endless human capacity for destruction and cruelty. Mostly I wanted to access for myself and others the mysterious, poignant, tender, sweet, funny, and helpful stuff in the Bible, to loosen and lighten it up.

Recently I spoke at the college I had graduated from—Allegheny

College in Meadville, Pennsylvania. I did so as an open lesbian alumna! At my lecture on "Outing the Bible," biblical literalists pounded me with a barrage of questions. They were outwardly polite, white, mostly middle-class students, wide-eyed with sincerity. I tried to understand their intensity and fear. For some of them, intellectual exchange and "agreeing to disagree" were tolerable. But others simply hammered at me rhetorically, as if trying to break me under the weight of their questions. As if just listening to them read from their Bible, I would fall down on my knees in front of them and repent! Students who I assumed (perhaps falsely) could tolerate ambiguity, fine distinction, and unresolved questions in other areas of inquiry could *not* do so with the Bible. The atmosphere became ritualistic, cultlike, as one young woman repeated over and over again that if one could *speculate* (I had enraged her by using the word) about homosexuals in the Bible, then, one could *speculate* about *anything* in the Bible! (Which apparently would ruin it!) When I replied that I didn't find the word *speculate* to be a bad word and asked just what was she so afraid of, her intensity increased. It was as if these young students believed the Bible to be a fragile magic snow castle ready to melt—or a row of dominoes ready to fall with the first invading question.

For me, the Bible is an elastic, resilient friend who bounces back and even talks back when I question it. I can still see how the "biblically impaired" male student shook with rage at my really rather harmless attempts to see gays and lesbians in the Bible. The demons of homophobia screeched at me through him that night.

It would be so much easier for these students if we gays and lesbians would just continue to hate ourselves and the Bible. If like Job's wife, these students, and all who believe the way they do, could just get us to curse God and die—no problem!

But it's not their Bible or their God to control. The Bible belongs to anyone who will love it, play with it, push it to its limits, touch it, and be touched by it—and the same is true for God. The Bible *must* be a holy text for gays and lesbians, because we are truly human, created by the God who created heaven and earth. We are at a critical moment on this question. Either we will believe what others have told us about the Bible, feel awful about it and ourselves (and possibly reject the Bible or devalue ourselves); or, we will dare to learn and study and struggle with our own canon. The choice is ours.

A Lesbian Hermeneutic of Suspicion

I am borrowing from Fiorenza in daring to speak of a "lesbian hermeneutic of suspicion." Lesbian and gay people, using all the tools of feminist and liberation scholarship, must dare to push against the biblical silences and clues about homosexuality. We must find the ways to expose the heterosexist biases of most Bible translations, and commentaries, and to be willing to discover the ways in which the Bible already provides us with all the necessary materials to develop a gay and lesbian interpretative method (hermeneutic).

In that vein, if it is true that "every interpretative method works to perpetuate some ideology," then it is fair to say that until very recently most, if not all, methods used to interpret the Bible have perpetuated the ideology of heterosexism.

For most people who have read or heard of the Bible, their unqualified assumption is that the Bible condemns homosexuality and homosexuals. People have the same certainty about this that they once had about the Bible's support for the subordination of women and the biblical justification of slavery and racism.

Part of the politics of biblical interpretation is the fact that some Bible passages and concepts get studied while others do not. What gets studied, published, recorded, and taught is what institutions and authorities (usually religious ones) will permit and fund. Basically, that is, what the dominant culture will support.

A hundred years ago, a daring group of feminist amateur Bible scholars wrote The Women's Bible. But, it took nearly one hundred years before male-dominated seminaries would finally support, permit, and fund women biblical scholars to study the Bible in a way that challenges thousands of years of misogynist assumptions and biblical interpretation. In a parallel way, one hundred years earlier, black liberation theology writers began to move beyond the reinterpretation of the "curse of Ham" in the book of Genesis. But it took a long time to fund African American biblical scholarship.

In comparison, it is only forty years since the publication of D. S. Bailey's Homosexuality and the Western Christian Tradition,[11] the first book ever to challenge the negative assumptions about homosexuality in the Bible. The birth and growth of the gay and lesbian secular and spiritual movement have begun to demand revision of traditional views of homosexuality and the Bible. Now, scores of books and hundreds of articles by scholars, historians, and literary folk have joined Bailey's first heroic effort.

However, even after forty years of biblical critique and research, the assumption in the popular mind still reigns supreme that the Bible condemns homosexuality. Most people, especially most Christians, are not aware that there is *any other point of view.*

This moves us beyond the politics of biblical interpretation to the politics of the church and its responsibility to teach what it knows.

From 1985 to 1987, I participated in a series of well-organized "consultations" jointly sponsored by the National Council of Churches of Christ in the U.S.A. and the UFMCC. These consultations were commissioned by the Governing Board of the NCC in the aftermath of their decision to "postpone indefinitely" their vote on UFMCC's eligibility for membership in the NCC. These three consultations were to be about subjects believed to be major areas of disagreement between UFMCC and member communions of the NCC (and, more to the point, among and between those communions). The subjects were biblical interpretations of homosexuality, the science of human sexuality, and ecclesiology (the study of the church).

We tackled the biblical consultation first. I served as one of two UFMCC persons on the steering committee for the consultations. Our preparation included gathering the names of requested scripture scholars "in the guild" who had published on this subject and who would be willing to speak publicly to the NCC and UFMCC. The idea was to get scholars on *both sides of the issue* in order to have *balance.*

After some time had passed, NCC members of the steering committee informed us that they were able to find several suitable scholars to speak on the side of supporting a revised view of homosexuality and the Bible but could find no one who would speak on the more traditional side of the issue. We in UFMCC responded by providing several names of scholars familiar to us who are known for their traditional views on this subject. The NCC folks countered by saying that none of those "scholars" was acceptable, as they were not represented in the "guild" of Scripture scholars or did not come from the churches of the NCC.

Finally, the steering committee proceeded by asking an Old Testament and New Testament scholar to be the presenters, Drs. Robin Scroggs and Bruce Schaefer. Both Scroggs and Schaefer presented information and conclusions that support UFMCC's position on homosexuality and the Bible. Dr. Schaefer said during his presentation that today (1987), *"no serious Bible scholar would make the statement that the Bible unilaterally condemns homosexuality."* That was the first time I ever recall any scholar making that statement. I thought it was probably the most important outcome of the consultation. Frankly, I thought it should be front-page news. But of course it never made it to the front page or even to the back page.

Our committee was permitted to report on the consultations to the NCC Governing Board, which we did. The board received our report and our very heartfelt request that the results of these consultations, especially the biblical consultation, be published, distributed, discussed in the churches, debated, challenged, and taught. The NCC then went through a painful leadership crisis, and the papers from our consultations were buried and ignored. To my knowledge, that was the first time in history that such a critical study of homosexuality and the Bible was presented and authorized at *that* level of church anywhere in the world. And yet the papers and findings remain suppressed to this day.

The leaders of mainline denominations and seminary professors from member churches of the NCC have *paid for* and *studied* this information about homosexuality for many years. Even conservative scholars like Richard Hays from Yale (notoriously homophobic in his biblical interpretation—I don't know if he is or was in "the guild") now admit that, for instance, the story of Sodom and Gomorrah is not and never was about homosexuality.[12] Yet the vast majority of Christians in and outside the churches of the NCC still believe outdated, erroneous, homophobic biblical interpretations. *The church leadership refuses to teach what it knows.* The violence and hatred perpetrated against gays and lesbians in our culture is silently—and sometimes not so silently—co-signed by the church. Church leadership knows that teaching the truth about homosexuality and the Bible will be controversial, difficult, and at first, costly. The fear of controversy, of loss of money, of criticism from the radical right keeps the truth locked up.

Bishop William Boyd Grove, chair of yet another NCC/UFMCC dialogue effort, said in one of our committee meetings that he thinks that homosexuality as an issue is like the little thread dangling from the lining of his coat. It doesn't look like such a big deal by itself, but he hears his wife saying, "Whatever you do, don't pull that thread!" Because if he does, the whole lining of his coat will fall out! Church leaders instinctively know perhaps that the issue of homosexuality is only the most visible issue in a connected fabric of issues about human sexuality that the church cannot bear to see unravel.

Meanwhile, gays and lesbians continue to be vilified in our culture on the basis of outdated and thoroughly disputed homophobic interpretations of a few mostly obscure passages of Scripture. We at UFMCC do not have the power on our own to overturn this situation, at least not easily and not as quickly as it needs to happen. The leaders of the churches in the United States and around the world must take responsibility for what they know.

And I guess I want them to fix it because those of us at UFMCC, in all gay and lesbian spiritual and religious organizations, are *tired* of trying to fix it and of not being believed. We are sick of apologetics, of having to say over and over again why we believe the Bible doesn't condemn us as a special class of sinners. I want *them* to do it, because we have much more important, pressing, exciting, and enjoyable Bible reading and studying to do!

So let's get down to it: a lesbian hermeneutic of suspicion is a method of biblical interpretation that will point out the connections among misogynist and homophobic and racist methods of biblical interpretation. It will ask questions about those traditional homophobically interpreted passages that we call our "texts of terror." It will ask why certain passages have or have not been studied. It will examine biblical annotations and question the use of certain words and phrases. It will search biblical dictionaries and commentaries to identify trends in interpretations, cover-ups, omissions, and silences. Also, it will begin to *unsilence* silent biblical characters, and it will be free to engage in wild, bold, shameless speculation about gays and lesbians in the Bible. And that's what I hope to *begin* to do in the rest of this book.

Making the Connections for a Lesbian Hermeneutic of the Bible

A lesbian hermeneutic of suspicion cannot be myopic, or afford to be done in isolation. We have to understand the biblical interpretive methods of the religious right, and how they have been used against us. We have to understand how Catholics have used the Bible, and how liberation theology and African-American biblical scholarship help us to rescue the Bible from our oppressors.

Fundamentalists have gone through some changes in the past twenty years in how they preach and teach the "texts of terror" about gay men and lesbians. It was a lot easier for fundamentalists twenty-five years ago. That was when gays and lesbians did not believe they could read the Bible for themselves and when there was almost nothing published to support a positive reading of the Bible for gays and lesbians.

Several years ago my friend, gay Presbyterian Chris Glaser, went undercover to an "ex-gay" conference in San Diego attended by five hundred very sincere folks. Chris, in reporting about this in *Frontiers* magazine and in conversations with me, said that there were no workshops about "Homosexuality and the Bible" at this conference. Instead, there were lots of testimonies from "healed gays" and seminars in bad psychology. Nothing on the *Bible?* Can it be that all the published critiques of traditional views of homosexuality and the Bible are becoming more difficult to refute? Have we begun to succeed in taking all the fun out of Bible study for homophobes?

I have noticed that both in articles by folks such as Richard Hays and in street-corner debates, the *soft sell* is very in. They've stopped talking about specific Bible passages (since we have credible responses now to Sodom and Gomorrah, Leviticus, Romans, and 1 Corinthians), and they're back to using pitiful statements like "God made Adam and Eve, not Adam and Steve." Well, true, God did make Adam and Eve. A charming heterosexual model couple!

My most recent street-corner encounter with fundamentalists happened in West Hollywood. But first, a little background information:

In the late 1980s, I got a call from Connie Norman. Connie is a mad and brilliant transsexual earth mother to all gay and lesbian, AIDS and justice activists, especially the young ones. Connie is someone who knows how to call out the troops for an action or demonstration. She has always been able to get my attention! She's a wonderful writer and a Los Angeles radio personality.

Our first serious encounter had happened the day that six or seven AIDS activists were attempting to fast on the steps of the Federal Building in downtown Los Angeles. Unbeknownst to the fasters, the federal government had recently changed its policy. Individuals could no longer fast overnight on the steps of the Los Angeles Federal Building (as Reverend Troy Perry had in 1977) because the feds didn't want homeless persons sleeping on their steps! So, the fasters (fasting for the immediate release of DDI, a desperately needed AIDS medication) were ordered to move.

Connie was calling every organization she could. I happened to be in my office and decided to drop what I was doing and join them. When I got there, the crowd was growing. I jumped in, and Bob Lucas, Connie, and I handcuffed ourselves to the building. We waited about five hours for the feds to come and arrest us. When they finally came to get us, they took me first. Connie knelt and began praying the Lord's Prayer. I felt like she was doing it partly for me. I'll never forget how it touched me to be supported in that way.

They dragged me for a bit, and the very butch female federal agent said in a commanding voice, "Nancy, just stand up!" I was too dazed and stressed to wonder how the heck she knew my name but not too out of it to disobey! They had run out of paddy wagons and were shoving us, handcuffed, into the backseats of patrol cars. Wayne Karr, AIDS activist and an outrageous person in his own right (who has since died of AIDS), was right behind me, not cooperating in the slightest. They had to drag him (handcuffed) all the way to the car. It was apparently too difficult to shove him right side up into the backseat. So they shoved him down with his face on the floor of the backseat and his feet in the rear window. Actually, most of his face was on my shoe. I kept asking him if he was all right. He laughingly said he preferred my foot to the floor of the patrol car!

So, when Connie calls, I know I may well be in for an adventure, and I try to remember to take fine or bail money with me.

This time she told me of some goings-on Friday nights in West Hollywood. It seems that a group of fundamentalists, identifying themselves with the fundamentalist Calvary Chapel in Costa Mesa (which turned out later to be not quite true), were out late on Friday nights handing out antigay literature, pamphlets that said cruel things about people with AIDS and how God feels about them. Connie said, "It's getting pretty heavy out here, and I think the kids"—the mostly younger gay and lesbians and AIDS activists, Queer Nation and Act Up folks—"need to see some collars out here!"

So I took a couple of UFMCC members and clergy with me on Friday night at about eleven o'clock to a corner of West Hollywood Park. There they were. We could hear the din. There were a handful of fundamentalists surrounded by a very loud, screaming crowd of queers. Apparently this had gone on for weeks and had started out with rational discussions in normal tones. But it had really escalated by now. As we approached, Connie saw me, grabbed me, and pushed me in front of the fundamentalists, saying, "Here's one of our ministers, talk to her!"

Frankly, it was hard to hear ourselves think. But we began to try to talk to them while also acting as a buffer between them and the screaming crowd.

I had to think fast about why we were there and how we were going to handle this. *Our* crowd (the queers) were so enraged and volatile that I knew someone was going to get hurt. And when that happened someone would be arrested, and they would be *our* someones. I knew we needed to defuse this situation and get these folks to leave the neighborhood. It was clear to me that the fundamentalist leader had some deep personal agendas that he was working out and had gotten some young idealistic fundamentalists to follow him out there to "save" these homosexuals. They felt like they were being "persecuted for Jesus' sake" by this angry crowd. I really believe they had no idea how hostile their activities were. By coming into the small neighborhood of West Hollywood—one of the *only* gay and lesbian-identified cities in the world, just a few square blocks of relative safety and openness—they were *violating* our sense of peace and safety. Safety from bigotry and insult, as well as from physical harm. The fundamentalists had invaded West Hollywood with judgment, condemnation, and pity, all "in Jesus' name"—with love!

I also surmised that a lot of the queer folks on the street were working out their issues on these fundamentalists. How many of these men and women were preachers' kids or were themselves from conservative religious backgrounds? Victims of religious abuse? Even for dedicated activists, it took a lot of commitment to be here every Friday night.

We tried to defuse things by standing between the two groups and engaging the fundamentalists. It unnerved them suddenly to have people talking to them who were not shouting, and who actually knew something about the Bible, and who had in common with them that we would say the words *God, Jesus,* and *Bible* without expletives attached.

I took on the leader and attempted to help him understand that Jesus *never* exercised his ministry in a way that made the materially or spiritually poor, the outcasts, feel *worse*. In fact, Jesus criticized the Pharisees who heaped their judgmentalism and narrow interpretation of God's law on the poor outcasts. The leader asked me if I thought the gay folks were behaving in a very *Christian* manner. I said, "No," but they weren't claiming to! And what kind of treatment had they received from so-called Christians?

By now, Richard Davis, Sandy Williams, Rev. Joseph Gilbert, and others of us had our hands full. The leader seemed more than a little shaken. He made noises like they might want to leave, and we got someone to call them a cab immediately. Then we escorted them to the main street. At one point, the leader attempted to put his hand on the shoulder of an angry young man, who screamed back at him. I took a big chance and with both hands grabbed the young man's shoulders and said, "Cool off, they're leaving." He turned to me with a look of joy and said, "How did you convince them that we are right?"

Well, of course, I hadn't done any such thing. I had only convinced them that this was not a safe or welcome place for their ministry. Freedom of speech does have its limits and responsibilities. Later the leader of the fundamentalist group tried to sue the police department and the city, saying that they had been battered in some way. I had to testify to the sheriff's department about my own observations to the contrary.

But the young man's response haunted me the most. It amazed and saddened me how much he wanted the fundamentalists to change their minds! For them to give him some kind of love, approval, or validation that he hadn't gotten or wasn't getting elsewhere. I was amazed that he would be so naive as to believe that rational discourse and debate about the Bible with such folks can have any real impact. There is this hunger for acceptance and legitimacy that underlies some—but not all—of the rage I saw that night and have seen many other times. That this young man wanted validation from fundamentalists shocked me.

Also, somehow, even though we were Christian ministers, the crowd trusted us. That also amazed me. We were *their* religious queers!

The issue of the desire or need for approval from religious authorities (fundamentalist or otherwise) is a very touchy one, especially in UFMCC where we do not want to be isolated, but to be a part of the broader Christian church. It is a narrow tightrope to walk at times. I worried that just by applying for membership in the NCC we in UFMCC were giving them the power to reject us, and thus giving their evaluation of us too much legitimacy. I worried that the seemingly inevitable rejection by NCC would only deepen our self-esteem issues as a church. We had to continue to exorcise from ourselves (especially those of us who dealt closely with the NCC) our own personal demons of self-doubt, to remember that our cause was twofold: expose their homophobia, and witness the miracle of the spiritual movement occurring among our sisters and brothers in the gay and lesbian community. Gaining their approval was *not* our purpose. But it was hard, sometimes, in the midst of the battle to keep that perspective.

Part of moving toward a positive lesbian and gay interpretation of the Bible means being willing to move ahead without the approval of fundamentalists or the NCC, and without converting them! No one is going to make this effort, this reclaiming of the Bible, easy for us. Nor can we make it comfortable for them—for fundamentalists, Lutheran bishops, Presbyterian pastors, or even the pope.

Catholic Encounters with Homosexuality and the Bible

In 1987, Pope John Paul II visited the United States. One of the big events was to be a worship service in a stadium in Columbia, South Carolina. This was the *Protestant* showcase service and all the leaders of the NCC, plus Southern Baptists and others were invited. All national Protestant church leaders were invited, and Rev. Troy Perry was on the list. We were never sure who made that decision in the National Conference of Catholic Bishops (what gay or gay-friendly person) but we were invited to participate in a procession of Protestant clergy into the stadium and to hear the pope preach. Despite Troy's previous negative experiences with the NCC, he just couldn't resist this. He asked me to go with him.

Now, as a lesbian pastor in a church that has its roots in the counterculture, I have an interesting history with just what *is* proper lesbian preacher attire! By 1987, I had gotten past the denim stage in the seventies and had since been wearing pantsuits and clergy shirts. I had even bought a more *dressy* suit or two to wear to the NCC meetings, mostly so that I could blend in a little better. I figured I was "different" in enough ways obvious to all of us that I didn't need to make a statement with my clothing. (Like a lesbian flannel clergy shirt or something . . .) However, the eighties saw the revival of skirts and dresses in a big way (thanks to Ronald Reagan and the conservative wave), and this did make me feel a little awkward at times, and pressured to dress differently. With the invitation to worship with the pope, it seemed as good a time as any to deal with the skirt thing.

By this time I was pastor of MCC Los Angeles. Sweet, sharp-dresser Lloyd King, a member of the church, now in his eighties, gave me some money so I could dress myself. I was shocked at the prices of skirt suits and dresses since I had last bought them (probably high school). So, I took the plunge and bought a suit, with a straight skirt and hemline below my knees. My lover Paula calls it my *nun* outfit.

Troy and I were both excited and nervous, not knowing what to expect at this event. We flew into Columbia, S.C., for an overnight. We saw no one we knew, and ate dinner together. Then I had to go to the drug store. And unfortunately I confided in him that wearing a skirt suit meant I had to wear pantyhose. And that I had not worn pantyhose in fifteen years and that when I wore them last, women shaved their legs. And I just didn't think I could wear pantyhose without shaving my legs! He thought that was hilarious. And proceeded to include this in his repertoire of Fellowship folklore: *how Nancy shaved her legs for the pope.*

Duly shorn, pantyhosed, and beskirted, I got in the car with Troy the next day as we drove to the stadium. When we got there, the rumor was that the pope was late because there was a hurricane in Miami. We were herded into a large room, where eventually nearly all the four hundred people in the procession were gathered. There were Catholics, Protestants, and Eastern Orthodox, clergy from the historic black churches, women and men religious. We had vested, and then we ended up waiting for four hours in the early September South Carolina heat. Just *fabulous* for me in skirt, pantyhose, and brand new low heels. To identify ourselves a little, Troy and I wore our buttons that said, "God is greater than AIDS." People would smile, introduce themselves sweetly, squint at our buttons, and read, "God is greater than AIIIIIDS," and turn away and quickly talk to someone else. There were a few friendly NCC folks, and a lot of unfriendly faces. The tension mounted as the temperature increased. I do not ever remember seeing so many police. The campus ROTC guarded us, assisted by the state police, local police, the FBI, and the pope's own secret service. It was a madhouse.

Finally *he* arrived, and the procession began, some people still giving us the "how the hell did you get invited" looks. We processed in. Troy and I ended up on opposite sides of the football field, with the crowds watching above. I ended up surrounded by the Orthodox clergy, of course. As we walked in, someone unfurled a gay pride sign in the bleachers.

The service began with an opening prayer by a woman in a clerical collar. She then walked off the podium—by prior agreement, we learned. The pope would not be on the same podium with a woman wearing a clerical collar!

Then came what was to be, for me, the highlight of the event, and the star of it was the Bible.

Helen Hayes read the first lesson, from the Hebrew Scriptures. She read Ruth 1:16–17.

> But Ruth said, "Do not press me to leave you or to turn back from following you! Where you go, I will go; where you lodge, I will lodge;
>
> Your people shall be my people, and your God my God. Where you die, I will die—there will I be buried.
>
> May the Lord do thus and so to me, and more as well." (NRSV)

I was stunned. I had been sitting there thinking, "What the hell am I doing here?" This pope has not been exactly a leader in the area of justice for women, gays, and lesbians! In fact, for someone so well educated, who had spent his early life in the theater, he seemed the very paragon of sexual repression.

But along came Ruth and Naomi that day in South Carolina. It was like the Bible itself was speaking to me that day, reassuring me. The Bible was secretly overturning the moment, speaking for itself. The story of Ruth and Naomi was *our* text! It is the most profound statement of committed love between two human beings in the Bible, and it is said between two women (more about this later!). There was Helen Hayes, reading this beautiful statement ("Where you go I will go, where you die, I will die"), right out there in front of the pope, God, and everybody. It was a profound victory for lesbian hermeneutics.

Then the pope himself read from the Gospel of Mark, chapter 3, verses 31–35.

> Then his mother and brothers came; and standing outside they sent to him and called him. A crowd was sitting around him; and they said to him, "Your mother and your brothers and sisters are outside, asking for you." And he replied, "Who are my mother and my brothers?" And looking at those who sat around him, he said, "Here are my mother and my brothers! Whoever does the will of God is my brother and sister and mother." (NRSV)

Again, the choice seemed strange. First of all, this is one of the passages where it is mentioned that Jesus has brothers and sisters. In Catholic doctrine, which teaches the immaculate conception of Mary and her perpetual virginity, Jesus is said to be without brothers and sisters. Even modern Catholic translations like the Roman Catholic–sponsored Jerusalem Bible claim that the word for brothers and sisters may also have been used to mean "cousins." No Protestant commentaries say this. Secondly, I had always seen this text as one of Jesus' harshest statements against the idea that one's biological *family* relationships should define one's identity. In fact, Jesus *redefines family* as *those who do the will of God!*

The pope then proceeded to use these two texts to preach a sermon that was essentially a campaign speech for *traditional family values*. He did have a really good subtext on the cross (he was, after all, in Baptist country). But most of the sermon was consumed by the "family values" stuff. Family values from whose tradition? Whose family? Both those Bible passages *critique* any "traditional" (really, modern!) understanding of family values. The pope essentially ignored that in his interpretation or lack thereof.

And then he blessed the children. Later I would write a short piece for *The Christian Century* about it. He blessed a couple dozen children that day, at least 10 percent of whom were gay and lesbian. I was thankful that at least the Bible provided a *balance* that day, and I prayed that when those children grew up, they would be included in the pope's version of family. The pope's sermon was so loaded with the "traditional family values" stuff that both Troy and I were expecting him to say something overtly homophobic. It never happened—and we hadn't planned what we would have done if he did. Would anyone on that big football field have taken notice—other than the FBI or the pope's secret service?

The pope had to rush off right away, being five or six hours behind schedule, so the promised reception line never happened. We went to the reception anyway and mingled with NCC leaders and Catholic bishops. A few of the bishops were extremely solicitous and knew right away who we were. One of them was well known to be actively homosexual.

African-American Lens on the Bible: Implications for a Gay and Lesbian Hermeneutic

The gay and lesbian movement in the United States has been largely *perceived* as a white male movement. This is at least in part because gay and lesbian white children, like other white children, are enculturated with sexism and white racism. Often, lesbian invisibility has meant that our specific issues as women get no attention in the "gay and lesbian" agenda. Likewise as with any movement, white people believe we have some divine right to rule, whether we acknowledge this or not.

This means that black gays and lesbians have had to walk a tightrope. To come out has often meant leaving home and family and culture behind. It has meant coming out into a white-dominated gay movement and having to work for change on both the *outside* and the *inside* of your movement. It has meant that black gay and lesbian people have often been asked to educate white leaders rather than being free to reach out to the black community. And in the black community, the movement for gay and lesbian rights has been seen as evidence of a "white man's disease." Racism in the U.S. has made overcoming homophobia in the black community more complex. In addition, the particular ways in which homophobia is related to sexism and the way that sexism and racism affect each other have made it hard for us to engage in dialogue about sexuality across racial lines.

Also, it is risky to *compare* oppression. Heterosexism and racism are not identical or equatable. I hear white gay and lesbian people express horror and disbelief that not all African-American politicians or church leaders support gay and lesbian rights, with the charge that the "oppressed have become the oppressors." Well, it isn't that simple. First of all, African-Americans do not have the power to reinforce their prejudices in our culture the way white people still do. Although anyone can have prejudices against persons of other races, in our world today, especially in the U.S., white people are more likely to have the power, wealth, and resources to make our prejudices count for something. White racism, as some have defined it, is the combination of personal prejudice with institutional privilege.

Secondly, there are many white gays and lesbians who have not really dealt at all with our racism (or sexism). We have *not* been willing to look at how we, as *oppressed* gays and lesbians, have often consciously or unconsciously perpetuated racism, sexism, and classism. Why do we not also see ourselves as "the oppressed becoming the oppressor" when we do that?

I have also heard or seen African-American leaders act shocked or horrified when gay and lesbian people talk about oppression. This is made worse when the stereotype of gays and lesbians as a wealthy white minority is proffered by gay activists. The economic oppression of gays and of blacks is not equivalent, but it is also necessary to challenge the "white wealthy" stereotype of gays and lesbians.

Nevertheless, I want to be able to acknowledge and make use of the work that African-American biblical scholars and historians of African-American biblical interpretation have done, in order to help develop a gay and lesbian hermeneutic of the Bible.

Michael Cartwright delineates some of the interpretative principles that have guided African-Americans' appropriation of the Bible as their text. I say "appropriation" because the Bible did not originate in African culture any more (or any less) than it originated in northern European culture. African-Americans had to come to terms with *adopting* the Bible as their text in the face of serious obstacles—more serious than those faced by gays and lesbians. I found these comments particularly helpful:

> Part of what distinguishes the African-American Christian tradition of biblical interpretation from other interpretative traditions is that reading—or literacy in the broadest sense—and the interpretative problems posed for African-Americans by racist interpretations of Christian Scripture have been linked to one another *almost from the moment African-Americans were taken from Africa as slaves.* Slaves were taught that the Bible "talked" to the master, but on those occasions when African-American slaves attempted to get the Bible to talk to them, they encountered silence. Given the fact that the slaves had been taught that "the Bible said" God had cursed them, it is no wonder that enslaved Africans concluded that the Bible would not speak to them because of the color of their skin.
>
> Nor, in retrospect, is it surprising that the slaves should begin to speculate about the existence of a "different Bible" in the face of uses of the Bible that legitimated the slavocracy of the antebellum South. Tired of listening to Euro-American preachers who appeared to read "obey your masters" on every page of the Bible, African-American slaves rejected their masters' interpretation of the Bible and the "slave ideology" by which it was legitimated. Instead, they gathered in "secret meetings" where they sang and danced and, in effect, reconstructed the Bible in relation to the spirituals and conversion narratives of the slave community and sermons of unordained slave exporters. The fact that these gatherings were illegal, and that they were also occasions in which slaves taught one another to read, simply underlines the degree to which the very act of reading the Bible was a threat to the slavocracy.

Given this racist ideology, it is amazing that more African-Americans have not rejected the Bible. But however tempting it may have been to rid themselves of the icon of their absence, African-American Christians have rejected this kind of "monologic" solution in favor of the reinterpretation of difficult texts. At the same time, "the black churches have never hesitated to *disavow* any interpretation of Scripture that would attempt to legitimate racism, slavery or any other form of human bondage." Based on this historical assessment, some scholars have been tempted to make formal claims about the text of the Bible: "there is no sacred Scriptures for blacks apart from the hermeneutic principles by which they are received and transmitted."[13]

One hundred years ago, much of the African-American focus on the Bible was apologetic, especially in refuting the racist interpretations of the story of Ham in Genesis and overturning the "Bible justifies slavery" interpretations of Philemon and other New Testament passages. Recent African-American biblical scholarship no longer sees the need to engage in that debate and almost seems to avoid it as a source of embarrassment.

Meanwhile, many black authors (starting with W.E.B. Du Bois), sociologists, and linguists have written about the "double consciousness" that existed in the mind of black slaves in the United States, as they heard about and then eventually read the Bible for themselves. They wrote about how slaves heard and used the text to speak with a "double voice" about their experience. James Cone, in *The Spirituals and the Blues*,[14] wrote about how the words to many spirituals conveyed double meanings. Hymns that praised heaven were really about praising the freedom that could take place by traveling north. Many spirituals are filled with images of crossing over, crossing rivers, traveling on trains, being bound for glory, about destinations and a happier future, about the suffering and struggles of this life. "There's a meeting here tonight" was more about secret antislavery meetings and plans to escape than about church services. The slave had to develop this double consciousness: the public, open language he or she used in the presence of the white slave owners; and the private, almost double-entendre language that could even be spoken in the slave owners' presence without them understanding. This was an encoded language, shrouding feeling and intention.

The Bible, as literature that expressed some powerful ideas to the slaves who bothered with it, became part of this double-voiced vocabulary.

Since most slave owners thought it was a *good* idea to "Christianize slaves" (in order to be able to control them more, with God on their side and the Bible to keep slaves in their place), slaves knew that "talking Bible talk" was relatively acceptable and safe.

But the Bible had and has its own agenda. It contains the stories of deliverance from slavery and oppression, expressed in spiritual terms such as "My Lord delivered Daniel, why not *everyone?*" The Bible spoke to the hearts of slaves its own unrepentant, uncontrollable revolutionary message: "Let my people GO!"

In UFMCC, we have compared being in the closet to slavery. Sometimes we have done this in a way that does not take into account the *real differences* in these two experiences. This is similar to the way people today use the term *closet* generically to mean "anything kept secret or hidden." Sometimes that usage feels as though it trivializes the painful experience of gay and lesbian oppression. So, too comparing the closet with slavery can result in trivializing the horror of being owned by another human being, held captive against your will, beaten at whim, wrenched from your family, lynched, murdered, with no recourse for justice.

Slavery is not just another form of oppression, and the closet is not just another *secret*. For gay and lesbian people, living in the closet, having to lie and cover up our sexuality has been soul killing and has often resulted in suicide, in lives of isolation, loneliness, and despair. It has been the source of enormous emotional, psychological, and spiritual pain. It has also been the cause of physical pain and discrimination. Gay people in the closet are more likely to engage in high-risk sexual encounters and may be targets for extortion or other threats. They are at more risk for gay bashing and job discrimination.

Slavery, as an imperfect analogy, however, can help us understand our situation and our relationship to the biblical text. Gay and lesbian people, too, have had to have a kind of *double consciousness*, a secret vocabulary, an encoded language for public and private use. We, too, have tried to live in this double consciousness in a heterosexually dominated culture. We, too, have our "texts of terror" that have been used to justify the homophobia of the church and culture.

It was an NCC official who first said in 1992 that the issue of homosexuality and the church is the "most divisive issue in the church since slavery." Then it became impossible not to use that analogy and take it to its logical conclusion:

Imagine if there had been a church council in the United States just prior to the Civil War. The church council consisted of free and slave-holding churches. For the "sake of unity" this council elected never to discuss the issue of slavery, for fear of offending each other's sensibilities. Most of the "free churches" did have African-American members, but these members were not in a position of power or leadership. In a few cases, African-Americans from free churches even represented their churches as delegates, but only with the clear understanding that they would never bring up the issue of slavery and that they would be as discreet as possible and would not be offensive to delegates from slaveholding churches. Blacks who were light-skinned or who could pass as white were preferred.

All is well until the day that the church of mostly freed slaves applied for membership. These were slaves of all hues, many with visible scars of body and soul. This "church of freed slaves" is a young church, still getting organized but growing by leaps and bounds as people begin to find their way to freedom. This is not a "quiet" church. They are loud and proud, angry and full of joy in their newfound freedom. They come to witness to the powerful, miraculous, redeeming love of the God of Jesus Christ, who has saved them and set them free. They want the whole church to hear of the wonderful things God is doing. How folks are healing from the devastating effects of slavery. How they are providing marriage ceremonies for men and women who had not been permitted to marry while enslaved. How God is healing their children and elders. How they provided for each other with "burial societies" because white people's mortuaries and cemeteries wouldn't accept them. How they were helping each other adjust to the new world of freedom, which still contained so much racism.

They came to this council to witness. And to be included, and to do that not only for themselves but for all the slaves they still knew in captivity, people who were held as slaves by some of these Christian folks. They spoke for the ones who did not dare to speak.

In fact, at the time they applied, there were many more slaves held by members of the churches that belonged to the council than there were members of this new church of freed slaves.

Some who agonized the most about this church of freed slaves were the few blacks who had achieved a little status and dignity in the "freed churches." They felt the most threatened by this ragtag, unruly bunch of radicals who were going to really *mess things up for the rest of us*. Why didn't they understand that these white folks still held *all* the power in the culture and that even the *good* ones didn't want to be pressured into change? God knows how they would *react!*

The slaveholding churches were firm and sullen: they threatened behind the scenes to pull out if this new church was admitted. And with them would go money and the prestige of the council. The representatives from slaveholding churches would never speak directly to the representative from the church of freed slaves—that would be giving them dignity and recognition! And the "free churches" felt they were in the middle. They did not want to "rock the boat" and threaten the fragile unity of the council. So behind the scenes, they acted disgusted and outraged at the behavior of the slaveholding churches but would never publicly confront or challenge them.

There was no way this council could admit a church of freed slaves without freeing their own slaves, without having to make a commitment *that slavery was wrong.*

So the council tried to ignore the church of freed slaves. They formed committees to study the issue, they tabled it endlessly, hoping the little church would have enough other issues to deal with that it would get discouraged and drop its request for inclusion. But the church of freed slaves just kept growing and growing and finding all kinds of ways to tell the council that as long as they shared in the same Body of Jesus Christ, the church of freed slaves was going to keep loving this council until it became free itself, or died.

This analogy has helped me spiritually and emotionally to work through some of the insanity that has occurred in UFMCC's relationship to the NCC over the last decade or so. As a church of "freed slaves," UFMCC is a living ecumenical witness to what a community for gay/lesbian/bisexual folks (including our families and friends) looks like when homophobia is conquered (at least externally). We terrify those NCC gays and lesbians in the closet; we anger the liberals who want us to love them for privately supporting us while publicly betraying us; and we exasperate those conservatives who are convinced we can't be Christians when we pray and sing and testify to God's love for our community.

In November of 1992, in Cleveland, Ohio, at the General Board meeting, the NCC voted narrowly not to accept UFMCC as an observer to the NCC. (We were already observers to the WCC.) At the time, even non-Christian organizations were so designated by the Council: the Unitarians (which include Christians, but do not have a trinitarian Christian doctrine), a Muslim group, and a Jewish organization all were observers of the NCC. There was in fact no criteria for observer status. We actually applied to be observers as a semi-graceful way of ending a long and painful (disgraceful at times) "dialogue to nowhere" that ended up being just a prolonged stalling tactic for not dealing with our membership application. We simply had no idea that asking to end all the silliness by settling for observer status would be controversial. But they debated for five hours about it, and voted no. No officer of the NCC spoke in our favor. From the floor, Dr. Paul Sherry, head of the United Church of Christ, along with the Methodists and a few others, pleaded for rationality. But to no avail. One young lesbian, a visitor (not from UFMCC) said, quite sincerely, "Even if you (the NCC) thought UFMCC was *of the devil*, wouldn't you want them to observe you so they could learn how real Christians act?"

At this point in the book, I'm happy to give you a choice. You can wander with me through the Bible, its translations and commentaries, looking for hints and clues, debunking the traditional views of homosexuality and the Bible. You can come with me and delight as I delight in critiquing the critiquers. Or you can just believe me that the Bible doesn't condemn homosexuality and that the biblical commentators are too chicken or too ignorant to say this, and turn to the next chapter!

DETOXING OR DEMYTHOLOGIZING THE "TEXTS OF TERROR"

Part of the difficult work of a lesbian hermeneutic of suspicion is to tackle head-on those "texts of terror" that reinforce the irrational biases of church and society.

Phyllis Trible, in her book *Texts of Terror*, takes on a very difficult area of feminist biblical interpretation: How can certain passages of Scripture that seem to justify violence and dehumanization of women be included in the canon? Are all parts of Scripture equally valuable or valid? How do we discover and discern the "canon within the canon"? And what is our stance toward obviously misogynist stories in the Bible?

The texts in the Bible that have terrorized gays and lesbians have been used, accurately or not, to justify the homophobia of the church and culture. Judges, legislators, and governors in our country *still* quote the Bible when justifying the denial of civil or human rights for gays and lesbians.

How can a group of people claim to be a legitimate minority group if the Bible says that God disapproves of or even hates them? People who may never dust off or read a Bible are just *sure* that it says bad things about gays and lesbians.

When I teach people at UFMCC about homosexuality and the Bible, I help them learn how to stand up to those who would make such claims. The first thing I suggest they do is to ask the question: "Where? Show me *where* the Bible mentions gay men or lesbians and condemns us." In about two-thirds of the cases, this will stump them right off the bat. We live in a very biblically illiterate society. However, if you are dealing with people who know the Bible (and fundamentalists are more likely to know chapters and verses), they will at least know about the story of Sodom and Gomorrah, and that it's in Genesis.

What is really enjoyable is for those of us who are gay or lesbian to be able to recite the passages that are our texts of terror *for* our *opponents*. It really throws them off! They can't believe that anyone who is gay has ever opened a Bible. And that we would not be afraid to know these passages and to discuss them. I've had fundamentalists *insist* on looking at my Bible to see if it's a "real" Bible or a special *gay* edition. (I wish!)

Interestingly enough, the New Revised Standard Version of the Bible includes the most amazing annotation as a comment on Sirach 22:3, which reads: "It is a disgrace to be the father of an undisciplined son, and the birth of a daughter is a loss." The annotation says of verse 3b, "This reflects the *misogyny* of the age."[15]

A remarkable thing, that the word *misogyny* actually appears in the text of the annotated Bible. Before I die, I would love to see an annotation to at least one of the texts of terror for gay men and lesbians that says, "This passage and its traditional interpretation reflect the homophobia of the age(s)." It will happen.

I do not want to spend time in this book going over the *explanations* about how to reinterpret these texts of terror. I would simply refer you to the best material available.[16]

Instead, what I would like to do is to take on the New Revised Standard Version of the Bible and the other biblical study aids and critique their handling of the texts of terror. This, for me, gets to some of the heart of the politics of biblical interpretation as it affects gay men and lesbians in the present.

Also, I have to confess a personal agenda in taking on this task: one of the most important reasons that I believe it has been crucial for UFMCC to be in study and dialogue with the National Council of Churches for more than a decade, despite their treatment of us, is because they *own the copyright* to the Revised Standard Version of the Bible (and the New RSV). This is very important because this is a very influential version of the Bible, and it grows out of the more liberal tradition of biblical criticism. If positive changes are to be made in the biblical text or its interpretation, they will most likely appear in this version first. Also, because the owners of the NRSV have a reputation for using the best information available, including modern critical tools and methods, and since they have access to the emerging critique of the texts of terror, they have *more responsibility* to reflect these critiques in the translation and annotation, even if doing so is politically unpopular.

If we use the logic of Elisabeth Schussler-Fiorenza's "feminist hermeneutic of suspicion," then what is *omitted* from a text or commentary may be as important, if not more important, as what is included. Both the presence and the absence of points of view, voices of characters, and commentary on both are important. The owners, publishers, and scholars who produced the NRSV know that a single word omitted, changed, or added to a text, or annotation to a text, is very, very important. Some previously marginalized groups (wmen/ people of color) have now found their way at least to some degree into the power structures that produce new Bibles. Gays and lesbians have yet to have that kind of access at that level. We need more lesbian and gay Scripture scholars to come out of the closet!

I believe that one can certainly see the influences of a mere twenty years or so of serious biblical reflection on homosexuality in the text of the New RSV. However, there are grave disappointments as well. I also hope to point out the serious consequences of what may seem like very minor inclusions, changes, or omissions from the text or annotations. This is the strange and sad politics of biblical translation and interpretation for gays and lesbians.

The Treatment of the Sodom Story in the Bible Texts and Commentaries

The story of Sodom and Gomorrah in Genesis 19:1–28 is the most familiar text used to justify homophobia.

The basic story line is that God sends two angels to destroy the "twin cities" of Sodom and Gomorrah because of some *great wickedness*. The city is the home of Abraham's cousin Lot, and in a previous chapter, Abraham intercedes with God about the fate of Sodom and Gomorrah for the sake of Lot and his family. The result of that intercession is that rather than just blow the city up outright, God sends the two angels to Lot to warn him and help him and his family escape.

In the process, the people of the city hear about the two strange visitors and threaten them with violence (possibly with rape). The angels blind the violent citizens of Sodom and Gomorrah and help Lot's family escape. *Then* they blow up the city.

This story has an interesting history of interpretation, first documented by D. S. Bailey forty years ago.[17] Basically, the story of Sodom and Gomorrah was not associated with homosexuality at all until the Jewish philosopher and biblical commentator Philo of Alexandria wrote his commentary in the first century (C.E.). Philo devoted many pages to enumerating and elaborating on the precise nature of the sins of Sodom and Gomorrah based on his own vivid imagination—and nothing more. His fantasy was apparently so compelling and thorough that it was *picked up* by the early church fathers and simply passed on for two millennia without being challenged. This could only happen because of homophobia. Basically, Genesis 19 was not studied very much for nearly two millennia, and since Philo's interpretation reinforced cultural prejudice against homosexuals, it seemed plausible. His explanations included graphic descriptions of homosexual acts (none of which are specifically referred to in Genesis 19) and accusations of bestiality (totally without any basis in Genesis 19).

The only possible link to homosexuality is the use of the verb *yadah*, translated "to know" (Gen. 19:5). This verb is used in only a few instances in the Bible to refer euphemistically to sexual intercourse. When the wicked folk of Sodom and Gomorrah want Lot to send out his guests that they may "know" them, this *may* have been a euphemistic reference to an "indecent proposal," or the threat of rape. Obviously the people's intentions were bad, whether or not violence of a sexual nature was the plan. And if these were men threatening to rape men, then that would have been homosexual rape—a common way that *heterosexual* men humiliated other men, especially in the context of conquest. Of course, there is the problem of the fact that Lot offers them his *daughters* and also that the guests were, of course, not men but angels. Neither of these facts supports the assumption that *all* the men of Sodom were homosexual rapists (a wildly bizarre assumption if you really bother to think about it). But, even if they *were* rapists, how does one make the leap from homosexual *rape* (not a sexual act, as we now know, but an act of violence, like heterosexual rape) as a moral evil to claiming that therefore *all* homosexual acts and relationships are wrong? One only makes that leap if one is homophobic!

So, how does the New RSV incorporate the research on homosexuality and the Bible that began forty years ago with D. S. Bailey?

What is most interesting are the annotations in the New RSV. The text remains essentially translated as it always has been, which is really not a problem! But the annotators say the following:

> 19:1–38: *The destruction on Sodom and Gomorrah* impressed itself deeply on later generations as an example of God's total judgment upon appalling wickedness (Deut 29.23; Isa 1:9; Jer 49:18; Am 4:11). 1. *Two angels,* see 18: 2–8, n. 4–11: Compare the crime of Gibeah (Judg 19:22–30). The episode is told to illustrate the sexual excesses of the Canaanites. 5. Know refers to sexual relations (v. 8), here homosexual (*sodomy*).[18]

The Bible is the best interpreter of the Bible, and the cross-references here (Deuteronomy and so on) are very interesting. In *none* of these references to Sodom and Gomorrah is there any remote reference to sexuality or homosexuality. There are, however, references to idolatry. In addition, one very important reference is omitted: Ezekiel 16:46–58. Only if you look up the annotations to Isaiah 1:9 and 10 will you find a cross-reference to Ezekiel. *This passage from Ezekiel is very important because it is the only passage in all of the Hebrew Scriptures that gives a definition of the sins of Sodom and Gomorrah!* One of the important things to note, in reading this passage, is that sexual impropriety, prostitution, and "lewdness" were repeatedly employed by the prophets as metaphors of Israel's unfaithfulness to God.

The passage from Ezekiel documents Jerusalem's *religious* apostasy and uses the metaphor of a "faithless bride" to do so:

> Have you not committed lewdness, beyond all our abominations?
> ... Your elder sister is Samaria, who lived with her daughters to the

north of you; and your younger sister, who lived to the south of you,
is Sodom, with her daughters. You [Jerusalem] not only followed
their ways and acted according to their abominations; with a very little time you were more corrupt than they in all your ways. As I live,
says the Lord God, your sister Sodom and her daughters have not
done as you and your daughters have done. This was the guilt *of
your sister Sodom: she and her daughters had pride, excess of food,
and prosperous ease, but did not aid the poor and needy. They were
haughty, and did abominable things before me; therefore I removed
them when I saw it.*

(EZEK. 16:46–58)

Several things are apparent in this passage and in the verses that follow: in no way is the "sin of Sodom" associated with sexual behavior of
any kind. The term *abomination* was a very specific word that referred to
idolatry, not literally to *sexual* sins. Sexuality is used as a *metaphor* for spiritual apostasy, but only as a metaphor. There is no suggestion that sexual
misconduct was the basis for God's judgment against Sodom and for her
consequent destruction. In addition, Ezekiel makes the point later on in
this section of chapter 16 that God says, "I will restore the fortunes" of
Samaria, Sodom, and Jerusalem. In any mention of Sodom and Gomorrah, I have never heard one biblical commentary ever mention that (1)
Ezekiel claims that the sins of Jerusalem were worse than the sins of
Sodom (were all of them homosexuals, too?) and (2) that Ezekiel prophesies the *restoration* of Sodom, along with others.

Why does the New RSV ignore Ezekiel 16 in its annotations to Genesis 19? I believe, in part, because Ezekiel 16 does not support the contention that this story is in any way about homosexuality.

I am particularly angry about the annotation to verse 5 of Genesis 19
(already quoted), which uses the word *homosexuality* when forty years ago
D. S. Bailey and countless others after him have pointed out that this passage is *not* about sexual relations (homosexual or heterosexual) but about
violence (and possibly rape). This is not a minor flaw. It is bigoted and
slanderous.

Furthermore, to perpetuate the association of homosexual sex with
the word *sodomy* is extremely irresponsible. And, by the way, this is a *new*
inclusion; it is not found in the old RSV. The word *sodomy* in English was
used in English jurisprudence to describe the homosexual act of male
anal intercourse and bestiality *based on the erroneous interpretation of*

Sodom and Gomorrah that the Jewish philosopher Philo and his successors in the church taught. Thus, the problem is circular: the word *sodomy* comes into the English language based on erroneous homophobic exegesis, and then the English word is used in the annotation of the New RSV to reinforce the association of homosexuality with Sodom and Gomorrah!

The consequences are that for the duration of the life of this translation of the Bible, gay and lesbian people will continue to be associated with this violent, negative story and will have this association used against us in the courts, the legislatures, the churches, and on the streets. It becomes a contributing factor toward gay bashing, having our children taken from us, and all forms of injustice toward gays and lesbians.

In contrast, the new *Anchor Bible Dictionary* has a five-page article on Sodom and Gomorrah.[19] The word *homosexuality* does *not appear in this article.* It states, "The transgressions of Sodom's inhabitants consist in sexual debauchery [is that a synonym for rape?], human hubris and violation of the (law of) hospitality."[20] The article does *mention* the history of interpretation, including references by rabbinical teachers to the ways in which the people of Sodom and Gomorrah "reversed" the laws of nature. And in those times, the "laws of nature" referred to the *human moral law,* not to the scientific concept of nature as we moderns think of it. Those reversals of the "laws of nature" included the folklore about Sodom and Gomorrah that their laws *were calculated to do injury to the poor and the needy.* They were a sort of ancient "Town Without Pity."

As good and more fair-minded as this article is, it is curious to me that the author does not refer to D. S. Bailey's book in the extensive bibliography. And although I am very appreciative that the author appears to be the first extensive commentator on Genesis 19 who does not perpetuate the association with homosexuality, I would have preferred it if he had *mentioned* that two-thousand-year association and why he decided *not* to perpetuate it. Silence, in this case, is better than slander, but it is not quite golden. It becomes the interpretation that dares not speak its name!

Sodom and Gibeah

The story of the rape of a concubine in Judges 19:22–30 is remarkable in two ways: how incredibly similar the story is to the story of Sodom and Gomorrah, and how differently the story is treated in its translation, annotations, and the history of its interpretation.

The *men of the city* of Gibeah are called a "perverse lot" in the New RSV, and as in the Sodom and Gomorrah story, they pound on the door of a man and demand to have access to a male guest (a Levite) in order to molest him. The interpreters in this case translate the same verb, *yadah* (to know) as "intercourse" ("so that we may have intercourse with him").

The annotation to these verses reads: "To forestall his own *rape* by the men of Gibeah, the Levite offers them his concubine. The text implies that the woman died as a result of her horror."[21]

It is fascinating to me that nowhere in the text or annotations does it suggest that these men of Gibeah were homosexuals or sodomites. Why not? It also uses the correct term for their intention toward the Levite and action toward the concubine: RAPE. Why isn't the word *rape* used in the annotation to interpret the Sodom and Gomorrah story?

Also, this story is practically unknown in the popular mind, unlike the story of Sodom and Gomorrah, although it is equally or more horrifying. In this story, the concubine is raped all night long and is in fact *murdered* by these men. The *threatened* rape of the two (male) angels in the story of Sodom and Gomorrah has excited more outrage (and homophobia) for two thousand years than the actual rape and murder of this woman. This is misogynist biblical interpretation.

One last word before we leave Sodom and Gomorrah (and unlike Lot's wife, let's not look back!): Jesus does make a reference to these "twin cities" in Matthew 10:11–16. In this passage, Jesus is sending out the disciples to preach the good news, "cure the sick, raise the dead, cleanse the lepers and cast out demons" (Matt. 10:8). He gives them instructions on how they are to travel and how to deal with their reception in the towns and villages they enter. To those who do not receive Jesus' disciples with hospitality, he gives the following warning: "Truly I tell you, it will be more tolerable for the land of Sodom and Gomorrah on the day of judgment than for that town" (Matt. 10:15). Jesus uses the famous story of Sodom and Gomorrah not to inveigh against any sexuality or lifestyle but to warn against inhospitality toward those he has sent.

The only other significant reference to Sodom and Gomorrah in the New Testament is in Jude: "Likewise, Sodom and Gomorrah and the surrounding cities, which in the same manners as they, indulged in sexual immorality and pursued unnatural lust, serve as an example by undergoing a punishment of eternal fire" (Jude 7).

Well, there it is, you say! *"Pursued unnatural lust"*—a reference to Sodom and Gomorrah that is implying homosexuality. Not so! The passage is in the context of the discussion of fallen angels, and the note on the words "pursued unnatural lust" says, "Gk: went after other flesh." In other words, an alternate translation of the Greek words *is:* "went after other flesh." The strangers who came to Sodom and Gomorrah were not men but angels. Verse 8 in Jude actually continues this thought: "Yet in the same way these dreamers also defile the flesh, reject authority and slander the glorious ones." The annotation in the New RSV states: "In spite of warnings, the heretics defy authority, revile *angels* [apparently those angels who are God's servants], and live licentiously." It's the threatened rape of angels, not homosexuality, that has Jude upset.

Other Texts of Terror

If we turn to the *Anchor Bible Dictionary*, it has the following notations under the heading "Homosexuality": See prostitution; punishments and crimes; Romans, Epistle to the; and sex and sexuality.

What this means is that the *actual word* "homosexuality" *does not appear in its original Hebrew or Greek equivalent in the whole Bible!*

Part of the reason for that is that the word *homosexual,* in English, did not come into existence until the nineteenth century. Any English translation of the Bible before that will not contain the word *homosexual,* and the New RSV only contains the word *homosexuality* in the annotations and in very misleading ways.

Was there a Greek or Hebrew word that is the equivalent of our English word *homosexual?* I don't know of one Hebrew word that describes us as a whole class of people, but there is such a word in Greek: *homophilia.* This describes not just sexual behavior but a relationship. *The word* "homophilia" *does not appear anywhere in the Greek New Testament.*

So, let's see what the *Anchor Bible Dictionary* has to say in these secondary references to homosexuality:

1. *Prostitution:* In the two articles that appear in the *Anchor Bible Dictionary* on prostitution, the word *homosexuality* is not used. However, there is some discussion about the existence or not of male cult prostitution and how that might have been related to

fertility cults, or how it might or might not have found its way into the life and culture of ancient Israel. Nothing helpful at all about homosexuality per se.

2. *Romans, Epistle to the*: There is a long article in the *Anchor Bible Dictionary* about Romans, but nowhere in it could I find the word *homosexual*.[22] It does have a short paragraph on Romans 1:18–3:30, which includes the second most famous "text of terror" for homosexuals, Romans 1:18–27, which reads:

> For the wrath of God is revealed from heaven against all ungodliness and wickedness of those who by their wickedness suppress the truth. For what can be known about God is plain to them because God has shown it to them. Ever since the creation of the world his [*sic*] eternal power and divine nature, invisible though they are, have been understood and seen throughout the things he has made. So they are without excuse; for though they knew God, they did not honor him as God or give thanks to him, but they became futile in their thinking, and their senseless minds were darkened. Claiming to be wise, they became fools; and they exchanged the glory of the immortal God for images resembling a mortal human being or birds or four footed animals or reptiles.
>
> Therefore God gave them up in the lusts of their hearts to impurity, to the degrading of their bodies among themselves, because they exchanged the truth of God for a lie and worshiped and served the creature rather than the Creator, who is blessed forever! Amen. For this reason God gave them up to degrading passions. Their women exchanged natural intercourse for unnatural, and in the same way also the men, giving up natural intercourse with women, were consumed with passion for one another. Men committed shameless acts with men and received in their own persons the due penalty for their error.

In the commentary it says that Paul is demonstrating that both Gentiles and Jews "deserve divine condemnation and punishment when judged on the basis of their 'works.'" The author of the article says that the word *them* in verses 23 and 25 refers to "Gentiles" (not homosexuals): "The Gentiles, though they 'knew God' (Romans 1:21a) did not give God the reverence and thanksgiving due him [*sic*] (1:21b). Instead, they became idolaters (1:21a–23), the result of which was all manner of sordid behavior that violates the divine will (1:24–31) and makes them worthy of divine condemnation" (1:32).[23] Is this why the *Anchor Bible Dictionary* makes the cross-reference to "homosexuality"? "All manner of sordid behavior"? Is Paul saying that this is a uniquely Gentile "sin"? Is it only about homosexuality? Homosexuality *under cover* of idolatry (and not other homosexual behavior)? *All manner* of sexual behavior practiced in the context of idolatrous worship and living? This is never clarified for us in the Bible or in the commentaries.

3. *Sex and Sexuality:* This fascinating article by Tikva Frymer-Kenskey says some very helpful things, first about the meta-physics of sexuality:

> In these laws of social control over sexuality and its conse-quences, we can detect a respect for the power of sexual attraction. Controlled and confined within the marital sys-tem, it reinforced the social order. Allowed free reign, it might destroy social arrangements and threaten the exis-tence of civilization. The metaphysics of sex, however, only finds explicit statement once in the Bible: "for love is as fierce as death, passion as mighty as Sheol, its darts are darts of fire, a blazing flame. Vast floods cannot quench love, nor rivers drown it" (Song of Songs 8:6–7...).
>
> ...There is no sexuality in the divine sphere. God, usually envisioned as male in gender, is not phallic; God does not represent male virility, and is never imagined below the waist.... This absence of sex from the divine realm is accompanied by a separation of sexuality from the realm of the holy.... Previous theories about Canaanite orgiastic rites or pagan sexual fertility rituals cannot be sub-stantiated. The separation of sexuality from the realm of the holy should *not* be seen as a polemic against pagan religion but as a result of the lack of sexuality in the conception of the divine. This created a vacuum in thinking about sex, one that was ultimately replaced by the negative Greek ideas about women and sexuality which entered Israel in the Hellenistic period.[24]

This is very interesting for several reasons. It is refreshing to read an account of the sexism in Judaism that blames the Greeks instead of just dumping it on Jewish thought. Also, of course, the Christian church came into being during that *Hellenistic period* in the life of Judaism.

This research also undercuts the notion that Jewish ideas about sexuality and homosexuality were a result of a *revulsion* toward pagan fertility-cult prostitution.

The comments in the same article about homosexuality are the only explicit ones in the entire *Anchor Bible Dictionary* and are as follows:

> Israel's intense interest in regulating sexual behavior is an aspect of its concern to prevent intermingling between individuals and groups who should be separate.
>
> ... Like sex with a daughter-in-law, sex with an animal is also called *tebel*, "(improper) mixing." Homosexual intercourse is not labeled *tebel*, but the extreme prohibition of homosexuality by the death penalty (Lev 29:13, Cf 18:22), *not inherited from any other* ANE *[Ancient Near East] laws*, is best explained as a desire to keep the categories of "male" and "female" intact. Anything that blurs the lines, such as cross-dressing, is also prohibited (Deut 22:5). Lesbian interaction, however is not mentioned, possibly because it did not result in true physical "union" (by male entry). The biblical view of creation is one of organization and structure; collapsing the categories of existence is a return to chaos. See punishments and crimes.[25]

Fascinating! Homosexuality (male) is an ironic exception to the rule of the prohibition against *intermingling*. In this case, the idea is to keep the genders "intact" by making sure the sexes intermingle! This, of course, would make sense in any patriarchal culture (which brings up the question, does it make sense in a non-patriarchal culture?). The penalty had to be severe because of course there were always a certain percentage of people who were naturally inclined not to stay "intact"! This desire to keep the male and female roles intact is, of course, the basis of sex-role stereotyping, the purpose of which is to keep women in their place. It is also interesting that "lesbianism" *doesn't count* because a penis is not involved. "True physical 'union'" is equated with *male (penile) entry*.

That reminds me of a story. Rev. Elder Jean White, pastor of MCC London, talks about viewing a TV show about homosexuality with her mother a few years after she had come out. Jean's mother finally turned to her and said, "Well, you can't really call what you women do together *sex*, dear, can you?"

Queen Victoria refused to sign a law prohibiting lesbian sexual relationships because she simply couldn't be persuaded that women did such
things, and if they did, how could it possibly count if there was no penis
involved?

So, homosexuality would "collapse the categories of existence and
"return us to chaos," "destroy social arrangements and threaten the existence of civilization!" This is *cosmic* homophobia expressed accurately
and well. This is the primal fear excited by the existence of homosexuals.
And what kind of "organization and structure," what kind of "social
arrangements" and "civilization" are we talking about? Patriarchal!

I do have to say that I appreciate the honesty of the writer in documenting how the importance of lesbianism was negated in ancient cultures, although it makes me furious. I could certainly have wished for
some theological or political insights about how this ignoring of lesbianism was related to the undervaluing of women in general. It really hurts
not even to rate a minor biblical condemnation in Leviticus or elsewhere!
Lesbian invisibility is about *female invisibility* in the Bible—and everywhere else.

Also, I find the constant pairing of bestiality and homosexuality to be
really annoying. I remember a tense moment in one of our NCC dialogues where an NCC staff member was commenting on the proposal of
one mainline U.S. denomination to refuse to baptize gay and lesbian people. Since this church practices infant baptism, we were all a bit mystified
about how the identification would be made. (Just refuse to baptize every
tenth child?) Nevertheless, she said, "If you will pardon the comparison,
what about murderers? The church doesn't say it won't baptize murderers." In one sense, I agree—point well taken. In another sense, "What the
hell do you mean, 'pardon the comparison?'" No, I will *not* pardon or
accept the comparison, thank you very much. Of course, if we are responsible for destroying "civilization" and "social arrangements," maybe in a
homophobic, patriarchal culture that is *worse* than murder. Especially in
a culture like ours that is addicted to violence, that *gets off on it*. So, who
are the real perverts, anyway?

Here's a really interesting bit of biblical trivia, besides: Exodus 20:13
is one of the Ten Commandments: "Thou shalt not kill." The Bible critiquing the Bible! Leviticus 20:13 says to kill queers; Exodus 20:13 says
don't kill—point that out to fundamentalists![26]

There are lots of actions that were deserving of the death penalty:
cursing your father or mother (Lev. 20:9); adultery (Lev 20:10); being a

medium or a wizard (Lev. 20:27); prostituting yourself, if you are the daughter of a priest (Lev. 20:2); sacrificing your children to the God Molech (Lev. 20:2). I think of the bumper sticker I have seen that says, "Kill a Queer for Christ," or "Death Penalty for Homosexuals,"or "AIDS: God's Gift to Sodomites." You *never* see one that says, "Kill an adulterer for Christ," or "Curse your parents, go to the chair!"; "Hang all psychic readers and advisers." Not that I would want to see them, but this does point out that gays and lesbians get selectively targeted for Levitical battering.

Back to the New RSV and how it treats us gay folks. There is no annotation on Leviticus 18:22, the first prohibition against homosexual (male) relations. Perhaps we should be grateful about that! But the annotation for Romans 1:24, 26–28 states, "They [the annotations don't say this, but "they" means Gentiles] violated their true nature, becoming involved in terrible and destructive perversions; God has let the process of death work itself out. 26–27: See 1 Cor. 6:9n."[27] In this commentary, the word *homosexual* is not used, but there is an unnecessary reference to another "text of terror" whose only connection is that Paul is also the author. The language describing the "sin" in 1 Corinthians 6:9 has nothing in common linguistically with Romans 1:18–27, except in the history of biased interpretation, and in the prejudiced minds of the commentators.

The translation and annotation of 1 Corinthians 6:9 are perhaps the most disturbing, because they ironically are the only comments that take into account any of the scholarship of the last forty years. They take it into account and then blow it!

So, 1 Corinthians 6:9 states, "Do you not know that wrongdoers will not inherit the kingdom of God? Do not be deceived! Fornicators, idolaters, adulterers, male prostitutes, sodomites, thieves, the greedy, drunkards, revilers, robbers—none of these will inherit the kingdom of God" (NRSV).

For me, the most grievous and painful error in this translation is the use of the term *sodomite*. It is the first time of which I am aware that an English translation of the Bible has used this term—which we have already established is a gross misusage, based on an erroneous interpretation of the Sodom and Gomorrah story! So now for the first time in the history of the English translation of the Bible the word *sodomy* is legitimized as being *about* homosexuality. The words *male prostitutes* and *sodomites* are English translations for two Greek words: *malakoi* and *arsenokoiti*. Much has been written about these two words. They do not appear with much frequency in the Greek language or lexicons, so translators have always had to guess at their meaning. In many cases, the two words were combined and translated "homosexual" (as in the previous version of the RSV). It is possible that these words did refer to a specific kind of homosexual behavior, *which may or may not have been practiced by homophiles* or the social equivalent of what we today call gay men. In any case, the annotation to 1 Corinthians 6:9 does nothing to clarify it: "6:9: Male prostitutes, young men or boys in a pederastic relationship; sodomites, the older homosexual; see Romans 1:26–27; 1 Tim. 1:10; possibly 1 Cor. 11:4–7 is pertinent."[28]

First of all, the opinion that these two words mean "a young boy prostitute" and "an older homosexual" john (or heterosexual john who is wanting homosexual sex) is a *guess*. The annotation should say that. Secondly, the equation of *sodomite* with "older homosexual" is misleading and damaging. This annotation now leads us to the last "text of terror," but before we go there, what about the cross-reference to 1 Corinthians 11:4–7?

As we turn to that passage, we see that the context is one of the more troublesome texts for women. It describes a "divine" descending hierarchy from Christ to man to woman:

> Any man who prays or prophesies with something on his head disgraces his head, but any woman who prays or prophesies with her head unveiled disgraces her head — it is one and the same thing as having her head shaved. For if a woman will not veil herself, then she should cut off her hair; but if it is disgraceful for a woman to have her hair cut off or to be shaved, she should wear a veil. For a man ought not to have his head veiled, since he is the image and reflection of God; but woman is the reflection of man.
>
> (1 COR. 11:4–7)

Well, I'm confused, what about you? Among other things, we realize that this is why Paul has never been very popular with feminists!

What do the annotators have to say about this passage? More about the "misogyny of the age"? Nope. Here's what is said: "Reflecting the first-century culture, a man dishonors Christ by worshiping with his head covered; a woman dishonors both her husband and Christ by worshiping otherwise. 4–7a: Confusion of gender, see 6:9n."[29]

So, the implication (it's implied, not stated!) is that this is some weird first-century custom, and just don't worry your heads (male or female) about it. However, the *deadly* reference is this "gender confusion" inserted into the annotation. The implication is that this "male prostitution/older homosexual pederastic sodomy" referred to in 1 Corinthians 6:9 is about gender confusion. Well, I think *they* are confused. This comment assumes a theory of psychology, *not in evidence*, namely that homosexuality is tantamount to *gender* or *gender-role confusion*. Frankly, that is outdated, bad psychology and irresponsible Scripture "scholarship."

Last but not, I'm afraid, least, we have 1 Timothy 1:10: "fornicators, sodomites, slave traders, liars, perjurers, and whatever else is contrary to the sound teaching" (New RSV). There is no comment on this verse in the annotations to the New RSV.

I do like the appearance of the words *slave traders, liars,* and *perjurers* in this verse, however. All who sought to justify slavery conveniently forgot this verse, I guess. Also, the church has lied and perjured itself in the ways in which it has dealt or not dealt with sexism, slavery, racism, and homosexuality. So I guess we're all in the same boat. In actuality, of course, the only time 1 Timothy 1:10 is ever dredged up is in the service of gay bashing.

So, I would give the translators and annotators of the New Revised Standard Version only a D-minus on their scholarship and sensitivity to the emerging critical issues related to homosexuality and the Bible. Time for a new New RSV!

My friend Chris Glaser shared a quote from an unnamed source one year on his Christmas card that said, "Jesus, save us from some of your followers." (Especially "liberal" Scripture scholars.)

Of course, I've picked on the liberals quite a bit. The New International Version of the Bible, for instance, translated 1 Corinthians 6:9 as "male prostitutes or homosexual offenders" — much worse than the New RSV. In 1 Timothy 1:10, the same word is translated "perverts," with no explanation for the different translation.

In the *Vines Expository Dictionary of New Testament Words,* the Greek word *arsenokoiti* appears with no definition. But the Greek word *malakos* has an interesting, somewhat balanced exposition:

> *Malakos:* soft, soft to the touch (Lat. *mollis,* English mollify, emollient, etc. are from the same root), is used (a) of raiment, Matt. 11:8 (twice); Luke 7:25; (b) metaphorically, in a bad sense, 1 Cor. 6:9, "effeminate," not simply of a male who practices forms of lewdness,

but persons in general, who are guilty of abdication to sins of the flesh, voluptuous.[30]

I think it is really a far cry from this Greek word to the statement that all homosexuals and all homosexual behavior are repugnant to God. But, all you voluptuous people, watch out!

And with that, it is time now to leave the texts of terror and move on to new frontiers of gay and lesbian biblical exploration.

4

Outing the Bible: Our Gay and Lesbian Tribal Texts

In this chapter, my hope is that I will go too far.

We've come a long way in a few years in the gay and lesbian community. However, in terms of boldly and comfortably claiming our presence, as if we *really have a right to be included*, we haven't gone far enough.

My experience is that as far as the world and the ecumenical movement are concerned, we have already gone too far just by virtue of showing up.

Being the first open lesbian in many settings has taught me a lot about how provocative our mere existence seems to be. Minority groups are often perceived as more threatening or "larger than life" to the dominant group. The dominant group has all kinds of fantasies about what *they* will do if *they* outnumber or overpower *us*.

Early in the life of UFMCC, women were a small minority. If there were ten men and two women in a room, most men thought of it as *pretty well balanced!* I remember when Troy Perry took my lover Paula and me to a popular gay bar in Hollywood after a big UFMCC event in about 1980. Troy wanted especially to impress Paula, and he told her the bar was about "fifty-fifty" (meaning 50 percent men and 50 percent women). When we got there, there were hundreds of sweating, discoing gay men, two straight women, one possible lesbian, and a drag queen. Troy was flustered and apologetic, and Paula never let him forget it. I watched Troy struggle to understand if this was just an *unusual* night at the bar or if his perception had really been that far off. He never forgot that lesson about perception.

Often, in efforts at dialogue between UFMCC and others, we've been in settings where gays and lesbians were a small percentage of the total group, but were perceived as "overpowering" by the heterosexuals. This is the same kind of phenomenon that often happens in racial contexts.

I used to joke with NCC leaders about our meeting locations. During the planning process for structured consultations, we would have two meetings per year in an airport hotel in Newark, New Jersey. Most of the NCC people came from the East—actually from Manhattan. MCC headquarters are in Los Angeles. I told them that meeting in New Jersey was just *their* idea of "meeting us halfway"! (Hey, it worked for them!)

We have always had to travel further in our consciousness, patience and forbearance, energy, money, and effort to participate in the larger culture. So have all marginalized people.

In this chapter, I am not willing to meet anyone halfway. So, come along if you dare. You've read the warning label!

I don't want to apologize or be subtle. I don't even want to have to be very careful. A bold, proactive reading of the Bible has offered me and others new life as lesbians, gays, and bisexuals. When we are willing to read the Bible *from below,* from our vantage point, the Bible comes alive with new relevance.

What if we just *assumed* that lesbians, gay men, and bisexuals were *always* in the Bible? What if we just accepted the fact that our counterparts followed Moses and Miriam in the Exodus, wandered in the wilderness, and walked with Jesus by the sea of Galilee? We were there! Even when we were silent or closeted about our sexuality. Even if many people in those ancient cultures repressed their sexuality or never expressed it (which is doubtful!), we were there.

It is time boldly to "liberate" some biblical gay, lesbian, and bisexual characters and stories from ancient closets. It may seem unfair to "out" these defenseless biblical characters, but I'm tired of being fair. Centuries of silence in biblical commentaries and reference books have not been fair. A passionate search for biblical truth about sexuality must be undertaken. It is time for shameless, wild speculation about the Bible and about *human* as well as *"homo"* sexuality. Our speculation will not destroy the Bible. If we are wrong about some of our speculation, no one will die. In fact, some people who thought they deserved to die just for being gay or lesbian may actually begin to believe that there is hope for them—and live.

Biblical scholars have always found a place for speculation and imagination when reading the Bible. Thousands of books and stories have been written that expand on or amplify the Bible. These writers do not claim to be infallible, and neither do I. They imagined, wrote, speculated out of their deep love and involvement with the characters and messages of the Bible. All of these are a part of my motivation, too, and I, too, am motivated by the needs of my own community.

The Jewish tradition of *midrash* is very relevant here. Rabbis and other Jewish writers have always claimed the right to *expand* on a given text. To give voice to those who do not speak; to imagine, in a textually consistent way, what they would have said. Allowing the silences to speak is one of the powerful methods of a feminist hermeneutic of the Bible.

It is time for us to let the gay and lesbian and bisexual characters and inferences have voice, life, and dimension.

Does the Bible actually include references to or stories about gays and lesbians *consistent with what historians and anthropologists know about sexuality during biblical times?* The answer is yes. Some stories are incontrovertible. Others are compellingly gay or lesbian. And there are other characters, stories, and images that are curiously suggestive of same-sex relationships. All of these can empower lesbians and gay men to embrace the Bible joyfully.

Gay and lesbian people have long had the "opportunity" to develop our capacity for forgiveness. We are one of the few minority groups (the only one) whose members do not necessarily share their minority status with their families. Many gay men and lesbians have been rejected, punished, and excluded by their families and churches, as well as by the larger society. In order to live, gay men and lesbians have had to learn how to let go, grieve, and forgive.

In order to embrace the Bible joyfully, many people will have to *forgive* the Bible, as well as forgive those who have used it to hurt and punish and ostracize them.

I've seen gay and lesbian people open a Bible fearfully, as if it would physically hurt them to read it. They have *Biblephobia*. For gay and lesbian people who grew up thinking that the Bible was a source of spiritual authority, the word of God, and the story of Jesus' love, the experience of being verbally abused with a Bible was devastating. It was an experience of betrayal. It was no longer safe to open a Bible, to read it, or even, some-times, to own one. And along with this pain came the loss of all the *good stuff* that the Bible had provided.

For other gay and lesbian people, the Bible was never particularly inviting. It was mysterious, intimidating, old-fashioned, male-dominated, hard to read, so they never tried. And if they had ever thought of trying, they sure stopped thinking that way when they came out.

So, what many gay and lesbian people have heard of the Bible is someone else's interpretation. Warmed-over, leftover, biased views of the Bible are a constant undercurrent in American popular culture.

I remember the moment when a person training to be a deacon at MCC Los Angeles suddenly realized that the Bible had a story line. She had always thought of the Bible as a set of instructions, "pearls of wisdom," lists of laws, and so on. Nowhere had she ever learned or heard that there was a *story* that connected all the books and characters of the Bible. I used diagrams, charts, and very *compressed* lectures to help people get the *big, sweeping picture* of the Bible's story line. When she realized this, she was delighted! It was exciting—there was actually a story here that could somehow relate to our story.

Overcoming the fear and hurt and learning to forgive are necessary elements in a gay and lesbian appropriation of the Bible. Obviously, not everyone will want to do it.

As I was preparing to preach a sermon series on "Outing the Bible" at MCC Los Angeles, some of our members took flyers into the street of West Hollywood. The flyers said:

> God doesn't approve of gay and lesbian lifestyles, right?
> THAT'S BULL!
> Come and hear . . .

At first, some of the people receiving the flyers thought that mem-bers of our group were fundamentalists—until they read it carefully! How-ever, even some of the gay men and lesbians who knew that our group came from MCC reacted with hostility just to the mention of the words *God* and *Bible*. People from our church were cursed as gays and lesbians on the street ripped up flyers and shouted, "F—— the Bible!"

Every time something like this happens, I try to teach MCC Los Angeles people not to take it personally and, instead, to utter a prayer.

First of all, a person who would react that way is hurt and enraged, possibly a preacher's kid or a survivor of some authoritarian, homophobic religious abuse. Also, we can say a prayer of thanksgiving. As hard as this is to say, because I also love the Bible, I believe it is better for these people to say, "F——the Bible" than to *believe the crap* other people tell them about the Bible. And even though they rejected the message today, their angry reaction ensures that they will never forget that they encountered a gay or lesbian person who somehow feels there is still something of value in a relationship with the Bible. Perhaps at some future date, when they are ready or are more needy than angry, they may remember and reach out and be able to claim or reclaim a healthy relationship to whatever religious tradition or text is theirs—or make their peace with it and move on.

A Lesbian and Gay "Nation"

Rev. Freda Smith, the first woman ordained in UFMCC, has said many times that UFMCC is the "most exciting church since the Book of Acts." Sometimes we identify very strongly with the intensity, challenges, and dilemmas of the first Christian communities.

That desire to be compared with the early church typifies a very *American* view of church. American sects, as well as many earlier Reformation churches, often have seen themselves as recreations of the "primitive church," and UFMCC is *not* the first church to make this kind of claim for itself. The longing to recapture that experience has its own history in the life of the Christian church. We long for a "primeval" Christian experience that predates the time when the church and the remains of the Roman Empire merged. The imperial church has been much maligned, especially by sectarian Protestants and, more recently, by liberation theologians, for its *institutionalism*, its unchecked wealth and power, its consequent secularization, its loss of urgency, intensity, and vision. The church is often no longer the church for the poor, the outcast, the marginalized—no longer like the disciples who risked everything to cast their lot with this Jesus. However, most Protestants, even sectarian ones, have developed their own forms of institutionalization, rigidity, and materialism!

Unlikely as this may seem to some people, there are some ways in which MCC shares some of the features of this early church—although we must always be aware of over-romanticizing ourselves *or* that early church.

In the early days of UFMCC, we never called ourselves a denomination. Denominations were what we had left behind—those narrow dogmas, doctrines, divisions, parochial loyalties. We were an *ecumenical fellowship*. In fact, *the Fellowship* is an inside affectionate term we use for our "denomination." In many ways, we are a post-denominational denomination. The term *post-denominational* has been in vogue in church circles for some time now. It reflects the reality, for example, of the present-day church in China: in surviving the Cultural Revolution, the Christians in China abandoned narrow and confining denominational differences in favor of a nationwide church. Some church historians believe that denominational ties and distinctions, in the U.S., especially, are fading as we approach the third millennium. The issues, doctrines, and practices that brought about denominational distinctions no longer matter to most people. That trend had made UFMCC's ecumenism understandable and attractive to many people.

On the other hand, UFMCC behaves a lot like a denomination in that we do have a style of organization that includes a modified form of hierarchy; we do have a very simple statement of faith; and we, like other denominations, have a headquarters and endless meetings! So, we've been a little ambivalent about our status as a denomination. Partly our identification as a denomination is a way in which we are trying to appear less sectarian, less marginalized, and more "mainstream."

But UFMCC, today at least, is still very young in the formation of its theology, its style of polity and worship. We were created not out of a theological dispute per se or as a break-off from one *particular* denomination or branch of the church family tree. Instead, we were *called out* from all denominations out of a desperate need, representing all races, classes, walks of life, ages, and lifestyles. Sometimes people in UFMCC can hardly believe whom they are sitting next to in church. It is one of the most difficult aspects of UFMCC to manage at times, and one of the most inspiring and attractive (to some!). Most UFMCC churches still do not own their building (although that percentage has increased greatly, especially in the United States in the last five years), and those that do own buildings do not always own *church* buildings. We still meet in office buildings, other churches, funeral homes, bars, private homes. Most of our churches still struggle to pay the rent and a part-time salary for a pastor, most have limited resources and a devoted core of committed leaders and members. Over the years, dozens of churches have been burned or vandalized. We've experienced lots of different kinds of persecution. This has also helped us to "recognize" ourselves in the Book of Acts.

There has also been a sense of the miraculous that reminds me of the first church. Troy Perry's book *Don't Be Afraid Anymore* documents this wonderfully.[1]

The first-century church existed within the context of a common language, and Hellenistic culture, and safe travel. All these helped the church to grow. UFMCC is a church that has grown up in the fertile context of a great, global gay and lesbian community in the midst of its worldwide awakening. The Book of Acts is an account of an early church that attempted to preach and embody an "unhindered Gospel" (Acts 28:31). UFMCC today is a powerful *ecclesiastical* movement whose first audience is the gay and lesbian community, most in need of an unhindered Gospel.

Reading the Bible and preaching at UFMCC means that I am forever comparing our experience to the experience of the early church. In the story of Peter and the Roman centurion Cornelius (a Gentile), Peter (a Jew) is given a divine vision from God accompanied by a revelation that "God shows no partiality, but in every nation anyone who fears God and does what is right is acceptable to God" (Acts 10:34–35).

The Peter and Cornelius story is just ripe for gay and lesbian exegesis! Peter grew up in a Gentile-phobic culture. And for good reason. In the Hebrew Scriptures, every time the Jews ran into trouble, it was because of their association with Gentiles (and Gentile gods and religious practices). So, the easiest way to handle this problem was just not to associate with them: don't eat their food, don't eat with them, don't marry them. However, there were also prophetic voices in Judaism that expressed countervailing opinions: David's great-great-grandmother Ruth was a Moabitess! Jonah, the reluctant prophet, is chastised by God for his unwillingness to preach salvation to the Ninevites. Isaiah prophesied of a time when Gentiles would be included in the true worshiping community (Isa. 56). The earliest Christians—all Jews—just assumed that one had to be a Jew in order to be a Christian. Nothing else seemed remotely conceivable. In fact, it was probably *heretical* and *blasphemous* to think otherwise!

Then Peter has this "rooftop vision" one afternoon. A huge sheet of all kinds of animals, clean and unclean (kosher and non-kosher) are spread out in front of Peter, and God tells him to *kill and eat*. This happens three times. The thought of eating non-kosher animals is repulsive to Peter. It violates every cultural and religious sensibility he has been raised with. He has been taught to believe that to do so would be to dishonor God and break God's law.

And now he hears *God's voice* saying, "Don't call anything I have made unclean" (Acts 10:15).

Right after he has this mysterious vision, Cornelius sends for him. The "unclean" Gentile asks to hear the good news of Jesus. Peter has no trouble making the connection. He understands that the vision was about the universality of God's love and commitment to every "nation."

The word *nation* is actually the Greek word *ethni* from which we derive our word *ethnic*. The terms refers to a *race, culture,* or *people.* Peter makes the connection that among every race, culture, or people, those who fear God and "do what is right" are eligible for baptism, for inclusion in the people of God.

This brings us back to the gay and lesbian tribal identity issue, only now, we can see it in a biblical context. Is the gay and lesbian community just a political lobby for homosexual behavior, or are we an *ethni*? Certainly there are heterosexual people who engage in homosexual behavior, and gay and lesbian people who may never have sex at all. Are we a kind of behavior, or a kind of people for whom homoerotic attraction is one characteristic?

An *ethni* may be defined by a common history, vocabulary, dialect, culture, institutions (schools, libraries, clubs, churches, synagogues, social organizations, businesses), heroes, political leaders, scholars, values, and the ability to recognize each other even when submerged in the dominant culture. If these constitute an *ethni*, gay and lesbian people are included in the word *nation* used in Acts 10:35.

What evidence of the gay and lesbian *ethni* exists in the Bible? This is a complex detective story made more difficult by thousands of years of heterosexist bias in secular history and biblical scholarship.

ADAM AND EVE

Before we get into a gay and lesbian discussion of biblical theology, I feel as though I need to give at least a nod to Adam and Eve.

My recent experiences with fundamentalists in debating homosexuality and the Bible are that once we have explored and resolved all the texts of terror (and they are surprised that we have read them and can intelligently refute their claims that these verses provide a biblical justification for condemning homosexuality), the fundamentalists usually retreat to the most desperate argument, "What about Adam and Eve? Huh?"

OK, let's look at this story of the mother and father of us all, Adam and Eve. First of all, the first two chapters of Genesis give two distinct traditions about creation, both of which refer to the creation of humans. Much has been written on the theology and grammar of sexuality in those stories: most notably, Phyllis Trible's *God and the Rhetoric of Human Sexuality*.[2]

Scholars have long demonstrated the connections among various creation stories in the Ancient Near East. It is believed by some scholars that Israel borrowed and adapted traditions from surrounding cultures in the telling of both creation accounts in Genesis. Similarities to the creation stories of other indigenous peoples have also been analyzed. Justo Gonzales theorizes that "Genesis 1 and 2 [are] two different stories of creation placed side by side. They represent different tribal traditions."[3] In the past, these stories have been labeled by "author" (*J* and *E*), as if the differences were about individual authors' styles. Gonzales's observation makes more sense in a culture that values the tribal identity more than the individual's identity.

These, then, are not gay and lesbian tribal creation stories! If we are truly to *universalize* them, we must not see Adam and Eve as exclusive in their natures but inclusive. Another way to explore this is to ask the question, Does the fact that God's creation of humans (and other species) includes gender differentiation automatically mean that sexuality is and must be monolithically heterosexual? We do not make the claim that all of human life is simply a *clone* of Adam and Eve. God does seem to like variety as an aspect of creation: human beings are incredibly differentiated into racial, ethnic, size, shape, hue, and other physical and intellectual characteristics. Why would the fact that God created human beings as men and women mean that human beings were to have only one type of sexual identity? Why is it that we cannot see sexuality as a complex, interesting part of the variety of creation?

There is the argument about the "mechanics" of sex, as I call it. One churchwoman said to me, "But, see, look at human anatomy and what *fits* where!" This is the "penis-in-the-vagina" theory—the be-all and end-all of human sexual possibility.

I don't think it is our fault that some people lack sexual imagination. Frankly, lots of body parts can fit quite nicely in lots of places. And I'm sure it is wonderful that for at least some heterosexuals, the *fit* of their penis and their vagina is quite pleasurable and that as the Bible says, "It's good!" But there are endless ways—erotic, sensual, pleasurable—in which human beings can touch each other for their mutual health and enjoyment.

Let's face it: good old Adam and Eve have produced gay and lesbian children! And the fact that we are gay or lesbian does not negate our maleness or femaleness, despite what the annotators of 1 Corinthians 6:9 in the New RSV think! (See chapter 3.)

More threatening and perhaps also making this more complicated is John Money's theory that gender, like sexual orientation, is actually not dualistic but exists on a continuum! There are people (hermaphrodites, transsexuals) who are toward the center of the continuum, and the rest of us are more or less male or female. The need for mythology and strong social sanctions to keep the gender differences "intact" is really understandable. If gender is more truly a *combination* of social construction, genetics, and physiology, then maybe the fundamentalists and patriarchs *do* have something to worry about. Maybe God didn't invent patriarchy, or rigid sex roles. Maybe those gender roles are not given, but change over time. Maybe the world never was monolithically heterosexual.

But let's get this "straight"—that isn't our fault. Adam and Eve, presumably Semites, had black, white, brown, fat, skinny, tall, short, smart, stupid, lovely, hateful, straight, bisexual, gay, and lesbian children. So don't blame us. Blame Adam and Eve. God may have indeed made "Adam and Eve, and not Adam and Steve"—but Adam and Eve made all the rest of us!

A NATION OF BARREN ONES AND EUNUCHS

One way to begin to get a handle on biblical views of a gay and lesbian anthropology is to try to understand biblical concepts of immortality.

The Hebrew Scriptures are not very clear about any consistent concept of life after death. The *Anchor Bible Dictionary* says:

In the cosmology reflected throughout most of the Hebrew Bible,
mortal humankind belongs on earth, not in heaven, at death
descends below to the netherworld known as Sheol. Psalm 115
expressed this succinctly:

> *The heavens are the Lord's heavens,*
> *but the earth he [sic] has given to human beings.*
> *The dead do not praise the Lord,*
> *nor do any that go down into the silence.*
> *But we will bless the Lord from this time on and forever.*
> *Praise the Lord!*

Generally speaking, just as there is no coming back from the dead,
there is no idea or expectation that humans can go to heaven, a
place reserved for God and his [sic] angelic attendants. This means
that any report of a human being ascending to heaven would be
seen as not only extraordinary, but often even as an intrusion or
invasion of the divine realm.[4]

The concept that immortality might consist of "going to heaven" did
begin to enter later Jewish thought and early Christianity, probably
through Hellenistic influences. And contemporary American Jews and
Christians often have similar ideas about heaven or the afterlife.

However, for most of the duration of biblical Judaism, the primary
way one could achieve any sense of "immortality" was through one's
descendants, one's children. Through them, you, your life, and your people lived on.

The cultural values of biblical-era Jews (and of Jews today) were
more communal than those of Western Christians. The individual was not
so important in himself or herself; he or she was important *insofar as he or
she belonged to a people,* to a community. One way to express this belonging was through the bearing and raising of children.

The worst fate that could befall someone in such a culture and religion was to be *cut off* from one's people. There were three primary ways in
which one could be cut off: by being exiled for certain crimes or afflic-
tions, by public execution, or by dying without leaving any children.
Those who were cut off were thought of as having been "cursed."

Conversely, prosperity and having many children were viewed as
signs of God's favor and blessing (see, for example, Psalms 127:3–5 and
128:3–6). The entire story of Job is a wrestling with these very ancient

concepts of curses and blessings, possessions and children as signs of God's favor.

In this context, female barrenness was considered to be the result of God's curse. A woman's self-worth and her worth in the society were directly connected to her ability to give her husband heirs. The immortality of both of them was at stake! The Bible is full of stories of women who desperately prayed to God to open their wombs. Sarah's inability to conceive children for Abraham led to her suggestion that Hagar become the first surrogate mother in the Bible.[5] Rachel's grief over her initial childlessness and Hannah's prayer are also well-known examples. (See Psalms 113:9, Genesis 30:1, and 1 Samuel 1:10.) Luke opens his Gospel with the story of childless Zechariah and Elizabeth and how God blessed them with a son, John the Baptist, in their old age.

In addition, barrenness became a metaphor used by the prophets to describe Israel's pitiful condition when its people felt abandoned or cursed by God. Isaiah 54 begins with a powerful recasting of this metaphor:

> *Sing, O barren one who did not bear;*
> *burst into song and shout,*
> *you who have not been in labor!*
> *For the children of the desolate woman will be more*
> *than the children of her that is married, says the Lord.*
> *Enlarge the site of your tent,*
> *and let the curtains of your*
> *habitations be stretched out;*
> *do not hold back; lengthen your cords*
> *and strengthen your stakes. . . .*
>
> *Do not fear, for you will not be ashamed;*
> *do not be discouraged, for you*
> *will not suffer disgrace;*
> *for you will forget the shame of your youth,*
> *and the disgrace for your widowhood you will*
> *remember no more.*
>
> (ISA. 54:1–2, 4)

Isaiah's prophetic message uses the metaphor of barrenness to represent Israel's condition: the "shame of [her] youth" represents pre-exilic apostasy (faithlessness) and "widowhood" is a metaphor for the Exile. Women were "disgraced" by widowhood because it was considered an indicator that they had done something to put them in disfavor with God. It was financially and socially devastating to be widowed, and even though it might have happened because of God's displeasure, Israel was also commanded to *care* for the widows and orphans in its midst (which, according to the prophets, they did better at some times than at others).

In this recasting of the metaphor, Israel is restored, and like a barren, widowed woman with no hope of children, she is visited with God's favor and now becomes the mother of many children, even more than the children of "she who is married." She is vindicated.

Two chapters later in Isaiah 56, Isaiah uses the term "dry tree" (in Hebrew, a feminine word that implied barrenness) in association with the word *eunuch* (verse 3). In verse 5 of Isaiah, the term "cut off" is used in association with the word *eunuch*. The way in which these terms and metaphors are mingled and associated (in nearby chapters and in the same verses), suggests that the term *eunuch* in Isaiah (and perhaps elsewhere, as we shall see) may really be a generic term used to refer to men and women who did not or could not produce children and were consequently "cursed" and "cut off."

The main reference in the Torah, the law, that was the basis for the exclusion of eunuchs from the Temple is in Deuteronomy 23:1. It reads: "No one whose testicles are crushed or whose penis is cut off shall be admitted to the assembly of the Lord." Leviticus 21:17 says only those who are "unblemished can present themselves before God." This verse was apparently applied to eunuchs, who in some ancient pagan religions were temple priests, and it also may have referred to children who were born of incestuous unions.

But in the marvelous fifty-sixth chapter, Isaiah proclaims an inclusive covenant that promises that eunuchs and barren women, along with Gentiles, will someday have the right to full participation in the blessings of God and in the worshiping community. In this case, Isaiah stops speaking metaphorically and speaks quite literally to two groups of outcasts vis-à-vis temple worship:

> *Do not let the foreigner joined to the Lord say,*
> *The Lord will surely separate me from his* [sic] *people"*
> *and do not let the eunuch say, "I am just a dry tree."*

For thus says the Lord:
To the eunuchs who keep my sabbaths,
who choose the things that please me
and hold fast my covenant,
I will give, in my house and within my walls,
a monument and a name better than sons and daughters;
I will give them an everlasting name
that shall not be cut off. . . .

These I will bring to my holy mountain,
and make them joyful in my house of prayer;
their burnt offerings and their sacrifices will
be accepted on my altar;
for my house shall be called a house of prayer for
all peoples."
Thus says the Lord God,
who gathers the outcasts of Israel,
I will gather others to them besides
those already gathered."

(ISA. 56:4–5, 7–8)

The word *accepted* that is found in the seventh verse has the very same root (using the Greek Septuagint version of the Hebrew Scriptures) as the Greek word *acceptable* in Acts 10:34–35. The context there is that story of Peter and Cornelius already discussed, in which Peter announces that "in every nation [*ethni, people*] anyone who fears God and does what is right is *acceptable* to God." So the connection of Isaiah 56 and Acts 10 is established in the word usage and theology.

My argument (and others have made this argument before me) is that the prophecy in Isaiah 56 is about the hope for future inclusion of those who were previously excluded from the worshiping community. Those who were outcasts and cut off because of their Gentile status or because of their sexuality will now be included. Eunuchs and barren women, I believe, *are our gay, lesbian, and bisexual antecedents*. I also believe it is amazingly simple to demonstrate this.[6] One very obvious point eluded me for a long time: it is in the actual words and structure of this section of Isaiah 56. In speaking about eunuchs, Isaiah says that God says "I will make you a monument better than sons and daughters."

If eunuchs were only males, or castrated males, then why would the words for both sons and daughters be used here? Eunuch is obviously a generic term for something!

In the typical style of the "politics of avoidance," the New RSV makes only this comment about the passage in Isaiah 56: "God himself [*sic*] will honor faithful eunuchs." A very tepid comment, to say the least, which gives no help in understanding the term *eunuch* or why Isaiah would be bothering to mention them in such a dramatic way. Isaiah is proposing changing very precious and sacred boundaries about the definition of Judaism.

Who were the "eunuchs" of biblical times?

Until a few years ago, I would probably have said that the only eunuch I'd ever heard of in the Bible was the nameless Ethiopian eunuch baptized by Phillip on the Gaza road in Acts 8. Most people aren't even aware of that story. I also assumed that the term *eunuch* had only one definition: a male who had been castrated.

But the Bible is virtually swarming with eunuchs! And there is *more than one* definition or understanding of what the term *eunuch* actually means.

Under "Eunuch," the *Anchor Bible Dictionary* says, "*Eunuch*. See Palestine, Administration of Post-exilic Judean Officials" and "*Eunuch, Ethiopian*. See Ethiopian Eunuch."[7]

Let's begin with "Palestine, Administration of." As technical as this passage is, I think it is very crucial in making my argument:

> 4. saris - Eunuch. Its Akkadian origin is sa-resi, "he who is chief." In
> 1 Kings 22:9 the saris is exactly the kind of official for minor errands
> which concerns us here. But he is usually a much higher and foreign
> official; as in Genesis 37–38; Esther 1:10–11; and 2 Kings 18:17.
> Though such an official was often called "eunuch" in the Orient,
> BDB is rather outdated in assigning this as its principal meaning and
> relating it to admittedly demonstrative verbs for castrate in Syriac,
> Aramaic and Arabic. Hence, it will prove relevant to the long-stand-
> ing debate as to whether Nehemiah (1:1) was really a eunuch, as in
> the corresponding Greek (2 Esdras 11:11). . . . Even if Nehemiah was
> called "eunuch," this term, like our "chamberlain," may have really
> signified some administrative office. If so, it would seem to have been
> of a higher and more privileged rank than the local officials being dis-
> cussed here.[8]

I have a theory about the role of eunuchs, especially in the Hebrew Bible: that eunuchs often appear on the scenes as *messengers* and *go-betweens* and are often involved in palace intrigue in the Jewish or foreign royal courts.

This theory or observation, perhaps more than any other, correlates to Judy Grahn's and Mark Thompson's theories of gay and lesbian tribal identities. If gay men, particularly, were *berdache* (go-betweens, mediators between earthly parties and between heaven and earth), shamans, and magicians in ancient cultures, why wouldn't they also show up in that role in the Bible? They certainly do. And in the Bible these people are called eunuchs. The eunuchs in the Joseph story and the Esther story are notable in this regard. And this is certainly the role of Nehemiah, which the NRSV says was as "a palace servant of Artaxerxes I at Susa in Elam,"[9] winter residence of the Persian kings. The word *eunuch* (*saris*) appears seventeen times in the Hebrew Bible, and there are other references to persons in similar roles. Furthermore, the *eunuchs serve a subversive role in the palaces of Israel's enemies*. They act as a kind of palace double agent, they are spies and sources of information (palace gossips). This reminds me of the old insider gay aphorism: "Telegraph, telephone, tell-a-queen!"

In some cases, these eunuchs actually go against their own bosses (and kings) and rescue the prophets, kings, queens, or spokespersons of God. One really important example of this is the Ethiopian eunuch in Jeremiah 38:7–13. At the risk of his own life, Ebed-melech, the Ethiopian, "a eunuch in the king's house," rescues Jeremiah by pulling him out of a cistern. Jeremiah, the unmarried prophet, was being held there, waiting to be murdered by his own people. Ebed-melech becomes the agent of God in rescuing Jeremiah. Interestingly, the New RSV has this to say about Ebed-melech: "Ironically, Jeremiah was delivered from murder . . . by a foreign court official (who was not necessarily a eunuch physically)."[10]

So, if he was not *necessarily a eunuch physically*, in what sense was he a eunuch? How does the New RSV know of more than one kind of eunuch? And why the association of eunuchs with castrati? One documented fact is that there were boys who were raised to become court servants or officials, and they were castrated so they could safely administer the palace household and be trusted not to impregnate the queen or princesses. They were castrated in order to preserve social order, to safeguard caste and class, through preserving the royal bloodline. Such castrati sometimes would still have heterosexual sex without ejaculating sperm, although many became functionally homosexual. It may also be that young men who were noticed to be gay were also groomed for these positions because it would be obvious that they would not be interested in impregnating the queen or princesses. If many ancient cultures managed to acknowledge the special gifts of gay and lesbian people, why not the cultures of the ancient peoples who are referred to in the Bible?

So, the term *eunuch* may have referred to a role that was *stereotyped* as one meant for castrati, gay men, or the occasional safe, highly efficient, trustable straight man. There are, as we know, occasional heterosexual male interior decorators and hairdressers—they're just not very common! In fact, the modern association of castrati with gay men may simply be a homophobic one—that is, all gay men are socially "emasculated," in modern cultures in particular.

Once we expand the definition of *eunuchs*, they of course become potentially a larger group of people. Isaiah, in chapter 56, chose two groups of people to symbolize the future expansion of the "people of God," thereby including those who had previously been excluded: eunuchs and Gentiles. If eunuchs were only castrated males, that would seem to be an awfully small group of people to prophesy about. Also, the New RSV annotators obviously agree that some eunuchs were "not eunuchs physically." It would be interesting to know why they think this particular *saris* in Jeremiah was not a castrati kind of eunuch (do they think he was also not gay?). Is it because they think a castrati wouldn't be that important an official? Or wouldn't he have been *butch* enough to be able to get Jeremiah out of the cistern? And it is clear in any case that whatever the sexual orientation of eunuchs, Isaiah viewed them as people who are *barren*, who do not reproduce, and who are therefore *cut off*.

The stories of Ebed-melech and of other faithful eunuchs before him make Isaiah's prophecy easier to understand. God wants to honor eunuchs, foreign and domestic, who have themselves already been faithful to God! God is overturning the restrictions on admission to "the people of God" based on physical characteristics, sexual status, or ability to reproduce.

I will demonstrate that this prophecy is actually fulfilled in the New Testament, as is the prophecy of the inclusion of the Gentiles. But I have never seen anywhere, except in writings by gay or lesbian theologians, even the barest research on the connections among the various references and prophecies about eunuchs in the Bible.

One of the most startling references to eunuchs in the New Testament was made by Jesus. He speaks about eunuchs in a passage that is one of the most *under commented on* in all of the Gospels: Matthew 19:10–12. These verses occur in the context of a discussion about divorce. Jesus is taking a hard line about divorce, and the disciples complain, saying, "Well, if you're going to be that strict about divorce, maybe it's better not to marry!" To which Jesus replies that this injunction against heterosexual divorce does *not* apply to everyone:

> For there are eunuchs who have been so by birth, and there are eunuchs who have been made eunuchs by others, and there are eunuchs who have made themselves eunuchs *for the sake of the kingdom of heaven.* Let anyone accept this who can.

It is amazing to me that: neither the story of Phillip and the Ethiopian eunuch, nor the story of Ebed-melech in Jeremiah, nor Isaiah's prophecy in Isaiah 56 are cross-referenced in the New RSV with Matthew 19—or in *any* Bible or standard commentary! These are the politics of biblical interpretation at their most subtle and at their worst. Such gross omission and silence obscure the possible relationship of these passages.

Furthermore, I have never seen any commentary on Matthew 19 that acknowledges that Jesus spoke of a *typology* of eunuchs. Obviously, Jesus knew that there was *more than one way* to become labeled as a eunuch. The annotation in the New RSV states simply, "Jesus recognizes a place for voluntary celibacy in the service of God's kingdom."[11] Voluntary celibacy? That's all? What about the other two categories? Do the annotators think they are self-explanatory? OK, suppose we agree that "making themselves eunuchs for the sake of the kingdom of God" is about voluntary celibacy and that, perhaps, "being made eunuchs by others" covers the castrati, but who are *"eunuchs from birth"*?

If "eunuchs from birth" are hermaphrodites or those with birth defects that affect the male genitals, just how many people are we talking about here? (Statistically, hermaphodites occur in less than one in one hundred thousand births.) It is unlikely that Jesus met more than ten thousand people in his lifetime—and even that estimate would be pushing it. The likelihood of him coming across such a person is remote. So, who are the "eunuchs from birth"?—those to whom the rules about heterosexual marriage may not apply? I have a clue, and I think John

McNeill, in his book *The Church and the Homosexual,* was the first to say it: gay and lesbian people!

We used to see a pamphlet—produced, I think, by Evangelicals Concerned (a gay and gay-friendly evangelical group started by Dr. Ralph Blair)—that said on the cover, "What Jesus Said About Homosexuality." You would turn to the inside, and there was a blank page! On the back page it said, "That's right, he said absolutely nothing." We thought that was cute and comforting. Thank God, at least Jesus kept his mouth shut about us. Big sigh of relief.

But I think it's not true. I think Jesus spoke about us and to us in Matthew 19. What this passage says to me is "Let anyone accept this who can": "Yoo-hoo! Homosexuals, listen up! This one's for you!" So he did speak about us, to us, and said, "I know who you are, and you are included, too."

But the real capstone in this chain of prophecy and fulfillment lies in the story of Phillip and the Ethiopian eunuch (Acts 8:26–40).

What is fascinating about this story in Acts is that it is the story of yet another Ethiopian eunuch, and I find no commentary anywhere that acknowledges that there are two Ethiopian eunuchs in the Bible. Bible commentators who spend paragraphs on obscure and remote associations *never* link these two characters. I think it's *eunuch phobia.* For that matter, the racism of the white-dominated biblical "scholar guild" could mean it is also *Ethiopian phobia.*

There are contrasting views of cultural "stereotypes" of Ethiopian eunuchs: Herbert Lockyer states that Ebed-melech was *"a credit to his class[!]"* (not race, but *class*).[12] Lockyer seems to have information that eunuchs were considered a *class* or *caste* of person. In addition he states, as a generalization: "The Eastern Eunuchs were a *pitiless, cruel race,* whose delight was to wound and vex."[13] Well, that sounds like some drag queens I've come across! "Priscilla [Ebed-melech] Queen of the Desert" eunuchs were a *bitchy* class? He also called him "the benevolent eunuch" in a way that sounds an awful lot like the "Good Samaritan," meant to be an oxymoron.

Beverly Roberts Gavents also writes about the Ethiopian eunuch of Acts 8 in the *Anchor Bible Dictionary.* She says:

> What has puzzled interpreters is that Luke identifies this particular Ethiopian as a eunuch, which means that he *cannot have been a*

proselyte to Judaism (cf. Deut 23:1 and Joseph Ant. 4:290–91), despite the fact that he has been to Jerusalem to worship and is reading from a scroll of Isaiah as he travels (8:27–38). . . . Interestingly, Luke himself does not comment on the restrictions about converting eunuchs, which may suggest that Luke is less interested in that feature of the story than he is in some others. For example, eunuchs frequently held places of respect and trust in Eastern courts, as does this one, and the identification of this figure as a eunuch may simply reinforce the reader's impression that he is an *unusual person*. . . .

Within the story, the Ethiopian's actions underscore this portrayal of him as an intriguing, romantic, even exotic personage.

The Ethiopian, coming as he does *from the end of the earth*, stands at the threshold of the worldwide mission. . . . He prefigures Cornelius. . . . Small wonder the early church writers pass along a tradition that the Ethiopian [eunuch] returned to his own country and preached a gospel there.[14]

This author thinks that the Ethiopian's "eunuch-ness" is just incidental and just serves to make him more exotic. This is a profound trivialization of the meaning of this story.

Gavents does not pick up that in the story the eunuch is reading the *Book of Isaiah*. He in fact is reading from Isaiah 53:7–8 (awfully close to Isaiah 54 and 56!), which among other things details the fate and destiny of the Suffering Servant, whom Christians identify with Jesus, the Messiah. In that description (53:8), Isaiah states:

> *By a perversion of justice he was taken away.*
> *Who could have imagined his future?*
> *For he was cut off from the land of the living,*
> *stricken for the transgression of my people.*
> (ISA. 53:8)

It is not *incidental* that Luke quotes this passage of Isaiah or that the eunuch wanted to understand it. The term "cut off" is a reference to the curse that was placed on anyone who was *exiled, executed by capital punishment,* or *did not reproduce.* The Ethiopian eunuch was reading a prophecy of a Messiah *with whom he could identify!* Someone who, like him, was cut off, not able to be a part, not able to enjoy the gift of immortality.

The eunuch had reason to believe that there was hope that those who had been cut off—who had not been eligible—would now be eligible. When he asked Phillip what was to prevent him from being baptized (he was ineligible before on *two* counts: being Gentile and being a eunuch), Phillip is silent in the text and simply baptizes him. And we don't even know his name. The nameless eunuch, the patron saint of Ethiopian Christians, a black gay man, becomes the first African Christian, and the most clear and complete fullfillment of the prophecy of Isaiah 56, that God's house would become a "house of prayer for all people."

The Wise Ones

My favorite eunuchs of the Bible are too obvious to be believed. The wonderful story of the magi in Matthew's narrative of Jesus' infancy is a tale of eunuchs. It doesn't say there were *three* wise ones; postbiblical legend invented that number. Matthew's second chapter is devoted to these mysterious foreign strangers who visit the infant (or toddler) Jesus.

Our Christmas crèches always combine the Luke and Matthew infancy narratives, which are almost mutually exclusive in their content. We just put everyone (shepherds, angels, wise men) there together at the manger at the same time.

Matthew 2 tells a story of what the New Oxford Annotated Bible calls "three wise men, a learned class in ancient Persia."[15] They were Zoroastrian priests, astrologers, magicians, ancient shamans from the *courts* of ancient Persia. They were the equivalent of Merlin of Britain. They were sorcerers, high-ranking officials, but not kings—definitely not kings. But, quite possibly, they were *queens*. We've always pictured them with elaborate, exotic, unusual clothing—quite festive, highly decorated and accessorized! But, not until I recognized that they were probably eunuchs did I realize that never *once* did I imagine that their wives accompanied them on this trip! Deep down, I never thought of them as having wives.

Also, the wise eunuchs, shamans, holy men were the only ones who had the forethought to go shopping before they visited the baby Jesus! This seems to me to be an obvious gay clue!

They also have shamanistic dreams. They deceive evil King Herod and actually play the *precise* role that many other prominent eunuchs play in the Bible: they rescue the prophet, this time the Messiah of God, and foil the evil royal plot against God's anointed. It's a classic gay/eunuch drama!

I mean, who were those guys? They get a whole chapter in Matthew and then disappear forever from the scene (another classic eunuch trait). They are foreigners. They are pagans. They are "queer"! They are heroes, and their images grace millions of homes, windows, churchyards, chancels, children's pageants, musicals, and hymns every Advent and Christmas. Just think of all those children in their father's bathrobes in Christmas pageants every year, trying to portray three queens in semidrag! Jesus had gay *fairy godmothers* who dropped in on him and saved his life, so he could save ours. What a great book! For a fairly complete listing of eunuchs in the Bible, see the appendix at the conclusion of this book.

JESUS: DE FACTO EUNUCH

Jesus Christ, whom Christians claim is the fulfillment of the Suffering-Servant prophecy of Isaiah 53, was "cut off" from his people in two ways: he was executed as a criminal, and he presumably died without heirs. He was a functional, if not physical, eunuch (like Ebed-melech?). The life, death, and resurrection of Jesus Christ, furthermore, redefined for the new emerging Christian community the way in which one achieves eternal life. No longer was eternal life achieved through bearing children but through one's identification with the risen Christ.

The whole "family" and "family values issue" is critical in looking at the issue of gays and lesbians in the Bible. The belief that there is an "ideal" or "normal" family and that everyone who doesn't "fit" that family model is somehow lacking is a politically motivated sham.

As we pointed out earlier, when confronted by his biological family (mother, brothers, and sisters), Jesus pointed to his disciples as his new family and said, "For whoever does the will of God is my brother and sister and mother" (Mark 3:31).

The Bible, in fact, knows almost nothing of the post-Reformation ideal of monogamous, lifelong, romantic heterosexual marriage. Heterosexual marriages, in fact, were not performed inside Christian churches until the second millennium. The Bible includes examples of marriage relationships that are based on political and property considerations; ones that are the product of international politics, that are essentially business transactions; as well as polygamy, extended families, Levirate marriages (in which a man was obligated to marry his brother's widow when he died), and other lifestyles. The antimarriage bias in the New Testament and the negative emphasis on sex of early Christian theologians (we can probably blame this on the Hellenists, too!) are well documented by experts in human sexuality.

Virginia Mollenkott has a wonderful appendix to her book *Sensuous Spirituality* that lists eighteen "diverse forms of family mentioned or implied in the Hebrew and Christian Scriptures." The appendix then goes on to include twenty-two "additional forms of family mentioned or implied in the Hebrew and Christian Scriptures suggested by participants at Families 2000"—a conference *sponsored by the National Council of Churches of Christ* (Chicago, April 1991).[16]

The myth—actually the *lie*—that said *the* approved form of biblical family consists of a romantic, lifelong monogamous heterosexual couple (with 2.3 kids) is amazing in its persistence and its powerful influence. Only something like 11 percent of families in the United States live in such a configuration. The way the rest of us live—in what are called "alternative families" (even though they are alternatives to a small minority lifestyle)—is actually much more like the varied family configurations of the Bible!

The so-called nuclear family is an invention of post-Reformation, industrial Western society. Yet at least in the United States, people who pontificate about family values and who put down the rest of us have been able to bully the politicians, the leaders of our country, and have misused the Bible to do it.

One way to get at this is to ask the question, Where in the Bible do you find a clear, incontrovertible example of that "nuclear family"? Every family in the Bible seems to have its *unusual* aspects or complications. The only heterosexual *couples* explicitly mentioned in the whole New Testament that I am aware of are Joseph and Mary (not by any means an *ordinary* relationship); Priscilla and Aquilla (if, that is, *Aquilla* is truly a male name); and Peter and his wife, but only by inference (since Jesus heals Peter's mother-in-law, we assume he was married or widowed). There are no other heterosexual couples actually identified in the entire

New Testament. Paul does complain at one point that some apostles get to bring their wives along on missionary trips, and this indicates that some of them were married (1 Cor. 9:5).

I always thought it was interesting that Paul feels the necessity to say, in 1 Timothy 3:12, "Let deacons be the husband of one wife." In the New RSV they translate it differently for the first time (although they acknowledge the literal wording, they give no explanation for their revised translation). It now reads, "Let deacons be married *only once*." In any case, the fact that Paul has to say this meant that Christians either *did* marry more than once (enough so that Paul would have to make special mention of this restriction for deacons only) or that the people who were being evangelized in the Hellenistic world (outside of Palestine) were still practicing forms of polygamy, which the church had not entirely outlawed. Why else would Paul feel compelled to mention it?

This is just one example of the ways in which we need to read *between the lines* and ask questions about the inferences about marriage in the Hebrew and Christian Scriptures.

WHAT KIND OF FAMILY DID JESUS HAVE?

There have been some books that speculate about Jesus' marriage and family but not very many.[17] Most people's superficial view of Jesus' family life is that Jesus grew up in a small town with his mother and father and (if you're not Catholic) with brothers and sisters; that Jesus' father probably died before his public ministry began (although this is never stated, it is a widely held assumption). The prevailing assumption is also that Jesus was celibate all his adult life—he never married—and he considered his mother and Nazareth his home base.

Besides Nazareth, there are two other places that are referred to in the Gospels as Jesus' home: Capernaum (Mark 2:1) and the home of Mary, Martha, and Lazarus in Bethany.

In a different way, the Temple in Jerusalem is also home for Jesus. In the only story of Jesus' childhood in the canonical Scriptures, Jesus gets separated from his biological family as they are returning from Jerusalem to Nazareth. They go back to Jerusalem to look for him and finally discover him, after three days (an interesting parallel to the resurrection), talking to the teachers in the Temple. Jesus is in his *Abba's* house (aramaic for "Father" or "Daddy," and some even say "Mommy") and feels at home there. The story records his mother upbraiding him for worrying them and "treating us like this." Is Jesus apologetic? Sorry for worrying and alarming them like that? No. His answer is actually quite surly (or perhaps even *snotty*): "Why were you searching for me? Did you not know I must be in my Father's house?" (Luke 2:49).

Jesus, at age twelve (a typical preteen in some ways), thinks his parents *just don't get it*. In fact, the Bible *says* they didn't understand him (the battle cry of adolescence!)

But this may also be a clue that Jesus' familial relationships were already a little strained—not "ordinary." In my lighter moments, I imagine this as every parent's nightmare: not only is your adolescent a know-it-all and doesn't want to be seen with you in public but on top of that, your kid really *IS God (or the Messiah)!*

One of the areas that intrigues me is the relationship of Jesus to his father Joseph. Only Matthew includes anything about Joseph: in that Gospel, Joseph plays the role of the faithful Jew, obedient to God's demands, a protective agent of the Messiah (a little bit like the role of a eunuch). Luke includes Jesus' parents in the story of his boyhood, but only Mary speaks.

The assumption that Joseph has died by the time Jesus begins his ministry is an interesting one. If Joseph was in his twenties or thirties or older when Jesus was born, his dying is very plausible. One also wonders if Jesus waited to begin his ministry until after his father died, and if so, why? What was their relationship like? Was Joseph still alive during part or all of Jesus' ministry? Was he disapproving? Joseph just *disappears* in the New Testament—vanishes without a trace like so many fathers (and like a lot of the eunuchs). Jesus fits the old psychoanalytical (and erroneous!) profile of a homosexual man: an absent father and an overprotective, domineering mother!

Why is it that scholars have never pursued the subject of Jesus' relationship with Joseph? What kinds of issues might this raise that would be difficult or challenging to our traditional views of Jesus' family life? Especially since it is still taboo in orthodox circles to see Joseph as Jesus' biological father.

Gay men and lesbians can easily understand Jesus' problems with his family's lack of understanding of his identity as the Messiah. Gays and lesbians, unlike racial and ethnic minorities, often find themselves feeling and being different from their family members. Not sharing your identity or minority status with most or all of your family members is very isolating and alienating..

In "coming out" as the Messiah, Jesus experienced alienation from his biological family, at least at first. We lesbians and gay men understand this very well.

So, Jesus had four homes: with his biological family in Nazareth, in Capernaum (we're not sure why); in the Temple (God's house is his home); and with Mary, Martha, and Lazarus. In another sense, however, Jesus is *homeless*. He is at home nowhere. "Foxes have holes, and birds of the air have nests, but the Son of humanity has nowhere to lay his head" (Luke 9:58). Jesus began his life *away* from his home in Nazareth, unable to find "room at the inn" in Bethlehem. There is a tension between Jesus being at home in lots of places (no one home or family structure could contain him, could be adequate for him, could completely claim or own him) and his never quite being at home anywhere.

We get a little view of family life for Jesus in John 2. Jesus' mother attends a wedding in Cana, nine miles northwest of Galilee. There is no mention of his father. (Dad hated weddings? Was he dead, or ill, or a workaholic?) This could have been the wedding of a cousin or other relative or of relatives of friends from Nazareth. Jesus *and the disciples* are invited. I wonder if those who are giving the wedding feast invited only Jesus, but he asked if the disciples could come. Or they invited Mary and Jesus, and she told them, "Oh, he'll only come if he can bring the whole gang!" Part of the style of Jesus' ministry and life was that these disciples were now a part of his extended family and social life as well. Verse 12 amplifies and corroborates this "blended-family" reality of Jesus' life:

> After this [the wedding in Cana] he [Jesus] went down to Caper-
> naum with his mother, his brother and his disciples; and they
> remained there a few days.
>
> (JOHN 2:12)

Capernaum is on the northern shore of the Sea of Galilee, so they were having a few days *at the shore*. Maybe to do a little fishing, resting, and strategizing. At this stage the family and disciples are still somewhat blended, in contrast to later stories (like the one in Mark 3:31) where Jesus' biological family seems to have been *replaced* by this *family of disciples.*

But even as we try to understand the disciples as Jesus' primary community or family, there are myths and assumptions to overcome. Jesus did call twelve male disciples to be the core of this new community. However, in many places in the Gospel the term *disciples* has a broader meaning that includes all those who followed Jesus—those in the crowds and the "camp followers." Many scholars believe that the limiting identification of the "twelve disciples" was written back into the Gospels. One passage from Luke 8 adds some very important information to this picture of who was providing support for the blended family or movement of disciples:

> Soon afterward he went on through cities and villages, proclaiming and bringing the good news of the Kingdom of God. The twelve were with him, as well as some women who had been cured of evil spirits and infirmities: Mary, called Magdalene, from whom seven demons had gone out, and Joanna, the wife of Herod's steward Chuza, and Susanna, and many others who provided for them [other authorities say "him"] out of their resources.
>
> (LUKE 8:1–3)

Now, let's see if we understand this! Jesus was traveling around the countryside (staying in homes, camping out?) with twelve men, one of whom had a mother-in-law and presumably a wife; but in addition, women traveled with them. One of these women had been healed of what would today probably be labeled a severe psychosis and was probably still recovering from years of social ostracism, pain, and rejection. Then there was Joanna, the wife of a man whose job is called "domestic administrator" (a court official, a eunuch?), and *many* others (women) who supported them (or "him," meaning Jesus) financially. Well, no wonder his family began to wonder if he were crazy; no wonder they came to get him! In a society that strictly regulated social contact between women and men, this was more than highly irregular. Married women without their husbands, who were there because Jesus had healed them. Probably some of them were *in love* with him, deep into what psychologists would call "transference," grateful to have been helped by a gentle man who actually noticed them and cared that they were suffering. Also, single, abused, and abandoned women, recovering from mental, spiritual, and physical illnesses. Probably many of the men were following him for the same reason. All of them wanting Jesus' attention, wanting to be a part of the new community.

The fact that Jesus accepted the money or other kinds of support from these women is also amazing in his cultural context. Imagine the scorn he and both the male and female disciples had to put up with for that alone! And *all* the men were benefiting from the support of these women. Imagine what names they were called.

What do we think Chuza's "domestic administrator" thought or said when his wife came to him and said, "See you later, honey; I'm emptying our bank account and going off with some women friends to follow Jesus and his disciples. Be back in a few weeks, maybe." Do you think he said, "Have a wonderful time, you're in my prayers, I think I'll ask Chuza for a donation"? I doubt it. What did other family members think? What were the consequences of the fact that Jesus and his followers broke many societal rules to do this ministry?

And just what was life really like on the road? Even if the understanding was that the members of this new family group were to be sexually faithful to whatever husbands or wives were back home (who may or may not have been filing for divorce!) or committed to an ideal of celibacy if they were single—the social, emotional, and sexual dynamics, the attractions and jealousies must have been incredible to try to manage. And the sleeping arrangements. And the day-to-day issues of being part of an eclectic, co-sexual nomadic community that did not have any of the same structures that these folks had been used to all their lives. It is unrealistic and naive not to consider these issues. Also, there must have been tremendous excitement, urgency and gratitude for the kind of loving fellowship that we only get glimpses of. All these people were there because they had been *touched by Jesus* and invited to go along. We read of others whom Jesus heals who ask to be allowed to come along, but Jesus tells them to go home instead. Was this sometimes because the traveling road show was getting complicated—too complicated to include more people?

Jesus also had a way of engaging complete strangers in an immediate, intimate way. The Gospels talk frequently about him feeling love and compassion for strangers, seeing into their hearts, feeling sorry for the lost and lonely crowds.

Were there children in his community? We certainly do read of the children who come to be blessed and the male disciples who want to shoo them away. But were there eventually children who actually traveled with Jesus' new community? If there were "many women" as it says in Luke 8, then I have to think there must have been some children traveling with them. It's hard to believe that they would have all been willing or able to leave the children behind. What was it like for these children? Or for the children whose mothers or fathers did leave them behind to be cared for by single parents or other family members?

Clearly, there are many unresolved issues about Jesus' home and family life. How much have traditional theologies read their own cultural mores and biases and lifestyles back into New Testament times? Certainly, I will be accused of doing that! However, all biblical commentators and certainly most preachers do that frequently. Dr. Thomas Hanks, a Presbyterian missionary in Argentina who is also a member of Metropolitan Community Church, has this to say in the *Anchor Bible Dictionary* about these biases.

> Liberation theologians have scarcely even raised any question about New Testament perspectives on despised sexual minorities and uncleanness (Countryman, 1988). Medieval monks assumed the New Testament to represent the perspective of continent bachelors; Protestantism has tended to assume that everyone except Paul must have had a wife and children. The failure to challenge sexual and family ideological assumptions has been a glaring weakness in theological efforts to delineate New Testament perspectives on oppression and poverty (Greenberg, 1988)[18]

It is very important, in a lesbian hermeneutic of the Bible, to "challenge sexual and family assumptions," especially about Jesus. A monolithically heterosexual, or even asexual assumption has dominated the interpretation of Jesus' life, ministry, and personhood for too long. For too long Jesus, and other New Testament characters, in particular, have been portrayed by the church as biblical versions of "genitalia-free" Barbie and Ken dolls. For Jesus to be accessible to new generations, in a new millennium, we will need to have the courage to read the same texts with new eyes, without those limiting assumptions. We must be willing to see ourselves in Jesus' experiences and choices about family and relationship.

At this point, I want to move on to the exploration of the people who I believe were Jesus' adult family of choice.

THE BETHANY COMMUNITY:
JESUS LOVED MARY, MARTHA, AND LAZARUS

We turn now to what J. D. Hastings, in an older commentary entitled *Greater Men and Women of the Bible,* called *"That most interesting of all New Testament households, the Bethany family."*[19] Hastings also calls Bethany Jesus' *"home away from home."*[20] Bethany was less than two miles from Jerusalem. There is some dispute among Bible scholars about whether or not there are two Bethanys. In any case, Jesus is said to have been baptized at the Jordan River near Bethany, and he actually ascended into heaven just outside of Bethany. In the Synoptics (the Gospels of Matthew, Mark, and Luke) Jesus made Bethany his "headquarters" during his final week (Mark 11:11–12; Matt. 21:17; Luke 19:24). Jesus was anointed there, either by a nameless woman at Simon the leper's home or by Mary at the home of Mary, Martha, and Lazarus. Bethany was the *last station for pilgrims on their way from Jordan to Jerusalem.* And in John 12, it is the "launching" place from which the crowd marches into Jerusalem on Palm Sunday.

I have sometimes wondered if we might someday find a long-lost "Bethany gospel" that might solve some of the mysteries of the Bethany community and of Jesus' relationship to Mary, Martha, and Lazarus, his "adult family of choice." Perhaps John's Gospel really is (in part) a Bethany Gospel.

On the one hand, Mary, Martha, and Lazarus are the *only persons mentioned by name* whom Jesus *loved.* The others are the "beloved disciples" (more about that later) and the nameless "rich young ruler" who turns away from Jesus' invitation to follow him.

John McKenzie, in the *Dictionary of the Bible,* says that there is an "old unsolved problem" about Mary, Martha, and Lazarus that seems to relate to differences in the Synoptic and Johannine traditions.[21] John's Gospel treats the story of the raising of Lazarus from the dead (John 11) as the pinnacle of Jesus' ministry. It is his most impressive miracle, on the one hand, and it seals his fate, on the other. It is the longest account of any miracle, and it contains a great deal of detail, dialogue, and symbolism, in typical Johannine fashion. Also, after the resurrection of Lazarus, crowds begin to form in Bethany to see Lazarus and Jesus, and the Pharisees begin to seek Lazarus's life as well as that of Jesus (John 12:10). Jesus and Lazarus become paired as dangerous threats to the religious establishment. It is that post-resurrection-of-Lazarus *Bethany crowd* that marches into Jerusalem on Palm Sunday.

In contrast, the Synoptic Gospels (Matthew, Mark, and Luke) *do not even mention Lazarus*. Luke has Jesus tell a parable, "The Rich Man and Lazarus" (Luke 16) that is about a poor fictional character. Most scholars believe this character is totally unrelated to the brother of Mary and Martha.

Even more curiously, Luke does in fact mention Mary and Martha in the famous story in Luke 10:38. He oddly omits any mention of Lazarus. In this account, Bethany is not mentioned, just "a certain village," and Martha is named as the householder. Why the mysterious reference to location? In John 11, Mary and Martha are well-known persons who live in Bethany. *Who's Who in the Bible* comments, "It is strange that there is no further mention of Lazarus and his family in the history of the early Christian church at Jerusalem."[22]

The story of the raising of Lazarus is corroborated by one non-canonical source, the Secret Gospel of Mark, a Gnostic Gospel. Eastern Orthodox tradition says he was shipwrecked and became the bishop of Kitionum on Cyprus. Western Christian sources say he became first bishop of Marseilles and that Mary and Martha became missionaries to France.

Some scholars theorize that the sources of the Synoptic Gospels represent a kind of cumulative "anti-Lazarus" feeling, brought about by the idea that his resurrection caused the hastening of Jesus' death. Other scholars theorize that John exaggerated this story, that it is not as reliable as other miracle stories in the Gospels, and that it is meant to be a symbolic story, with Lazarus as the representation of all Christians who will die and be raised with Christ.

One very fascinating aspect of all this is the connection to the mystery of the "beloved disciple."

I found Vernard Eller's book, *The Name of the Beloved Disciple*, published in 1987, to be totally credible, and it convinced me that Lazarus *was* the beloved disciple.[23]

Tradition favors the view that John (son of Zebedee) was the beloved disciple. In fact, the identity of the beloved disciple is never overtly stated; it is only implied. There is a connection to the probably pseudonymous author of the Book of John.

Eller's arguments are very well made. He gives ample evidence for the *unlikeliness* of John as the beloved disciple and makes a good case for

Lazarus. Eller hypothesizes that Lazarus, like Nicodemus and Joseph of Arimathea, was a member of the Jewish intelligentsia and therefore a great threat, as Jesus' disciple, to the religious establishment. Consider these points:

1. The term "beloved disciple" is *only* used in the Gospel of John (which was not actually written by the disciple John), and the term only appears *after* the resurrection of Lazarus. It first occurs in the description of the Last Supper, where the beloved disciple *lies on the breast of Jesus*. A very poignant scene, if this is the newly raised Lazarus. Eller points out that this would increase the jealousy of the twelve disciples toward Lazarus. Also, in the story of the raising of Lazarus, Lazarus is refered to as "he whom you [Jesus] love" (John 11:3).

2. Eller develops an elaborate schematic diagram that shows how the fourth Gospel has carefully paired a Mary (Mary-L) with Lazarus in certain episodes and thereafter pairs a Mary (Mary Magdalene) with the beloved disciple in other episodes.

3. Eller connects Lazarus and the one labeled "another disciple" to the disciple who had influence with the family of the high priest during Jesus' trial (John 18:12–27).

4. Eller proposes that Lazarus and Mary *Magdalene* were offering Jesus' mother a new home in Bethany after Jesus' death and resurrection (John 19:23–37).

5. Eller has a theory about Galilean disciples and Judean disciples being in ethnic regional competition and often being paired for balance. This would fit if Peter and the beloved disciple (Lazarus, not John) rushed to the empty tomb together (John 20:1–18).[24]

Eller's contention is *not* that Lazarus is a plausible guess but that Lazarus is the *best* guess among all the possibilities to be the beloved disciple.

This brings up some other issues for us, then, in understanding the story of Jesus, Mary, Martha, and Lazarus.

First of all, only Mary and Martha speak: Lazarus never says a word, even as the beloved disciple. From an older commentary by Alexander White we read:

> Lazarus' . . . name is never to be read in the New Testament till the
> appointed time comes when he is to be sick . . . to die, and to be
> raised from the dead for the glory of God. *Nor is his voice heard.*
> *Lazarus loved silence, he sought obscurity. He liked to be overlooked.*
> *He revelled in neglect.* . . . *The very Evangelists pass over Lazarus as if*
> *he were a worm and no man.*[25]

Obviously, Whyte's writing is archaic, but he does make some interesting observations about Lazarus and his silence. It is as if Lazarus is
almost in some kind of a closet, isn't it?

Years ago, West Hollywood Presbyterian Church, inspired by Chris
Glaser, founded the Lazarus Project, an outreach to gay men and lesbians. They used the name Lazarus because they compared the experience of being in the *tomb* to the experience of being closeted. Also, when
Jesus raised Lazarus, he used the words *"Come out"* (John 11:43)!

However, it is quite another thing even to begin to suggest or think
that Lazarus might have been homosexual. Perhaps he loved Jesus, had a
crush on Jesus. We don't really know how old Lazarus was. Did he and
Jesus have a platonic but distinctly homosexual relationship? How did he
die the first time? The second? Was he the victim of a gay bashing? Did
the authors of the Synoptic Gospels want to disguise and cover this up?
Was the Gospel of John more free of "homohatred"? Were suspicions of
"homoerotic" particular friendships and unusual "family" arrangements
part of the reason people were attracted to the Jesus movement—and part
of some other people's desire to persecute them?

Was Lazarus silenced for Jesus' protection or for the protection of
the early Christian church leaders and authorities? Was he silenced "for
his own good"?

What if Lazarus could speak? In the traditions of Jewish midrash and
of feminist biblical interpretation, it is fitting and necessary to let the
silenced in the Bible find their voice. What do we imagine Lazarus felt,
thought, and knew? What must it have been like to be in a tomb for four
days, actually to hear Jesus' voice, to respond, and be willing to receive a
second chance? And then to be immediately thrust into the middle of a religious and political drama that would result in your being simultaneously a
local celebrity and hunted down by the religious and political authorities?
To lose this friend so soon, who only days earlier had raised you from the
dead? To stand by his cross and watch him die, while you were helpless?

And what if you were also secretly—or not so secretly—in love with this friend? And what if you knew *he loved you, too*—that you were "the one whom Jesus loved"? What if Jesus raised Lazarus partly because he could not go through his last weeks without Lazarus's support, company, love, and friendship?

How did the disciples feel about Lazarus's closeness to Jesus in those last weeks? And was Lazarus's identity and memory *erased* from the Gospels of Matthew, Mark, and Luke because of the jealousy of those (Galilean) sources? Or because of overt or covert homophobia?

What was the family structure of Mary, Martha, and Lazarus? In Luke, there is no Lazarus. There are just Mary and Martha. In John 11:2, *Mary* is the one who says that Lazarus is her brother: "Mary was the one who anointed the Lord with perfume and wiped his feet with her hair; *her brother* Lazarus was ill." What if all three of them were not biological siblings? What if they were siblings in a looser sense? Perhaps they were stepsisters and stepbrothers. Perhaps Martha was a stepsister to both of them.

There are lots of examples, sociologically and historically, of people calling each other relatives when in fact they are not related by blood. During several of the waves of U.S. immigration, people helped each other get into the country by saying that they were relatives when they were not. People often lost contact with their biological families and "adopted" each other as family both to get into the country and to serve as a buffer from this loss, from the isolation and loneliness. Also, in the South and rural areas of the U.S., people speak of "shirttail relatives": people who are distantly related in ways much too complicated to figure out. Because of family secrets or scandals, people may not want anyone to find out! So, they're just *relations* in some kind of way. Maybe Jesus was a "shirttail" relative of either Mary, Martha, or Lazarus, and that's why it wasn't so scandalous for him to stay at their home. I think of how Native Americans refer to human beings as "all my relations." Remember that John the Baptist was a "shirttail" cousin of Jesus as well. This is a very typical rural understanding of "relations." This was Jesus' style.

Until the nineteenth and twentieth centuries, the only way in which lesbians ever lived together was by calling themselves "sisters" or "cousins"—and they have, by the millions, over the millennia. Recently, I came home to find a young man doing some repair work on our house. My lover Paula and I do not resemble each other in the slightest. Yet when I arrived at my home, he said, "Gee, are you and Paula sisters?" He said this because he sensed there was a relationship and because we lived together. Almost every lesbian couple I know gets referred to as "sisters" at some point by people just meeting them. If I had a need to be closeted and if Paula and I had just moved into a new neighborhood, it would be so easy to just say yes to anyone who asked if we were sisters. I've heard of and known many women who have done that. Once that "relationship" is established, who would question it?

When I was at the World Council General Assembly in Australia, MCC folks there organized all the gay and lesbian WCC delegates we could find and then asked for a space in which to hold a worship service. While leaving the assembly site to go to the service, a German woman delegate stopped me and asked if I was going to the service. She had her bicycle with her. I told her yes and that most of those going were gay and lesbian. "No!!" she said. And I told her the good news of the Gospel being preached to gays and lesbians and that we had an MCC in Hamburg. She then told me of the underground organization of lesbian pastors in the State Lutheran Church in Germany, called the "Mary and Martha Society." So, obviously other lesbians have identified with their story as well!

Maybe Mary and Martha weren't lovers. Or maybe they were distant cousins *and* lovers. Maybe Lazarus was Mary's brother, and he was Martha's brother in the same way that Paula views my biological brothers as her own.

Maybe Mary and Martha did live in a little obscure village (in Luke 10) and then moved to Bethany. Or maybe Bethany was their home, but Luke was trying to dissociate them from that *rowdy* Bethany crowd! (Home of the Lazarus stories, the "beloved disciple" stories, and other "messy" material he would rather not include.)

And what if Mary Magdalene and Mary the *sister of Martha and Lazarus* were the same woman? Many think that Mary Magdalene was a prostitute, although the Bible never says that. We do know that Mary Magdalene had been possessed of "seven demons." She would be labeled mentally ill today. Could it be that her fear and oppression as a lesbian caused her to have symptoms of mental illness, which Jesus healed? Was it possible that they felt safe having Jesus in their home because he knew, and he loved them? The Bible also never mentions Mary Magdalene being married. And it would make sense for her, as a disciple, to be sitting at Jesus' feet and to anoint him. To be the one who ran to his tomb, who saw him first, and then ran to tell Peter and the "other disciple" (Lazarus, her brother?).

It is amazing how many lesbian women have occupied positions of prestige and importance in little towns and villages all over the world.

They were often considered wise spinster women (that is, women who engage in *spinning cloth to make ends meet*). These independent women were teachers, leaders, healers. Their sexuality was not usually questioned (except in the tragic times of witchhunts). No one thought about them being lesbian, either. They just were. All of us over forty in the United States grew up knowing such people, who were our parents' ages. And our parents remember them, too, from their childhood. We have always been here, without the labels, closeted and secretive about sexuality. Here were two unmarried women, living together, called "sisters." And at least sometimes, a brother named Lazarus lived with them. And sometimes a *brother* named Jesus came to stay with them.

Did anyone ever question Jesus' actually staying in a home with two unmarried women and an unmarried brother? Two spinsters and a bachelor brother? Two barren women and a eunuch?

Even the *Anchor Bible Dictionary* notes, "For apparently unmarried women to have received a teacher into their home and engaged him in a dialogue represents an *unusual social situation in first-century Palestine.*"[26]

I had never seen anything close to an adequate treatment of the question of the identity of the beloved disciple until Eller's study. And I feel quite certain that homophobia has contributed a great deal to the lack of desire on the part of mostly male biblical scholars to explore Jesus' special relationship with a particular man. It is interesting to me that Eller can write a whole book on the subject and not even feel he has to explain away any possible homoerotic possibilities.

This is not, after all, the disciple who *loved Jesus* but the one *whom Jesus loved*. What do we really think of Jesus' having one person in his life whom he loved in a special way? Obviously he loved the other disciples, and his mother, and his family, and the crowds, and strangers, and even his enemies. Then why mention a *special* or *particular* love in his life? This love must have been different in some sense. One may argue a great deal about whether Jesus may or may not have ever had sexual contact with anyone. However, if he was *fully human*, he had hormones, sexual organs and a normal system of sexual arousal. He would have had to have had romantic, erotic, or sexual feelings and impulses, whether or not he ever acted on them.

How is it possible to read over and over again about this man whom he loved and not imagine that there might have been at least some dimension of passion and eroticism connected to his feelings?

And if gays and lesbians are 10 percent of the population, then 10 percent of Jesus' followers were gay or lesbian. Ten percent of the twelve disciples!

I believe that the most obvious way to see Jesus as a sexual being is to see him as bisexual in orientation, if not also in his actions. If our sexuality is most healthy when it is connected, not disconnected, to our values, to intimacy, to our feelings of love and connectedness with others, then the bisexual option sounds the most fair and likely.

I know that saying that Jesus was bisexual in his orientation is really going to send some people into orbit (even some gay and lesbian people)! But *it is very important to deshame the fact that Jesus, as part of his humanness, part of the concept of incarnation, was sexual.* And that this is not a statement about sexual behavior only but about orientation and the erotic, emotional component of many of his relationships, which may or may not have been overtly or "actively" sexual. To deshame Jesus' inherent sexuality, to acknowledge that feelings and fantasies were a normal and natural part of his experience of being human, of being male, is one way the Christian church can help begin to deshame its own members. This *revolutionary* concept that Jesus must have been a sexual being does open the door to speculation about the direction of his sexuality and speculation about his behavior. And opening this door does startle and alarm people.

It does seem as though Jesus is much harder on the sins of hypocrisy, self-righteousness, and greed than he is about breaking sexual morals or laws. He seems frankly a little *wimpy* about sexual sins (saying simply, "Go and sin no more" when saving a sexual sinner from the death penalty, meanwhile pointing out *everyone's guilt,* in John 8). With the possible exception of the teaching on divorce, he doesn't harp on and on about sexuality or sexual sins. Prostitutes loved him. A lot of them still do. They may never trust the church or Christians. But somehow Jesus is a safe, acceptable friend.

At seventeen, Ritchie was already a hardened street hustler. His trademark was his yellow or red very tight bell-bottomed jeans; if he was wearing these, it meant he was working that day. Ritchie loved the idea of MCC and was glad we had come to Worcester, Massachusetts (around 1974). He would often bring younger street kids to us—ones he thought were too naive or not smart or desperate enough to make it on the streets. One time he brought us a thirteen-year-old who he was sure had no idea what street life would be like. We borrowed a car and took the kid to Father Paul Shanley, the street priest, in Boston.

Ritchie was quite sociopathic in many ways. And as such people often are, he was also charming and likable. Even then, when we knew so little, we knew that when Ritchie brought us those kids he was really bringing us his younger self. We were not there when Ritchie was thirteen or fourteen or even fifteen years old, when we might have been able to help him. He was now convinced that at age seventeen, it was too late for him to change.

He always had a cheerful, self-sufficient demeanor. He was tough, the expert, never needing anything for himself. Ritchie would occasionally come to church, which he wasn't sure he liked. But, he really loved Jesus. Church (especially a "gay" church) was OK, but Jesus was better. And he thought of himself as someone who occasionally helped Jesus out by bringing these kids to us. Every now and then, Ritchie would slip, and we would see a needy little boy who desperately wanted mothering or fathering. Then he would have to disappear for a while or do something awful to act out or make us angry with him.

I've thought a lot about that "kid relay" we had: from Ritchie, to ourselves and MCC Worcester, to Father Shanley. Each step up the relay we were taking care of the lost and needy children within us all.

I doubt that Jesus consciously knew about the complex psychology (in much debate) of prostitution and its relationship to early childhood sexual trauma. But it is as if he sensed it. He knew not to injure further those who were "sinning" because they were *already* so hurt and broken and hopeless, or shut off from their own self-worth. I know that not all prostitutes see themselves this way. But I do want to make the claim that Jesus' capacity to be compassionate and merciful toward women and men who broke the rules sexually was the result of the facts that he was himself a sexual being and that he had been a child.

SAME-SEX RELATIONSHIPS IN THE BIBLE

A lesbian hermeneutic of the Bible will begin to tell "our stories" with new boldness. There are many important stories in the Bible of persons of the same sex who had passionate, committed, long-lasting relationships. Most of them are just mentioned in passing, or are barely mentioned (the women missionary couples Paul refers to, Paul and Silas, Paul and Barnabas, Paul and Timothy, Paul and John, Mary and Martha, Jesus and the beloved disciples, Jesus and Lazarus—maybe the same couple?). But there are two same-sex couples whose relationships either take center stage in a biblical drama, or whose relationships are the main subject of a biblical drama: David and Jonathan (in 1 Samuel), and Ruth and Naomi (in the Book of Ruth).

Saul, Jonathan, David

Jesus Christ is called by Christians the "Son of David" because King David became the *model* for Messianic hopes. If we think of Jesus as bisexual in orientation (while bypassing speculation on his behavior for the moment), this certainly makes sense, as David is probably the most clearly bisexual figure in the whole Bible.

The authors or editors of 1 and 2 Samuel really must have been palace insiders. They have incredible insight, palace gossip, and details about the early kings of Israel especially. The stories, in particular of Saul, Jonathan, and David (and his sons), read like a Greek tragedy. I think the writers were possibly palace eunuchs, those invisible officials and servants who always had their ears to the wall and their mouths shut. Also, 1 Samuel's account of the triangle among Saul, Jonathan, and David is filled with homoeroticism. And the descriptions of David physically are among the only descriptions of their kind in the whole Bible. They stand out for that reason. The author was very attuned to David's ample beauty.

Tom Horner, in his book *Jonathan Loved David*, was really the first to make this case. He does so primarily from a literary, critical, and historical point of view.

The David and Jonathan stories contained in 1 Samuel chapters 18–25 are among the oldest writing in the Old Testament. They were written in much the same way that classical Greek history was written. The stories are ones of "warrior lovers," common in the Ancient Near East. In patriarchal cultures, men and women lived separately. All men, whatever their sexuality, were expected to marry and have children. But many men also engaged in homosexual sex—some occasionally, some regularly. Some of these men were bisexual, and some were more serious and romantic about their male lovers than about their wives or female lovers.

The concept of warrior lovers was considered noble and normal. The adventure and *glamor* (a gay sexual word, actually)[27] of going to war was viewed erotically. And there was no shame connected to homoeroticism.

The only shame might be if you wanted to get really serious about a male lover for life. That was considered *feminizing*, and was to be avoided. Male, "boys-will-be-boys" homoeroticism was normal, fun, but not to be overly celebrated or acknowledged. This is still true in many cultures today.

David's classic beauty first attracted Saul in 1 Samuel 16:14–23. It says that "Saul loved him greatly" and that David's musical abilities calmed and relieved Saul. It would not have been unthinkable for Saul to have had David as a *boy lover* during this time, either occasionally or for a period of time during David's teenage years. This story was recorded before the Levitical code was written down or accepted by Israel, which explicitly prohibited such relationships.

This eventually became a tragic triangle. David had actually already been secretly anointed by Samuel to replace Saul as king. Saul began to get jealous of David. To make matters worse, Saul's son Jonathan, who was supposed to succeed him as king, was totally *smitten* with David and wanted David to succeed his father. This meant that Jonathan was playing the more *passive* role in this romance, even to the point of giving up his crown for David (1 Sam. 18 1–4; 1 Sam. 20:30–34).

This, of course, infuriated Saul all the more. The account of Jonathan's first meeting with David could hardly be more explicitly homo-erotic:

> When David had finished speaking to Saul, the soul of Jonathan
> was bound to the soul of David, and Jonathan loved him as his
> own soul. Saul took him that day and would not let him return to
> his father's house. Then Jonathan made a covenant with David,
> because he loved him as his own soul. Jonathan stripped himself
> of the robe he was wearing and gave it to David, and his armor, and
> even his sword and his bow and his belt.
>
> (1 SAM. 18:1–4)

Tom Horner documents how this account compares with similar kinds of relationships described in Greek literature in particular and how it compares to classic homoerotic warrior literature. Jonathan's stripping of his robes and armor may be a sign of sexual as well as political submission, something that must have infuriated Saul. Tom Horner details all the correspondences in the story of Jonathan and David linguistically and literarily with other homoerotic literature.[28]

I think it is amazing that the New RSV comment on this passage says only, "A deep friendship arose between David and Jonathan."[29] Ah, yes! Very deep.

Saul is very threatened both by David's success as a warrior and his relationship with his son. The New RSV, in its annotation to 1 Samuel 20: 1–42, notes that this passage is "an independent tradition of the break between Saul and David, incompatible with much of Chapter 19. David is represented as still a member of the king's household, and Jonathan seems unaware of Saul's hatred of David. The break between Saul and David was so significant that many different stories about it were told."[30] And I think some of the "different" accounts are told from the *insiders'* point of view, and these are the ones that have the romantic, sexual dimensions.

In one account of the conflict between David and Saul, David tells Jonathan, "Your father wants to kill me." Jonathan says, "No, it can't be true," and then betrays his father to help save his lover (and the future king of Israel). David gives Jonathan an out, saying, "If you don't want to betray your father, just kill me!" Jonathan is grieved by the suggestion and then makes a "sacred covenant" with him, which includes these words:

> "If I am alive, show me the faithful love of the Lord; but if I die,
> never *cut off* your faithful love from my house, even if the Lord is
> to *cut off* every one of the enemies of David from the face of the
> earth." Thus Jonathan made a covenant with the house of David,
> saying, "May the Lord seek out the enemies of David." Jonathan
> made David swear again by his love for him; for he loved him as he
> loved his own life.
>
> (1 SAM. 20:14–17)

Notice the use of the term "cut off" and how Jonathan's request is to be included in David's family eternally. Jonathan wants his eternal life to be connected to David's family and his descendants. It is amazing to me that most biblical scholars cannot even bear to think of this relationship as homoerotic. I have seen a few notes and comments that were actually apologetic: "Well, we know this sounds awfully homosexual, but it just can't be. It can't be because David, the greatest king of Israel, the forerunner of the Messiah, could not have been *queer!*" Actually, David seems very bisexual in his romantic interests. It is possible that Jonathan was more truly gay and more in love with David than David was with Jonathan. After all, David needed Jonathan's help. There follows, in 1 Samuel 20:35–42, a very intimate account of another secret meeting. It says, in part:

> David rose from beside the stone heap and prostrated himself with
> his face on the ground. He bowed three times, and they kissed each
> other, and wept with each other. David wept the more.
>
> (1 SAM. 20:41)

There is no comment at all on this verse in the New RSV. The note
to "David wept the more" says, "*Meaning of Hebrew uncertain.*" In the old
RSV it says, "Until David recovered himself." In another note it says that
the literal meaning is possibly "David exceeded himself." Others say that
it may mean he was "overcome." Overcome? With feeling? Passion? Tom
Horner says this may be a euphemism for sexual arousal.

In any case, if this had been an encounter between a man and a
woman scholars would not hesitate to acknowledge and write about this
most explicit of romantic and sexual relationships. Even the new *Anchor
Bible Dictionary* homophobically refuses to entertain any possibility that
David and Jonathan's friendship was also homoerotic. As if, of course,
homosexuality would make it bad, dirty, and not about *friendship*. As if
homosexual lovers are not friends.

In addition, there is an incredible section of the narrative in which
Jonathan is questioned by Saul about David's whereabouts. Saul realizes
that Jonathan is covering for David and curses Jonathan's mother and says
he should be ashamed of his relationship with David. Saul, in his own
homophobia and denial, sees his son as the more "passive" partner in this
romance because of Jonathan's submission to David and to David's agenda,
and he is trying to humiliate Jonathan about it. Jonathan's response is to get
up from the table in anger and go to his room and not to eat for two days
because he is grieved for David and because his father has disgraced him
(1 Samuel 20:30–34). How clear can it be? Anyone who has ever come out
to their parents knows about these scenes! Saul blames Jonathan's mother,
and Jonathan pouts in his room while lovesick over David.

King David, as a young warrior, was the love of Prince Jonathan's
life. Centuries of homophobic Bible commentaries have kept them in the
closet too long!

But just in case you still have any doubt, here is the clearest evidence. It is David's lament for Saul and Jonathan, both killed in battle:

> *Saul and Jonathan, beloved and lovely!*
> *In life and in death they were not*
> *divided;*

they were swifter than eagles,
they were stronger than lions. . . .
How the mighty have fallen
in the midst of the battle!
Jonathan lies slain upon your high
places.
I am distressed for you, my brother
Jonathan;
greatly beloved were you to me;
your love to me was wonderful,
passing the love of women.
(1 SAM. 1:23, 25–26)

The New RSV makes no comment on these verses. If this had been a love poem from a woman to a man or a man to a woman, it would be noted. (Such as, "Gloria, Gloria, I am distressed for you; greatly beloved were you to me; your love was wonderful, passing the love of [those other] women!) Also, David here acknowledges his feeling of love for women (plural), and we surely have stories about David and heterosexual lust (Bathsheba). It seems too much to believe that David is not speaking here of his passionate, sexual feelings for Jonathan. If it were about a nonsexual friendship, then David would have spoken about how this love was special and *different* from his love for women. Instead he says his wonderful feeling of love for Jonathan, and Jonathan's love for him, *passes* or *surpasses* the love of women. He is *comparing similar kinds of love*, not contrasting them. Also note that the lament shifts at the end: the verses switch from the third person to the first person.

Then there is David's grief for Saul, mentor, king, benefactor, and possibly also lover. We must remember that in their culture, this would not have been scandalous and would not have impaired Saul's heterosexual image one bit. The depth of denial in Bibles, commentaries, and dictionaries about David and Jonathan is only one more clear indication of the depth of the homophobia in our history and culture.

Ruth and Naomi

David and Jonathan are one example of same-sex, lifelong relationships in the Bible. The other remarkable same-sex couple consists of Ruth and Naomi. Both of these couples provide the Bible's most moving models of committed love under stressful circumstances. In fact, of course, Ruth is actually King David's great-great-grandmother. Maybe homosexuality *is* genetic—at least in the Bible!

The book of Ruth is really a romantic novella.[31] In this story, Naomi, her husband, and sons move to Moab because of famine, and then her husband and sons die. Naomi's sons have married Moabite women. Now she is widowed with no heir—*cut off*. Her daughters-in-law, Ruth and Orpah, both love her. Naomi decides to go back to Palestine and encourages her daughters-in-law to return to their own kinfolk.

They are both reluctant to leave their beloved mother-in-law. Remember that in their cultures, women were segregated socially from men, so the women of the family were very close. They want to stay with Naomi, but she tells them she can't help them. Even if she were to remarry, she is too old to produce sons, much less sons for them to marry!

Orpah returns to her family. But not Ruth. It says that "Ruth clung to her" (Ruth 1:14). Then Ruth makes this moving vow (used for millennia in heterosexual wedding ceremonies):

> *Do not press me to leave you*
> *or to turn from following you!*
> *Where you go I will go;*
> *Where you lodge I will lodge;*
> *Your people shall be my people,*
> *and your God my God.*
> *Where you die, I will die—*
> *there I will be buried.*
> *May the Lord do thus and so to me,*
> *and more as well*
> *if even death parts me from you!*
> (RUTH 1:16–17)

Ruth returns to Bethlehem with Naomi. There, as two impoverished *barren* widows (one a foreigner), they glean in the fields of Naomi's cousin Boaz. (Another "shirttail relative" story!) Ruth then sexually seduces Boaz and manipulates him into marrying her. He has no obligation legally to do this, because although he is Naomi's kin, he is *not* responsible for Ruth. He is not *her* kin. But of course, Ruth and Naomi have a covenant and are *family*. Boaz is an honorable man, accepts responsibility for his "kinswoman," and marries Ruth.

There is never any remote suggestion of romance between Ruth and Boaz.[32] Boaz represents male privilege and is a benign figure. This novella is told very much from a woman's point of view.[33] Boaz is a "means to an end," the end being survival. Eventually, Ruth has a son. The novella ends happily with these words:

> Then the women said to Naomi, "Blessed be the Lord, who has not left you this day without next-of-kin; and may his name be renowned in Israel! He shall be to you a restorer of life and a nourisher of your old age; for your daughter-in-law *who loves you*, who is more to you *than seven sons*, has borne him." Then Naomi took the child and laid him in her bosom, and became his nurse. The women of the neighborhood gave him a name, saying "a son has been borne to Naomi." They named him Obed; he became the father of Jesse, the father of David.
>
> (RUTH 4:14–17) — *emphasis is the author's.*

The New RSV makes no comment at all on these remarkable words!

The women of the neighborhood give Boaz absolutely no role and recognition in this. Ruth is more to Naomi than *seven sons*. Ruth takes the role of husband and of son to Naomi, by *giving* her a son. She uses Boaz to do it, but Ruth's is the active role: she is the *hero* of the story. And Naomi is really the subject, the main character. Ruth is Naomi's *redeemer*, providing her with a child to care for her in her old age, preventing her from being *cut off*.

Clearly Ruth and Naomi's relationship is unusual and unique. The women in the neighborhood recognize it and admire, even envy, it. They are boasting about this woman who is worth more than seven sons (sounds like a dyke to me!). Ruth and Naomi act like a couple. Nowhere have I ever seen biblical commentators talk about the sex-role reversals, how the story plays off the traditional gender roles, or about the remarkable statement of committed love, *unto death do us part*, from one woman to another.

This is particularly significant in light of the way in which mother-in-law/daughter-in-law relationships are viewed in white Western culture. Mother-in-law jokes are common. Often, mothers are considered to be in *rivalry* with their daughters-in-law for their sons' attention or with their sons-in-law for their daughters' attention. The idea that a mother and daughter-in-law could have a deep love and friendship is remarkable. It is a *subversive* aspect of the text. The only acknowledgment of this I have read is in Mary Hunt's book *A Fierce Tenderness*,[34] or any acknowledgment of the *subversion* of male privilege and power in this story. Ruth gets what she and Naomi need from the system to survive: a husband and a son. But this is all done in the context of a women's community, where Ruth and Naomi are the central relationship.

Is it possible that Ruth and Naomi were also lovers? Perhaps Ruth was not really Naomi's daughter-in-law but an unmarried woman or widow who befriended Naomi. Maybe they made up the story about Ruth being her daughter-in-law in order to protect their relationship. *It's been done many, many times by lesbians who needed to lie to protect their secret.* In their case it was necessary for Ruth to be eligible to marry Boaz— Naomi's cousin, not Ruth's. Perhaps they *were* mother and daughter-in-law, but Ruth fell in love with Naomi. They could have had a deep platonic friendship that was also romantic in a homoerotic but not homosexual way. Many lesbians never had the freedom, courage, or opportunity to have a sexual relationship with another woman, though all their desires and fantasies were homosexual. Many women throughout history lived with a "roommate" all their lives in committed, faithful "Boston marriages," without daring to be sexual.[35]

The fact that no biblical commentators have been willing to explore the meanings of these same-sex friendships, romances, or relationships is powerful evidence of the overwhelmingly negative politics of biblical interpretation at work. In a culture that vilifies homosexuals as promiscuous, as unable to keep commitments, as faithless, these stories of committed faithful love, filled with risk taking, are moving, powerful biblical stories for gay and lesbian people. We must take them back.

The fact that there is not *one* example in the Bible of heterosexuals who express their undying commitment to each other in a way that can be used in heterosexual marriage ceremonies is certainly a major omission! Heterosexuals have ripped off our love stories for too long! I find myself fantasizing about going through every wedding liturgy in every Christian worship book with my ecu-terrorist scissors and cutting out Ruth's words to Naomi. *You can't steal them!*

Colette Jackson and I performed her play, *Bibles and Bulldaggers*, based on my queer interpretation of the Bible, at Highways Performance Space in Santa Monica in June of 1994. After the first or second performance, a young heterosexual couple came up to me shyly, saying how much they loved the play, especially the part about Ruth and Naomi — which I had explained in the talk-back with the audience afterward. They liked the passage from Ruth so much that they wanted *my* permission to use it in their wedding ceremony! I was so touched I almost started laughing, but I quite seriously gave them permission, but only if somehow they could indicate that these words were originally spoken from one woman to another. They cheerfully agreed to my "terms," thanked me, and left. I have fantasies of interrupting poor, unsuspecting heterosexuals at their wedding with "STOP, in the name of Ruth and Naomi, Jonathan and David! Stop stealing our stories while making *our* relationships illegal or characterizing them as immoral!"

More Gays and Lesbians in the Bible

Is that all there is? A couple dozen eunuchs strategically placed; barren women, Mary, Martha, Lazarus, and the beloved disciple; the wise men, and two famous same-sex couples? That's a good start, but I think there are a lot more. It is as if *they* keep appearing and appearing. The more we ask questions, challenge heterosexual assumptions, the more we see them emerge from ancient biblical closets.

What, for instance, do we think of Lydia in Acts 16:11–15?

It is interesting that in this story the narration of the book of Acts moves to the first-person plural, which means the author may have joined the missionary group on its way to Philippi. Lydia is reported in this story to be a wealthy, independent businesswoman. She owns a home large enough to house the apostle Paul and his friends. No husband is mentioned. She is someone who worships God, and she is either a Jew from the city of Thyatira (in what is now Turkey), a Gentile convert to Judaism, or a Gentile "God-fearer." Apparently there were not enough Jewish men to have a minyan on the Sabbath at the outdoor synagogue, but she assembles a group of God-fearing women to hear Paul.

Lydia becomes the first European Christian, and when she is converted, all her household is baptized. This makes her the equivalent of a *pater-* (or in her case, *mater-*) *familias*, the head of a household, which as a woman was unusual. The new church in Philippi begins to meet in her house (Acts 16:40). Lydia has gone against Jewish customs not only by speaking to Paul in public but by inviting him to speak to this group of women and then inviting him into her house.[36] In addition, Lydia's business is quite interesting. She is a seller of *purple dye*. Purple, of course, has ancient associations with magic, royalty, *and* gays and lesbians. The dye was made from certain mollusks. Homer, in the Iliad, mentions *two women* who were famous for the art of purple dyeing in *Lydia* (a city in Asia Minor), founders of a tradition of women makers and sellers of purple dye.[37] Lydia, the woman, was an inheritor of this tradition described by Homer.

I also had fun with Bible maps on this one! Did you know that the Isle of Lesbos does appear on every biblical map of Paul's travels? Lesbos had been home to the greatest lesbian poet of the Ancient Near East, Sappho, in the seventh century B.C. If you draw a straight line from Thyatira (where Lydia was from) to Philippi in Macedonia (where she met Paul), you will draw it right through the Isle of Lesbos! Perhaps Lydia had stopped at Lesbos on her way to Philippi. I wonder if the legendary two women who originated purple dye knew of Sappho or of what was called *Sapphic love?* Is there some kind of women's tradition, lesbian tradition going on here that is only hinted at by Homer and in the Bible?

Paul himself actually stopped on the Isle of Lesbos once! Except, in the Bible it is called Mitylene (the name of the capital city of the island). Acts 20:14 records this. I wonder if the name was changed in order to suppress the association of Lesbos with lesbians.

It is not clear whether or not women like Lydia would have known about Sappho or her lesbian community, named after the island on which they lived. What part of that Sapphic women's culture still existed, aboveground or underground in New Testament times in Lesbos, or Greece, or anywhere?

Uppity Women

It also seems to me that Jesus was often drawn to women who challenged him, who talked back to him, who were outside the ordinary social rules.

According to the story in John 2, Mary pressed her son Jesus to do something about their relatives who had no more wine for the wedding feast. Jesus (a little curtly, I think) told her that this was not the time for him to be "showing off" his Messianic powers. She ignored him and told the servants to "do what Jesus told them." She was pushy. Jesus responded by doing what his mother wanted: he fixed the problem (John 2:5–11).

Two chapters later he meets a lone Samaritan woman at Jacob's well. There, he engages in a theological dialogue with a woman who is clearly a sexual outcast. She's had five husbands and lived with a man who was not her husband in a small rural village. How many times a day, do you suppose, people called her the equivalent of "whore" and "slut"? While she was not a lesbian, she was a woman who broke the rules, sexually. According to Jewish law, Jesus should not have engaged her in conversation, because she was a woman, a Samaritan, and a slut! But he asks her for a drink, engages her not only in small talk but asks about her personal life and talks about theology. She talks back to him. He touches her spiritually and probably emotionally. He does not judge her or call her anything. He treats her respectfully, as if she has valuable thoughts. What adult man, do you suppose, had ever treated her this way (John 4:7–42)?

Not only that but after the disciples showed up, the Scriptures say that they couldn't believe he was talking to the woman, but they don't dare question him. Why not? What didn't they want to hear?

Then, they actually stay in this village for a few days. The Samaritan woman's outcast status is transformed as she becomes the center of attention in a positive way. She becomes the first apostle of the good news of Jesus recorded in the Gospel of John. Jesus meets with many of these villagers, who actually believe her concerning her experience with Jesus. Where do you suppose he and the disciples stay? What were the results of their visit? When Jesus left, did the villages still care how many husbands she had had?

In the Gospel of Luke (chapter 8:40–48), a woman who has been hemorrhaging for twelve years attempts to be healed by *unobtrusively* touching the hem of Jesus' garment. She does this, but Jesus is affected by her gesture. He describes it as "power going forth" from him. She has taken her healing from him, without his consent. Instead of being angry or feeling deceived or even *violated*, Jesus expresses awe and admiration for this woman's aggressive seeking of God's healing through him. The fact is that by touching a Jewish male while bleeding, she is making him ritually unclean. It is never clear to me whether or not Jesus abided by the law or not when he was touched by menstruating women or lepers or anyone "unclean." He would have been required to go through a process of ritual cleansing. It sounds as though when it came to healing, he did not keep these laws, any more than he kept the Sabbath laws. In any case, he showed encouragement and admiration for women who *took what they wanted from him.*

The most glaring example of this is his encounter with the Syro-Phoenician woman, recorded with some differences in Mark 7:24–30 and Matthew 15:21–28. Here, as Jesus is attempting to get away from the crowds, this Greek (or Canaanite) woman finds him. In all fairness, the guy could *never* get a vacation or be left alone. In Matthew's version, he refuses to speak to her at all at first. Finally, she is being such a pest that the disciples beg him to see her. Jesus then hears that her little daughter is possessed by a demon. Jesus refused to heal her at first, saying that he has come to the "lost house of Israel" and is not open to helping *her kind* of people. But she will not give up. Even if he was elitist, racist, even if she despised him, she would not give up for the sake of her daughter. So it says she kneels before him, even after he has rejected her, and begs him to heal her daughter. She talks back. She is aggressive, persistent, and will endure any shame from Jesus to save her child, including his saying, "Let the children [Israel] be fed, for it is not right to take the children's bread and throw it to the dogs [Gentiles, Canaanites?]" (Mark 7:27). Now at this point, I might have thought of some snappy rejoinder to that *dogs* remark and marched out of there. "Bitch! Are you calling me a bitch? I'll show you what a bitch I am!" But this woman is as single-minded as it is possible to be. She responds to him *from the social position of a dog* with relentless determination and says, "Sir, even the dogs under the table eat the children's crumbs" (Mark 7:28). Jesus then says, "*For saying that,* you may go — the demon has left your daughter" (Mark 7:29).

Jesus took no credit for a lot of the miracles that involved uppity women. He was almost a passive participant, a reluctant bystander to their process of claiming and receiving what they needed. It is interesting, though, that he would say, "For saying that . . . " Is that because she is like the woman who pesters the unjust judge "until she gets what she wants" (Luke 18:1–8)? Was Jesus rewarding her for her persistence, her refusal to back down? Was he simply in touch with what God had done, as she exercised her own faith by pestering him? Was he touched by the way in which she endured his abuse and then turned it around, perhaps hoping to humble him with her willingness to bear any abuse for her daughter's sake? He never claimed to heal her daughter. He announced the healing. This uppity foreign woman got his attention.

Luke, a more Gentile Gospel, does not record this story. The Palestinian Gospels have it, perhaps showing a developmental issue in Jesus' ministry: that he did not start out with an openness to Gentiles, women or men, even though Luke might want us to believe that.

In any case, women are touched and healed by him (sometimes) almost in spite of him, and he seems very attracted to uppity women who talk back. What kind of man would be attracted to such women?

The Lost Coin

For a more fanciful gay and lesbian exegesis, I like the parable of the woman who lost a coin and then finds it (Luke chapters 8–10). In a trinity of parables, Jesus chooses a shepherd, a woman (there is no mention of a husband—the story reads as if she is alone in her house), and a father to represent the God who seeks and finds the lost. The shepherd and the prodigal stories are the ones that we generally hear about in sermons. Jesus' image of God as a woman who has lost her coin gets precious little attention.

In this simple parable, a woman has ten silver coins, loses one, lights a lamp, and searches for it, sweeping the house, until she finds it. When she finds it, she calls together her friends and neighbors to rejoice. It is interesting that in this case, the lost coin represents her security and well-being in a culture in which women who were alone, barren, or widowed were always vulnerable. Money, any savings, would be her only hope in this case, and finding the coin is saving herself, perhaps even more directly than in the story about the shepherd or the father.

I wonder if Jesus was conscious of choosing a woman for this parable about a lost coin because its value would be greater to her than to a man in a patriarchal society? And he knew the politics of this situation would heighten the pathos of losing and finding a coin? It is this woman's independence and power that are at stake here, a point lost on male Bible commentators and preachers for most of two thousand years.

I am fascinated by the fact that there are ten coins. In one sense, a *tithe* has been lost. Gays and lesbians are about 10 percent of every population. Are we actually a tithe of humanity? Is there an economy in the creation of human beings that reserves 10 percent of us to be available in every "tribe" to exercise our particular tribal gifts? Are we a *lost coin* that God is joyfully *finding* and lifting up in our day? Isn't God thrilled that her gay and lesbian children are being found? Isn't there rejoicing in heaven over that (if not at the National Council of Churches of Christ or in evangelical TV programs such as "The 700 Club?") In a similar metaphor, are we not that *pinch of leaven* in the *loaf* of every culture? A necessary, particular ingredient?

The Gay Centurion

Tom Horner has documented the gay associations with the healing of the centurion's slave in Matthew 8:5–13 (and also in Luke 7:1–10).[38] The story is about a prominent centurion, loved by the Jews in his town, a supporter of the synagogue, who comes out to meet Jesus and plead that he will save his servant's life. In the version told in Matthew, the Greek term used for servant is different from the term used in Luke. The term in Matthew is one that was associated with a common practice among Gentiles in Jesus' time: he was a "slave boy," which meant a young male lover, who might have been a debt slave.[39] This relationship was common among Roman soldiers and would *not* have meant that the centurion was not also married. It would have been odd for the centurion to go personally to Jesus to plead for the life of a servant, even one who was "dear to him." The story makes more sense (and is more poignant) if this is a more intimate relationship. In the Gospel of John 4, there is a similar story about a "royal official" who pleads for the life of his son. The annotation in the New RSV says he is a "Gentile military officer" (another *eunuch?*).[40] This story is connected in the annotations to the other two in Matthew and Luke. It was the custom of Romans to adopt slaves as their sons when they were emancipated, especially slaves held in high regard or slaves who had also been lovers. This may be the same event reported differently in Matthew, Luke, and John. What is interesting is Jesus' nonjudgmental approach to this centurion's pain and love relationship. "When Jesus heard him, he was amazed and said to those who followed him, 'Truly I tell you, in no one in Israel have I found such faith'" (Matt. 8:10).

Women Partners in the New Testament

Women scholars are beginning to explore the patterns and possibilities of women partners in the New Testament, using Adrienne Rich's "continuum" concept of lesbian relationships. One such "couple" consists of *Tryphaena and Tryphosa*, mentioned by Paul in Romans 16:12. These are both Greek women's names. Also, *Euodia and Syntyche* are mentioned in Philippians 4:2; they were apparently having a conflict that was affecting their ministry partnership.[41]

Did the bias against heterosexual marriage among religious leaders select for gay and lesbian leadership in the early church? The celibate priesthood and the requirements for celibacy among the Roman Catholic religious has certainly selected for a higher percentage of gays and lesbians than the usual 10 percent. Many of these leaders are not celibate, as is becoming clearer through the incidence of AIDS and the coming-out stories of priests and nuns.

What About Paul?

Bishop John Shelby Spong, in *Rescuing the Bible from Fundamentalism*,[42] has made one of the more uncompromising cases for Paul's homosexuality. It does seem as though Paul has very little compassion or patience for those who are "troubled" by heterosexual lust. It is as if he cannot comprehend why some of the men have to marry, although he acknowledges that it is "better to marry than to be aflame with passion" (1 Cor. 7:9). Paul continuously has fights and emotional scenes with his male traveling companions. Clearly, Paul is happy to travel with men and often stays in the homes of wealthy, *independent* (lesbian?) women.

It is clear that Paul sees himself as a celibate, perhaps an *asexual* person. But his temperament, his emotional and affectional preference, seems to be toward men. He seems to fit a profile of a certain kind of "gay sensibility" (recognizable to gays and lesbians!). If being gay or lesbian is not so much about behavior but about a matrix of feelings, behavior, and culture, Paul was probably a repressed, closeted (even to himself?) homosexual.

The Color Purple

As we have seen in the Lydia story, there are interesting connections to the color purple in the Ancient Near East and in the Bible. Judy Grahn was the first to document seriously the extensive connections of the color purple to ancient concepts of magic, spirituality, transformation, change, royalty, spiritual power, and gays and lesbians.[43] If these connections are accurate historically and in terms of mythology and ancient symbolism, then what *is* the relationship of the color purple in the Bible to all these issues? Jesus wore the color purple to the cross. Purple cloth is associated with the Temple.

And what is the association of magicians and the occult with gays and lesbians? There have been a lot of assumptions about the role of magic in early indigenous Israelite religion.[44] Magic seems to have been an integral part of all religions, especially what we call *ancient* or *indigenous* earth religions. There has also been a lot of misunderstanding about the role of magic, and assumptions about magic and the occult *may or may not* be accurate or fair historically. Certainly, especially in conservative Christian circles, there is a near hysteria about magic and the occult that is based sometimes only on half-truth or on biases that may be rooted in cultural issues, rather than on genuine theological issues.

If gay and lesbian people have been associated with indigenous religion, with magic and the occult, for millennia, is this one reason for the intensity of homophobia in the Christian world?[45]

WHAT DIFFERENCE DOES IT MAKE TO SEE THE BIBLE IN THIS WAY?

I believe that it is essential for gay men, lesbians, and bisexuals to take back the Bible. If we are not included among the stories and characters of the Bible, then it cannot be our book. It is also important for heterosexuals not to see the Bible monolithically either but to see the people of the Bible as they must have been: as varied and complex in their sexuality as human beings are today.

Years from now, none of this will be shocking or unusual. Biblical annotations will include footnotes about us, not just in a negative way. More biblical commentaries and dictionaries will contain articles by feminists, gays, lesbians, and others doing important work in previously unexplored areas of the Bible and human sexuality. As gay and lesbian biblical scholars come out, do the scholarship, and pay the price, the texts will be healed. Meanwhile, we must boldly begin to ask the questions, make suggestions, and "go too far."

5

Outing the Sodomite

Until D. S. Bailey published *Homosexuality and the Western Christian Tradition* in 1955, the ancient philosopher and biblical commentator Philo was the single voice that had defined the "sin of Sodom." With the advent of a gay and lesbian religious movement in the late sixties, Bailey's writings were "discovered" by gay folks, and a new hermeneutic of the story of Sodom and Gomorrah, found in Genesis 19, began.

For nearly two millennia, the lie that the story of Sodom and Gomorrah was a story about homosexuality (or bestiality, or anal or oral sex, or *queer sex* of any kind) prevailed and validated homohatred in the Western world and every place in the world where Christianity had gotten a foothold. If God hates queers enough to blow up two cities because of them, then homophobic hatred is justified and maybe even holy! The story of Genesis 19 became a virtual religious *license to kill* those whom God deemed unacceptable. But with the onset of the gay and lesbian religious movement, we began to *read* D. S. Bailey and to write and teach ourselves about this tragedy of biblical interpretation.

Part of the tragedy has been that Philo's interpretation was allowed to stand unchallenged because homophobia and homohatred meant that scholars did not want to study Genesis 19 or other passages that purportedly dealt with homosexuality. I don't know what compelled D. S. Bailey to take a second look. But just a *superficial* examination of Genesis 19 revealed the problems in Philo's original interpretation. We began to educate ourselves and to attempt to educate other Christians. In the seventies there were literally a handful of other books and pamphlets (mostly produced by MCC and Evangelicals Concerned) that began to tell of this new interpretation of Sodom and Gomorrah. Today there are several library shelves of books, chapters in books, and articles—all third and fourth looks at Genesis 19 and other passages. Even conservative theologians today know that Genesis 19 does not support wholesale condemnation of homosexuality.[1] The biblical sources for proof-texting (quoting Bible verses out of context to prove a point) homophobia are dwindling, thank God.

The problem is, of course, that the most biblically illiterate people in the world, who barely know any of the Twenty-third Psalm or even two of the Ten Commandments, are just *sure* that the Bible and God condemn homosexuality—and they are the ones who vote.

When our MCC church was located on Washington Boulevard in Los Angeles, we were across the street from a gas station and minimart. There were several men who lived on the street, most of them addicts, who washed car windows at that location for spare change. Our church had a kind of symbiotic community with these guys, some of whom I came to know by name if they were able to talk at all. Church members were a good source of spare change and some of these men actually watched out for the church building. One was a young, handsome man named John. He was smart and manipulative and well spoken, and he always addressed me respectfully. (He'd probably grown up in church.) One day while I was trying to prevent him from washing my windows (the car was actually newly washed for a change!), he said, "Can I ask you something?"

"Sure."

He then told me he'd seen two women leaving the church walking arm in arm or holding hands. Maybe it was the first time John realized that there were gay people involved in the church, I'm not sure. He said that this bothered him, them walking down the street like that because wasn't it *against the Bible?*

Now, mind you, this man was a crack addict and a panhandler who spends half his life in and out of the county jail. He lies, steals, and is throwing his life away because he is sick with addiction. But he was morally shocked and offended by two lesbians he had seen touching each other in public (in a way that is acceptable for heterosexual lovers or spouses to show affection)! Not only that but he believed—he *knew*—that the Bible supported him in this disapproval! So I gave John a very short version of "Homosexuality and the Bible." I also told him I was a lesbian, and his eyes widened. He looked over his shoulder to see if any of his buddies were watching him. Then he spoke confessionally, and let me know that he had had homosexual sexual experiences. He was clearly conflicted about this. Somehow, deep inside of what is left of this man's personality and heart, he is sure God will forgive him everything else *but not this.* I shifted the conversation to say to him, "John, I just hope that whenever you have sex, you have safe sex and use a condom — do you understand what I mean?"

"Yes, ma'am," he said sheepishly.

I let him know that there were free condoms available in the men's rest room in the church. With that I got in my car and left him to sort it out for himself.

For days I thought about that incredible conversation. How did homosexuality get to be *the* unpardonable sin, worse than addiction (self-murder), stealing, lying? Is it the depth to which gay and lesbian sexuality and lifestyle threaten "heteropatriarchy"? Is the *ultimate* crime or sin against God the overthrowing (or even just the providing of an alternative to) the domination by men of women through sexuality? So that a poor, young black male crack user who long ceased caring about his own life, who has long since given up hope for anything but another day of survival and using, can *still* be shocked and frightened by observing two women breaking the alleged sexual norms of his day — and frightened by his own secret desires and sexual feelings? *How amazing.*

THE SIN OF SODOM AND GIBEAH

Much of recent gay and lesbian theology (and a lot written by our heterosexual allies) has begun the process of turning the tables on Sodom and Gomorrah. Since the 1970s, I have heard and preached that the sin of Sodom and Gomorrah was the sin of *inhospitality*, especially *inhospitality to strangers.* What gay and lesbian theologies have pointed out is that it is the church of Jesus Christ that for two millennia has been inhospitable, especially to gays and lesbians.

This works especially well in an exegesis of Genesis 19 if we view the pair of same-sex, male-appearing angels as gay! The two *gay angels* are the potential *victims* in the story, not heterosexuals.

I also think (and will elaborate on later) that it is just possible that gay and lesbian culture — or *sensibility*, if you will — include the spiritual gift of hospitality. And this is another lens on the tragic irony of the traditional interpretation of Genesis 19.

Actually, "inhospitality" is the understatement to end all under-statements as a way to describe the "sin of Sodom." It is a euphemism. Especially if we link the Sodom and Gomorrah story to the story of the murder of the concubine in Gibeah (Judges 22).[2] *The sin of Sodom, I believe, is the sin of ethnic and sexual violence.*

Rape, we have come to learn, is not a sexual crime or sin primarily. Rape is a means of physical, mental, and spiritual domination. It is an act of ruthless power: the annihilation of the "other."

As I look at the stories of Sodom and Gibeah, I see a pattern in the objectifying and demonizing of the "other," the stranger. In both stories, there is a punishment of the stranger, the other, the *different* one through physical brutality and domination. The other is consequently *dehuman-ized,* silenced, obliterated. This action is not personal, it is systematic, cal-culated. It is domination through violence whose intent is power or profit or both. This is the sin of Sodom and Gibeah.

Sodom and Gibeah are ancient stories of *ethnic cleansing* that we see replicated in our century in Nazi Germany, in the genocide of the Armenian people, in Bosnia, in South Africa.

Sodom and Gibeah are North Carolina, 1993. A UFMCC congre-gation bought a small building in a suburban area of Charlotte, North Carolina. The neighbors found out that there were "queers" on their street. During worship service, people appearing to be adults and claiming to be Christians stood outside the church and turned on power saws and power mowers to disturb a small group of mostly (not exclusively) gay and lesbian Christians who were praying and singing hymns. This is not just inhospitality, although it is surely that; it is violent, threatening, and vul-gar. Men with power tools in hand (how can we miss *that* metaphor!), stalking a small MCC church outside the door and windows of a sanctu-ary. It is a scene highly *suggestive* of sexual violence. In an updated way, it very nearly replicates the scene outside of Lot's house in Genesis 19.

Inside the church (like Lot's house) there were humans, and thank-fully, there were angels. No one was hurt physically. Thankfully, only months before MCC had been admitted to the North Carolina Council of Churches. This gave encouragement to the council publicly to con-front the homophobia of MCC's neighbors, which they did, and this helped defuse the violence.

There is another twist in the story. In many ways, the Council of Churches played the same role as Lot and his family in the story of Sodom and Gomorrah. They are basically good people, minding their own business, who live in an extremely violent culture, where sodomy (not defined as homosexuality but as sexual and racial violence) is rampant. In the Genesis 19 story, two angels (of the same sex!) appear at Lot's door. He has to decide whether or not to take them in. And what will be the consequences of offering them hospitality? Who was Lot afraid of? Who were some members of the North Carolina Council of Churches afraid of? Who was peering in at their window, spreading gossip about whom Lot let in that night? Who began fueling the chain saws, getting the crosses ready to burn in North Carolina? The crowd at Lot's door that night is the *same* faceless, cowardly crowd that has lynched black men and burned their homes, raped and killed black women, and that rapes women and bashes gays in our streets every day, in North Carolina, and all over this country.

So, like Lot, the North Carolina Council of Churches had a decision to make. Would they be willing to stand by these strangers, and at what cost?

Sodomy is the sin of the Virginia Court of Appeals in September 1993, when it removed a two-year-old from his mother's home because she, Sharon Bottoms, is a lesbian.

The irony in the case against Sharon Bottoms was that the child was awarded to the grandmother.[3] One woman responded in the *Los Angeles Times*: "The court in its wisdom has taken from a lesbian her adorable two-year-old and turned the child over to the heterosexual grandmother who bore and raised the lesbian daughter to begin with. Can we talk?"[4]

Sodomy is rampant in Ovett, Mississippi. Brenda and Wanda Henson, minding their own business, trying to live their quiet rural lifestyle, run a camp called Camp Sister Spirit for feminists. The *Los Angeles Times* reports that "they have been subjected to anonymous phone calls, threatening letters, jeers, and random gunfire from their neighbors. A bomb has been exploded in front of their gate, and a dead dog was found draped over their mailbox. The climate of intimidation has intensified with two meetings led by Baptist ministers to raise money to force the Hensons out of their former pig farm."[5]

Those women are no more harmful than the two angels who appear on Lot's doorstep. But somewhere deep in the consciousness of the Sodomites, they know that these two angels, like the lesbians of Mississippi, are bringing warnings, challenges of changes needed, changes that are coming. Their presence tests whether the people of the city are *righteous or not*. This is a test that sodomites, by definition, always seem to fail.

The *Times* also reported that "Paul Walley, a lawyer advising the groups attempting to purge Ovett of the Hensons, explained that 'the area is a conservative religious community that has a standard based on biblical morality. Residents of Camp Sister Spirit reject that standard and have a radical agenda that would seek to change our way of life.' Their biblical moral precedent is apparently not the injunction of Jesus of Nazareth to *love thy neighbor.*"[6]

SODOM AND GIBEAH AND THE U.S. MILITARY

Two modern stories clearly resemble those of Sodom and Gibeah, and both of them have occurred in the context of the changing nature of the United States military.

The first is the "Tailhook scandal." Stories of sexual harassment, like this one that occurred at a United States Navy event, are as old as the United States Navy. Nothing particularly new went on here except for the fact that women broke the silence. Another new factor is that women's roles in the United States Navy, as in the military in general, are *changing*. And many men hate and resist this change. Somehow, women's full inclusion in the military makes the military "less masculine," less a place of clear, unquestioned male primacy and privilege. In a culture that has been critiqued for its sexism, in which women are challenging male privilege more and more (and not always winning), for one of the "last bastions" of male privilege to be overturned is highly threatening. The Tailhook scandal was just one example of the explosion of sexual harassment cases brought to light in the early 1990s in the U.S. Tailhook occurred in the context of the Clarence Thomas/Anita Hill phenomenon. Women were speaking up—loud, clear, on television, in the Senate, and in the military and were willing to pay the price for it. It wasn't necessarily true that sexual harassment itself was on the increase, but that women were "mad as hell and weren't going to take it anymore."

When men are threatened politically by women, one of the tools of patriarchal oppression is harassment or sexual violence. Tailhook is a classic example of this. Military officials seemed shocked at the degree to which this boys-will-be-boys behavior was condemned. They seemed—and often still seem—unwilling to condemn it themselves or really to acknowledge that this is anything other than normal, rowdy, acceptable male behavior in the military. The fact that women were insulted, injured, and terrorized by their comrades and officers seemed of little consequence. Somehow the implication was that the changing mores and pressures of women's inclusion (*caused by women*) merited this kind of *backlash*. Somehow these guys just hadn't caught up with the new rules. What's the big deal? If women want change so bad, this is to be *expected*.

The other "defensive" tactic was to assure the public that this is not a common navy behavior—a defense known as *denial*. There was a pretense of shock and disbelief accompanied by an institutional version of feigned innocence: "We don't know *how* this could have happened!"

Like the concubine in the horror story of Gibeah, these women were objectified and used and then exposed to public humiliation as the price of finding any justice. It was a typical rape trial, only it was corporate and military.

There is another striking modern parallel, with some ironies, to the Sodom story. Alan Schindlar was a young navy recruit who agonized about his own sexuality. He was found murdered in a rest room outside a bar in Japan that navy men frequent. Later one of his navy comrades confessed to the brutal murder. Schindlar was beaten beyond recognition and genitally mutilated in the process. The murderer did not claim that Schindlar had approached him sexually or had made unwanted advances, which in some people's minds *would* have merited murderous retaliation. His murder was a seemingly *inexplicable* act of violence. Schindlar was not the aggressor. His only crime was to be suspected of being homosexual. The murderer had no explanation for beating Schindlar, other than that he was drunk at the time.

What is it about hatred of the other, those who are different in race, ethnicity, or sexuality, that inspires such brutal murderous rage? Why is it that rape and mutilation and torture so often accompany such murders? One thinks of the ethnic cleansing in Bosnia, which included so much rape and torture. It also brings to mind racist murders and lynching and their long history (which continues *today*) in the United States. Rituals of Klansmen have included *dressing up* for the occasion! One wonders about all the elaborate preparations that accompany a mob ganging up on one black man to beat him, humiliate him, torture him, and then hang him. There is a kind of special sadistic pleasure that surrounds this ritualized violence. It is like the pleasure the men of Tailhook took in harassing and tormenting those women.

What is it that makes this behavior pleasurable? Is it the need to dominate and control? The need to experience the powerlessness and helplessness of someone else over whom you have at least temporary power and to whom you can cause pain and harm? Some psychologists see this as the surfacing of suppressed childhood rage. The rage of children who are humiliated, beaten, raped, or persecuted and who cannot fight back. Under the "right" circumstances, this rage will pour out on someone who is seen as a potential victim.

It also seems to me that this kind of sadistic sexual or ethnic violence serves a more sinister political purpose, but those who *benefit* from this purpose are not usually the ones visibly doing the acting out. The participants are influenced and driven by forces behind the scenes that manipulate mass culture, that incite the rage of those who have *just enough* power to be able to subdue those *just below* them.

The story of the origins of the Ku Klux Klan in our country is the *classic* example of the way in which wealthy, powerful politicians and businessmen convinced poor and working class whites in the south that *their* class solidarity with blacks was worth trading in for "white privilege." It is a tragic story about how people who are under economic stress can be convinced that the only way for them to improve their lot is to make sure that someone is made to feel inferior to them.

This is the same story today of the growth of right wing militia groups in our country, who are frustrated by the gradual decreases in the standard of living, and who want to blame that on racial/ethnic minorities, "liberals," "feminazis," and, of course, homosexuals.

The comparison of Tailhook and Alan Schindlar's murder to Sodom and Gibeah is not neat or simple. In Gibeah there are no apparent consequences to the murder of the concubine. In Tailhook (as in Gibeah) women are harmed, some men were punished, but the punishment does not seem to be enough or to go *high enough* up the chain of command. On the other hand, in the modern story, it was the gay man who was murdered, not the woman (in *this* instance). The likelihood, however, is that as a gay man, Alan Schindlar was *seen* by his murderer and by other navy companions as a *man who wanted to be, or who was like a woman.* He was, therefore, betraying his gender. Any man who would want to be loved sexually by another man, who would presumably want to share love and affection with men, is betraying some image of men and masculinity, and this inspired an act of psychotic, murderous rage.

Some even believe that that murderous rage was justified—unlike the murderous rage of the Sodomites or the Gibeahites? And just what is God's response to all of this? In the story of Gibeah, God seems absent or silent. In the story of Sodom, God seems angry *at* the murderous, would-be rapists. This interpretation of God's role in what was a geological event (volcanic eruption?) must be looked at in the context of biblical and modern views of God's relationship to nature and natural disasters.

SODOM AND SEISMIC THEOLOGY

At 4:31 A.M. on January 17, 1994, all of us in Los Angeles and the surrounding region were jolted out of our sleep by a particularly violent earthquake. Years of earthquake preparedness and all the efforts to shore up buildings and infrastructures actually worked remarkably well. A similar size and type of earthquake in India in recent times killed ten thousand people. "Only" about sixty or so perished in what has been called the Northridge quake. Angelinos were unusually calm in the moment, and there was little criminal activity or exploitation of the event at first. (I can't say that about insurance companies or government agencies later on!)

About a month later I had a friend introduce me to California Institute of Technology's earthquake spokesperson, Dr. Kate Hutton. Kate is the calm scientist who often appears on behalf of Cal Tech on local and national television just after a quake. She is also an open lesbian. I have always found that endearing and reassuring in a strange kind of way: Kate's face, sometimes her hair still in the early stages of waking up, and her calm voice speaking with "lesbian authority" about the nature and size of a particular seismic event. Thank God someone understands this, and she's a lesbian! Also, she would often be attired in some kind of feminist or lesbian T-shirt. I would find myself squinting and trying to *read* it on the screen! Which year women's festival T-shirt is she wearing today?

So I got to meet Kate. I wanted to meet her because I was personally more traumatized by this earthquake than by previous ones, and I was trying to learn more about earthquakes, hoping that this would make them less frightening.

My approach to overcoming my earthquake fears is based on my goddaughter Rechal's methodology of facing up to major phobias. Rechal was frightened at an early age by the idea of sharks (she had apparently never actually seen one). At age five or six she would approach the lifeguard at the beach in Santa Monica and ask, "When was the last shark sighting here?" Then she began to read about sharks. She became so fascinated with sharks that she could tell anyone who cared to listen about the various typologies of sharks, shark habitats, just how dangerous they really are or aren't. She came to believe that sharks, in fact, were actually *very* maligned creatures and decided that she might want to become a marine biologist someday.

Not that I am about to become a seismologist. But I thought that maybe just viewing all the equipment and charts and graphs at Cal Tech and all the people at work assembling data on the computers would at least give me the illusion that someone (like Kate?) was "in control" of all this. Actually, in the course of our conversation, Kate told me that on a particularly slow news day after the earthquake, several news stations got together and asked her, "Did God cause this earthquake?" She told them modestly enough that that wasn't her field of expertise. So much for illusions of control.

The other reason I came to see Kate was to ask her a favor. Our church building had suffered severe damage in the earthquake. We were located just one and a half blocks from the section of the Santa Monica freeway that collapsed. The seventy-year-old dome of our historic building (once a famous restaurant located near MGM studios) fell into the street. Fortunately, at 4:31 in the morning no one was around. No one was hurt or killed. But the building had to be torn down. Since we had not finished all the renovation, and because it was an old brick structure, and even though we had invested over $100,000 in retrofitting, we were not eligible for earthquake insurance. It was a devastating loss—the second for our twenty-five-year-old church, which lost another building to arson in 1973.

So, I had a brainstorm. If other lesbians and gays were as reassured as I was by "Kate from Cal Tech," we could sponsor an event that would be a fund-raiser. She agreed to give an earthquake lecture sponsored by MCC Los Angeles for the community. Perhaps others, like me, would want to use Rechal's counterphobic approach to their earthquake jitters. Let's get lots more information from our favorite lesbian science teacher!

Plus, I was doing research on the emerging "earthquake theology." It was amazing, in the days and weeks and even months following the earthquake, the kind of earthquake theologies that appeared everywhere. Tony

Alamo, a notorious off-the-wall fundamentalist of sorts (a Hollywood fixture, really), printed a special pamphlet for the occasion, littering our windshields and the streets of Hollywood with his self-serving diatribe entitled simply "Earthquake." In it he claims that God got him out of Los Angeles and saved his life that day. Pat Robertson, Jerry Falwell, and others took great glee in letting us know that the earthquake was God's judgment on Los Angeles, particularly for the sins of abortion and homosexuality. Jerry, in fact, has a video titled *Hollywood, Washington, and Hell* illuminating the connections among the three. In fundamentalist theology, Hollywood was just getting what it deserved. (So what terrible evil and sin were going on in Northridge? Or did God just miscalculate by a few miles? Did God mean to *hit Hollywood* but hit Northridge instead?)

Does God Cause Earthquakes?
Spiritual Narcissism and the Alternatives

So, did God cause this particular earthquake, and why? Is Los Angeles a modern Sodom and Gomorrah, as Falwell is fond of implying? Did our earthquake preparedness efforts thwart God's plan to kill more of us, or was this just a warning to change our evil ways?

If for the fundamentalists this was the act of an angry, judging Father God, there were some equally firm speculations from a different theological viewpoint. A liberal feminist colleague and friend of mine referred to the earthquake as an expression of "Mother Earth's anger." I have heard this many times in many forms: that earthquakes, floods, and so on are a response to human pollution of the earth, air, and water. Perhaps this is happening because the earth is *sick* of us humans and is trying to warn us or stop us from destroying the environment. Sometimes this is explained scientifically (if we destroy the ozone layer, for example, then we are "reaping what we sow" in terms of cancer and other life-threatening consequences). Sometimes it is explained mystically (as in my friend's observation).

Was the earthquake about anger and judgment? This seems to be a common theme, even if there are different ideas about just *who* was angry and about *what* precisely. This is a sort of cosmic ACA (Adult Child of an Alcoholic) experience for human beings: we can never be quite sure which parent is going to be in what mood and just when will Father God or Mother Earth decide to fly into a rage and hurt us! And will they hit the right one or just the kid who happens to be within reach? (As Northridge was apparently in the way when God was after Hollywood?)

Are the gods crazy, angry, and how can we appease them? The more optimistic among us began reframing the earthquake as a *good thing*, and we had some great justifications. The minimal loss of life, for instance. Most of us (not *all*, however) were grateful for the timing, when so few people were on the freeways or in office buildings. Also, the search began for the *good results* that often come out of tragedies: people bonding and working together, new focuses on new issues. But this "it was a *good* thing" angered a lot of people who felt like they were not allowed to feel grief or anger if thousands were not killed in the earthquake. It reminded me of all the platitudes and clichés some people seem to need to say in the face of tragedies: "Only the good die young"; "God must have needed him or her more than we do"; "just have another baby right away"; "something good must be just around the corner"; "every cloud has a silver lining." Many people need to control what other people feel—the fear seems to be that if we *all* were to express our grief and loss as they are felt, the avalanche would overwhelm and destroy us. So we counsel each other to *stuff* it, to suppress it, bury it, but for God's sake, don't tell us about it!

Eighty churches were destroyed or damaged in Los Angeles during the Northridge quake. But I do not believe that any Baptists or Lutherans or Catholics worried that the earthquake destroying their building meant that God hates Baptists, Lutherans, or Catholics. Yet there *were* members and frequent attendees of MCC Los Angeles who jumped to the conclusion (which obviously already had a foothold in their consciousness) that God allowed the earthquake to destroy our building because *God hates homosexuals*. It was their own mini-Sodom experience, and it is not possible even to explain all the ways that this was played out in our church. Some people simply never came back to the church; others suffered silently, feeling guilty for some time until enough of us had articulated our fears and doubts to give them permission to express theirs as well.

I have heard psychologists talk about the fact that for many children who are abused, it is more comforting for them to believe that they *caused* or *deserved* the abuse they received than to have to face the possibility that Daddy or Mommy just beat them because they were *there* or were in the way of their rage. Children prefer to hold on to the illusion of logic or reasonableness rather than to know that they live with powerful adults who do terrible things for complex reasons that have nothing to do with them.

This is rooted in the kind of childhood narcissistic view of the world in which "I" am the cause of most things. Children often rely on a kind of magical thinking—the idea that if they simply wish or fantasize something, it *can* and *will* happen. This is why children often blame themselves if a family member dies or if parents get divorced. "It must have been my fault. I did something to cause this." Which means, of course, by implication: "I could have done *something* to prevent this." Which means "the universe is still *somewhat* in my control. If I change now, I can prevent this or other tragedies—if I am just clever enough, or good enough, or smart enough. And if I can't prevent these tragedies, it must be my fault."

Many adults have a very narcissistic spirituality. I believe that this is true partly because many adults' only context for theological reflection is through memories of their early childhood church or religious experience; consequently, when these adults think about God or spirituality, they have only a childhood vocabulary, with childhood images, stories, and experiences to rely on.

Those early childhood images are very powerful. They stay with us even when they are challenged by adult experiences. Many adults who understand (as much as any layperson can, in a scientific sense) the structure of the solar system or the galaxies *still* spiritually dwell in a three-story spiritual universe in which heaven is "up" and hell is "down." These world views (childhood and adult) exist side by side in our consciousness. What many adults do is to tell themselves they just don't believe in that "God stuff" anymore, that they are atheists or agnostics. The problem is, the spiritual narcissism persists beyond our desire to wish it away. When there is a crisis, sometimes older children or adults will unconsciously reach for the spiritual "toys" (or tools) that they think they have long since put on the shelf or in a closet.

An awful lot of adults simply stop growing in their spirituality. When push comes to shove, or the earth shakes, or tragedies come, all that is available to them is a very narcissistic view of God and the universe—the old worn-out toys.

We live in a world that is desperate for adult spirituality and reflection, which can move beyond and heal the latent spiritual narcissism that is *inadequate* for adult living. This explains the popularity of Harold Kushner's book, *When Bad Things Happen to Good People*,[7] and M. Scott Peck's book, *The Road Less Traveled*.[8] Kushner's title is interesting because it uses simple words and is a phrase that plays on a childlike question that all adults have and don't like to admit having: "Why do bad things happen to good people?" Kushner also deals very directly with the second reason I believe we are stuck in a narcissistic spirituality: religious leaders and institutions have failed miserably to foster *adult* faith.

Authoritarian religions are the most obvious about not fostering adult faith. They foster authority-dependent faith based on magical thinking. Fundamentalists and other authoritarian religion systems have a *stake* in adults staying stuck in spiritual narcissism: such persons need a religiously rigid system to hold back adult needs and questions. It is about power and control; it is politically motivated by the desire to keep religious authority figures (pastors, popes, TV preachers) in power.

On the other side of the spectrum, the more liberal churches and institutions have failed to capture the hearts and imaginations of emerging generations of adults in our quantum age. They do not strive to help adults wrestle in depth with issues of adult faith. This may be out of fear (that there are no answers, that evangelicals are right?) or laziness. It seems to me that most progressive churches seem kind of lost, paralyzed, or floundering, or trying to find something to hang on to, something to live for, die for. They are struggling to find some anchor of meaning in an age of holocausts, space travel, genetic engineering, sexual revolutions, and terrorism. The "brightest and best" minds and voices are *not* seeking the church for their vocational venue. At least not as a first career! The church seems like a joke to many, or like a senile parent we don't want to embarrass but we don't quite know how to be honest with him or her, and we don't quite know how to tell them to shut up at the dinner table. The best we can hope for is to restrain them so that they do no harm to themselves or others. But even that is not always successful. Not the kind of institution or profession you want to give your life to.

I think many adults feel spiritually orphaned or abandoned by churches all along the spectrum, as adults do by aging parents who are not dead but who are no longer capable or available (if they ever *were*). I see this all the time in gay and lesbian adults who are trying to find something that *works* spiritually, in the context of a community that turns them on without insulting their intelligence or treating them like children. Both Kushner and Peck's writings are popular not because of the answers they give but because they know *what the real questions are*.

Not everyone, of course, wants a grown-up faith. Many people are so wounded in their spirituality and psyches that they are begging for someone to take care of them, to give them simple answers, tell them what to do, fix it all, touch them, heal them. It is not easy to form a community with people who want a grown-up faith (but who also have occasional lapses into narcissistic, spiritual longings!) and those who are not strong enough or secure enough to tolerate a more challenging, less dependent faith. I remember one woman at MCC Los Angeles in the middle of a heated theological debate finally saying, "All I want to know about is the Jesus I learned about in Sunday school when I was five!" I understood her pain and her need. But to permit *only that Jesus* is to deprive the church of an adult faith. The truth is, all communities contain a combination of such folks, and all of us move along a continuum of spiritual maturity at different times in our lives. All of us have moments when we are more willing to risk our theologies, when we are open to new information. We all deserve to be met right where we are and to be loved and to be able to hear the Gospel and *grow* in faith at our own pace.

Sometimes it *is* the "little children" (adult or actual) who lead us. Several years ago, as our church began to grow, I was challenged about how my pastoral style would have to change if we were to "break the two hundred barrier," in the language of church growth (in other words, if we were to grow in attendance past two hundred to three hundred). What I was told and believe is true is that I would need to spend more of my time training and mentoring *other* leaders in the church who could share or actually do the pastoring, so that we could nurture and love *more* people.

This meant that I would have to spend 80 percent of my one-to-one time with leaders or potential leaders and only 20 percent of my time with rank-and-file members or with some of the more dependent and needy members of the church who seemed to take an inordinate amount of my counseling time. On the surface, especially to a woman pastor who is supposed to be accepting, warm, loving, and nurturing to the *whole world*, setting these boundaries seemed very *cold*. But I also knew that if the church were going to move beyond my limits and skills, beyond what I could handle by myself, I had to shift; we had to shift. I had to keep in mind what one teacher had told us: It is possible to give someone a great deal of love, support, and *focused* attention in just five minutes, especially by offering to pray for them.

Then along came my teacher in this matter. A very dependent voice on the telephone. A woman who had diagnosed herself as a multiple personality, a self-proclaimed victim of ritual abuse, who wanted me to become her counselor. I did not have the time or skills to do this. So I suggested something. I offered to pray for her once a week for up to five minutes when I was in town. I did this for a year. Debbie often talked to me in one of her alleged "alter" voices, in a childlike way. She often pleaded for more time and begged me to become her therapist or counselor. Over and over again I would tell her I was not able to offer her that, but this is what I could offer her: five minutes of conversation and prayer, once per week. Sometimes she would call the office several times on that day, and the office had to tell her I was not available. Eventually she was able to stop calling the office as much and only called a lot if I were late or had to reschedule our time. I was always calm and firm. I never went over five minutes. I always reassured her that God loved her and that I was not angry with her. These were my limits; I hoped that she found what I could offer helpful. She always had simple requests for prayer.

It was a long time before I realized that Debbie was *teaching* me about how to shift my style of pastoring; she gave me weekly practice in setting new limits while still offering what I could realistically offer and that in which I was very skilled. During this time, Debbie had one therapist and lost another therapist. She wanted me to fix that, to be her counselor or find her a new one. I calmly declined to help but prayed about it with her. She had financial problems. We discussed options, she had other resources, and we prayed about it. She often wanted me to comment on her diagnosis. That was also inappropriate, and I told her so. I stuck to the program through the constant testing and never changed the boundary. Praying always helped, and sometimes, truthfully, the prayer time was as important to me as to her, though it took me time to see that. That five minutes of prayer often *refocused* me in the middle of a hectic day. It also comforted me when I felt helpless about what I was or was not doing *for* Debbie.

About a month after the earthquake (and several other big losses in my life) I was sitting in my office when Debbie called. I didn't really feel up to it that day. The initial shock of the losses and the earthquake were wearing off. I was feeling inadequate that day and not really sure I was moving ahead in my own pastoring skills. Was I really going to be able to pastor this church? There were still people in the church who felt like I gave too much attention to certain *kinds* of people. People like Debbie. Depending on which group you talked to, you might get a different critique: to some, five minutes was not enough, and it was too much for others. All my people-pleasing issues were in full swing that day. I felt vulnerable, and it was one of those days, and Debbie was on line two. . . .

We talked, and she told me she thought she had a therapist lined up for one month from now, but couldn't I pleeeeease be her therapist? I calmly said no again; we made our next appointment, and I was ready to hang up. Suddenly an adult voice spoke to me on the line, Debbie's adult voice—one of the few times I ever heard it. "Reverend Wilson," she said, "I just want to thank you for all the time you've taken to talk and pray with me. I really appreciate it; you will never know how much."

I took that in and thanked her for being willing to accept what I had to offer. I was humbled, and I felt centered again.

The Measure of Mature Spirituality for a New Millennium

Mature spirituality is tested by several things, primarily how we deal with the tragic, how we deal with the poor, and how we deal with joy and sexuality.

Liberation theology speaks of "God's option for the poor," meaning the economically poor. "God's option for the poor" means that God loves all people, rich, poor, and in-between, but that God asks those who *have* to be in a constant process of conversion and solidarity with those who *have not*. In a world where desperate poverty causes unbelievable suffering, God calls us to change the world, so that their suffering is relieved.

It is dangerous to spiritualize the poor, as if there is not a special way in which we are called to show solidarity with those who are economically oppressed. Sometimes Christians have addressed spiritual or emotional "poverty," metaphorical uses of the word poverty, without ever addressing the causes or cures for economic poverty. This has become a rationale for not caring about the poor. It is important not to *substitute* the term *poor* (meaning spiritually or emotionally poor) for *economically poor*. On the other hand I do *not* think it is wrong to *expand* our understanding of the poor to include all who are oppressed—economically, politically, emotionally, and spiritually—while making sure that we understand the *serious differences* between literal and metaphorical poverty. Seeing the connection does not *have* to dilute the truth of God's option for the economically poor, if we are vigilant.

All gay and lesbian people experience oppression. Economic, race, or gender privilege may insulate some of us for a time or to a degree from that oppression, but not always and not forever. So, in the gay and lesbian community we are also poor, although some are poorer than others, and there are certainly the economically poor among us. Indifference on the part of some to the poverty of others is real in the gay and lesbian community.

But how a religion, spiritual path, or church responds to the poor is one measure of its authenticity, its maturity. Its refusal to ghettoize the poor, to keep them out of sight, its refusal to distance itself from the needs, cries, and gifts of the poor is a measure of how rich a spirituality this really is.

And this is not about romanticizing "the poor." Jesus said he came not for the well but for those who knew they needed a physician. He was not *excluding* the well but asking them to be willing to see what in themselves *still* needed healing, and how they could also join him in seeking those who already knew their need of a physician (of God).

When the church at large refuses to see gays and lesbians as the poor or to reach out, touch, include, and respond to us, it exhibits immaturity in its spirituality. When MCC or other gay and lesbian churches refuse to touch and see the poor among us (those with AIDS, HIV, those in prison, those who are economically poor), we betray the very vision that birthed us.

Also, the way in which our faith is able to embrace the tragic without explaining it away, minimizing it, or allowing it to be the *ultimate* truth is another measure of mature spirituality.

In being willing to deal with and learn from the poor and the tragic, we are engaging in a process of healing the spiritual narcissism that dominates so much of religious life in our culture in this century.

When the earthquake of January 17, 1994, hit Los Angeles, I was in bed sound asleep next to my lover Paula. When it began, I was terrified, sure that we were going to die and that the house was falling down on top of us. I grabbed Paula and would not let her go. She tried to get us both up and to some safer place, but I wouldn't cooperate. I was terrorized. And then I began thinking that probably other people were dying, and I prayed all kinds of selfish prayers that *everyone* would be all right. Although I said everyone, I think I really meant people I knew. My father had died the month before, along with nine other people I knew (mostly of AIDS). The thought of thousands of deaths, of friends or family or church members dying, seemed beyond my capacity to handle. So, though I was praying for them and considering the possibility that some had been injured or died, I was also being totally selfish. I say this without shame, simply as an experience of myself under stress.

The moments after the quake were deadly silent—except for car alarms going off everywhere. There were no lights or phone, only a radio. The aftershocks came quickly and were terrifying.

I said, "Oh, God," about a hundred times. I kept telling Paula I loved her, afraid I would never have the chance to say so again or she would never have the chance to hear me again. It was apocalyptic, like the end of the world. Weird to have survived it at first. Like we were in some old rerun of the *Twilight Zone.*

Gradually, information began to arrive in bits and pieces, and the light of dawn came filtering through. Phones worked intermittently. I learned that the church dome was in the street, and I headed off with Paula and Norm (who had almost single-handedly renovated the church) to the site. Driving through Los Angeles streets with no streetlights or signals was eerie, surreal.

As a person who has frequently been asked "why" questions by parishioners and others, I stifled that question in myself. Over and over I had been there with adults who were facing life's struggles with the question "Why?" and who looked to me. I had tried not to lie to them, to pretend to have answers I didn't have.

A few weeks later while halfway around the globe in South Africa, I happened to be reading a book about maps called *Mapping the New Millennium* by Stephen Hall.[9] Right in the middle of his book he deals with earthquakes. At first I just wanted to throw the book at the nearest wall. But I let myself read on. I had some vague notions about earthquakes—that they were a necessary evil somehow, a very natural phenomenon.

I had never thought or theorized much about earthquakes until I moved to California. In the mideighties, my friend Rev. Dusty Pruitt told me about one of my favorite "pop" theology authors, Agnes Sanford. In her later life, Sanford felt *called* to set aside her human-oriented healing ministry (people began to *irritate* her more and more!) and felt a call to pray for the San Andreas fault. She said that she felt she could do this with the clear understanding that earthquakes were natural and necessary but that she could pray for minimal loss of life and property damage as they occurred. Dusty and I observed ominously that earthquake activity began increasing after Sanford died! Dusty frequently wondered just who it was that was to take Sanford's place (her *mantle*) and why they weren't doing their job!

In Hall's chapter on mapping the earth's core and mantle, he comes very close to explaining the physiological "why" of earthquakes. The explanation involves the observation that the earth, contrary to what we may assume, is asymmetrical, even though it is more or less round. It is not perfectly round but *flawed.* These subtle imperfections, it now appears, are linked to the processes that make our planet, "almost alone in the only solar system we know, alive and dynamic and capable of reinventing itself.... If the internal properties of the earth were spherically symmetric, our planet would be tectonically dead. Asymmetry breathes life into the heart of the planet."[10]

Hall says that part of the job of the map reader is to drop old poses and look at familiar materials in unfamiliar ways. (Could this not also describe the job of a creative theologian?) Hall observes that the mantle of the earth, though solid, behaves geologically like a fluid; this "mantle operates as a large, single, indivisible convective cell," and this "convection causes the sea floor to spread, creates ocean basins, builds mountains, moves continents, ignites volcanoes, and triggers earthquakes: it is the pulse of a living planet."[11]

Also it appears that the *"enigmatic border* between the mantle and the molten core"[12] of the earth is the arena where the dynamics critical to the life of the earth take place. This is a *powerful* image of the nature of change and the origins of life and creativity.

I believe that both sexuality and spirituality are connected to that "enigmatic border" of our life and creativity. Sexuality is still a great mystery in many ways. Where else in human experience do the issues of genetics, biology, politics, psychology, ethics, poetry, and even metaphysics intersect? What does it mean to be a woman or a man, to be straight or gay or bisexual? The very first things that anyone wants to know about you or me when we are born is our gender and if we are *healthy*. Our gender and our health status shape others' and the world's and our own perception of ourselves from *before we are born*.

Whenever anyone challenges our deeply held assumptions about gender or sexuality, they drag us into that enigmatic border, and this terrifies us. People who do so are often ostracized, punished, or banished.

The same, I believe, is true with spirituality. Spirituality is the "enigmatic border" between the worlds—between heaven and earth. That inner space that we occupy simultaneously with our physical existence. The inner world of the "heart," "mind," or "spirit" that has fascinated human beings but has always to some degree eluded us. And we also refer to the world of the spirit as our "spiritual life." The word *life* is used both in the physical sense—as biological life—but also in this other sense, the sense of our "spiritual life."

What I began to grasp is that events like volcanoes and earthquakes are evidence of *tectonic* life. Also, it is the fact that our earth is a fluid, molten, unfinished core at the center, surrounded by a mantle that behaves like a living, indivisible convective cell, that creates the *biochemical preconditions for life to exist on our planet*. A "tectonically dead" planet cannot produce the conditions that make life sustainable. Neither is life sustainable without sexuality and spirituality.

Earthquakes are a sign that our planet is alive and can sustain life. The problem lies in the *interpretation*. As the earth shakes with new life, some of us are in the way. Buildings, freeways, human creations, infrastructures, plants, animals, and even humans get in the way of these awesome events, and sometimes they are damaged or die.

I meditated a great deal about this new (for me) information about earthquakes. I have not stopped trembling at the memory of the power of those forty seconds of terror on January 17, 1994. It is easy for me to understand how many people experienced it as some expression of divine or cosmic anger—God's or Mother Earth's. It was *so* powerful, it was hard not to personify it. But the geophysiology contradicts this. The powerful roar that I can still occasionally recall was not the roar of anger but the roar of tectonic birthing, *the roar of planetary life itself*. That *does* cause me to tremble!

Earthquakes are actually waves. These waves can travel even through the center of the earth and be felt. I can tell you that earthquakes can move through *our* core being as well. All our issues about life, death, mortality, priorities, all our "why" questions, all our fears, our needs, come sharply to the surface in the aftermath of an earthquake. For many people, the sense of physical betrayal (the earth is *supposed* to be solid, not fluid) triggers enormous feelings, memories. We ordinarily walk around with the illusion that the earth is steady, and it is not supposed to move, crumble, shift sideways beneath us. But that is an illusion. The earth is a flawed sphere hurling through space at fantastic speeds around a minor star. This sphere is not solid but molten at its core, allowing it to be constantly reshaped. This illusion of the static, solid ground is very like the illusion that we are *not* going to die or that we have a right to expect to live seventy-plus years or so. These are narcissistic illusions. They don't die easily—sometimes they only die with us.

This is the Big Picture for me. A very important way out of narcissistic theology is to keep seeking the bigger picture in order to understand more and more of what is really going on. At the end of the most violent century in human history, our planet manages to be tectonically alive and demonstrates that fact with particular fervor, it seems. Is this the creation and the Creator's response to what humans are doing (or not doing) on the planet, *simply to assert life*? This may be stretching things too far. Perhaps the assertion of life simply keeps happening, whatever we do or do *not* do.

I recall, however, that at the end of the Sodom and Gomorrah story in Genesis 19 there is the *rain of fire and brimstone*. Was that really a tectonic event? Was it a volcanic eruption (which is akin to earthquakes in its geological purpose)? Is God's response to the violence of sodomy (*not* homosexuality) to burst forth in life? We may attempt to *read into this* as human beings a kind of "micro justice" (justice pointed at individuals or small groups) that God is meting out in these events, but that thinking, that theology, is flawed. At best, I believe there is macro justice, but the micro issues are apparently left for us to sort out.

Job of the Hebrew Scriptures discovered that. His lifelong, comfortable, unchallenged narcissistic spirituality that assumed that God rewards the good and punishes the wicked with timely micro justice *bit the dust* when his world fell apart for no damned good reason that he could see. That experience was the beginning of spiritual maturity for Job. As it was for Rob Roberts,[13] as it is for all of us who struggle, suffer, and grow.

Earthquakes and Faith Crises Across Cultures

For many people in Los Angeles and at our church, the earthquake became a fundamental faith crisis. If we cannot count on God to keep the earth from shaking or to keep our church building standing upright or our homes or lives from being destroyed, what can we count on God for, anyway? I remember reading Paul Tillich's theology in seminary. He wrote about a God who is the "ground of our being." What happens to our faith in the ground of our being when the *ground* is shaking?! Tillich obviously had a seismically insensitive theology!

This faith crisis was acted out in many ways in our church. People who believed they had long ago left behind the *judging* God suddenly found themselves wondering if God were exercising a fundamentalist-style micro justice in toppling the building of a gay-and-lesbian-owned church building. There was almost a kind of morbid glee when our members learned that other predominantly *straight* churches had been destroyed, too! What a relief, we weren't *singled out!* Other members found themselves still unable to return to church.

An African-American member of my church talked poignantly about how in the African-American community, church has always been the "safe place." For many African-Americans (and for poor folk of different ethnic backgrounds), the church was sometimes the only piece of real estate they ever owned or hoped to own. MCC, like the historic black church, is the "historic" church of the gay and lesbian community. For African-Americans the church was, and sometimes still is, everything; it was where community meetings were held (when they couldn't meet legally in other buildings). It was *theirs*; no one could take it away from them. It was where they discussed voting and politics; it housed the burial societies; it was a place where you could always get help. African-American gays and lesbians at MCC Los Angeles had a different historical perspective, a different lens, perhaps a more intense spiritual and political symbolic investment in the church building than other members. Church structures are not *supposed* to fall down. If *they* fall down, the community is *exposed* and vulnerable in devastating ways.

MCC Los Angeles members who owned their own homes generally did not take the destruction of the church so personally, unless they were African-American or had other complicating issues. Thus, the destruction of our building challenged our multicultural community in new ways. We had to communicate more in order to understand each other's particular pains and sorrows.

Latinos and Latinas had yet other concerns. Many of them are immigrants from countries that experience devastating earthquakes, where there was little money for the kinds of seismic preparedness that had been possible in Los Angeles. They had been through experiences where hundreds and even thousands had died in similar earthquakes. They *knew* not to trust the ground. They, of all groups in Los Angeles, took the longest time to reenter their homes, even if they had not had any damage. It took some of the Hispanic members of MCC Los Angeles a very long time to come back to church with any sense of safety, if they ever could. On top of the lack of safety in a culture that is increasingly anti-immigrant, now not even the church was a safe place.

Race, culture, and class privileges made the earthquake less traumatic for some than for others. But even the *most* privileged among us knew that all the retrofitting, all the money and power and education in the world amounted to *nothing* in comparison to the force of this event. For most of us, it was the most powerful external physical force we had ever experienced.

Seismic Sexuality

Life at its core depends on the asymmetry, the messiness, the incompleteness, the imperfection of the geophysical nature of the planet. What an incredible concept. How are we to understand this theologically? It is as if the planet responds passionately to the asymmetry. In many ways, I think it is interesting to consider this possibility: that volcanoes and earthquakes are, metaphorically speaking, the *sexuality* of the planet. The life urge, the urge to connect, to give birth, to conceive, to change, to grow, to affect and be affected. That is sexuality. That is life.

Are the tectonically unstable and sensitive places or "hot spots" on the planet, like the ring of fire around the Pacific rim, akin to a kind of *erogenous zone* for the planet?

I believe that the third challenge of a mature theology is its capacity to celebrate and embrace sexuality, joy, *embodiedness*, and the big picture.

It is very hard, in our microworlds and with our individualized concerns, to celebrate earthquakes as an expression of the planet's will to *live*, its expression of something like our sexuality. But I do think that's what earthquakes are, metaphorically speaking. Sometimes our human creations and structures do not take the earth and its will to live (a really big picture) into account. Most of the people in Los Angeles who died in the earthquake died in one building that was demonstrated to be unsafe or on freeways that were not as safe as they were thought to be. People also die from earthquakes, floods, and tidal waves where no human ingenuity could have saved them. Sometimes, as small frail life forms, *we are in the way*, in much the same way, perhaps, that the very small life forms that are sometimes in our way are thought to be of no account or worth, and we poison, kill, or sweep them away without a thought.

I am still sometimes haunted by a memory of the aftermath of the Mexico City earthquake in 1985. One of our church members was killed, and others saw death and injuries on a scale from which they have never quite been able to recover. A few days after the quake, we had an ant attack in our kitchen, as happens in Los Angeles when the weather is very dry. The sight of thousands of ants crawling over the kitchen counter repulsed me, as it does many people. I grabbed the bug spray and began to kill them. Suddenly I realized that for *them*, this was a terrible disaster—a lot like an earthquake or flood, perhaps. I felt helpless and horrible. I did not want to feel this connection *at all*. I wanted to dissociate from these tiny creatures, from any sense of their world or existence. They were in my way. I could so easily regard them as nonlife, to be disposed of at my will, disregarded. I wanted so much *not* to feel it, not to connect them to the human beings in Mexico, to my own humanness, to my own existence and stark vulnerability as a *life form*. It infuriated me that I could not close my mind to these thoughts, and I felt just a little *mad* for a while. I felt grief and shame and helplessness. For a long while I tried other ant control methods, some of which I still use, such as keeping little pans of water outside the house, outside doors and windows near their entry points. This seemed to help, at least for a while.

A big picture and a very tiny picture intersected at that moment in a powerful way for me. What about our human desire to control, exploit life—does all life have inalienable rights? When we speak of reverence for life as a value, what kind of life are we talking about? What are the limits, if any? What do I do with all that bug spray? (It is probably bad for the ozone layer anyway!) How far do I have to go in sharing the planet and with which species?

The Bible and Earthquakes

There are about twenty-five references to earthquakes in the Bible. Some of these references are not necessarily *theological* at all, as in this reference from the first verse of the first chapter of Amos:

> The words of Amos, who was among the shepherds of Tekoa, which he saw concerning Israel in the days of King Uzziah of Judah and in the days of King Jeroboam, son of Joash of Israel, two years before the earthquake.
>
> (AMOS 1:1)

The earthquake. Zechariah mentions the very same earthquake in 14:5, as if all persons reading this will simply know or remember a particular earthquake called "The Earthquake." Anyone alive and near Los Angeles on January 17, 1994, will remember *the* earthquake. Until, of course, something greater in our disaster memory replaces it as a dating device. The earthquake during Amos's lifetime must have had devastating effects to be so singularly remembered. The Oxford Annotated Bible simply comments, "The earthquake, mentioned again in Zechariah 14:5, cannot be precisely dated." Time came when the memory faded and life went on. Sometimes earthquakes, then, are simply recorded as an alternative method of dating a person or events.

There are two categories of the *theological* uses of earthquakes in Scripture. One category I would call *earthquakes as evidence of God's self-expression*. Sometimes earthquakes (accompanied by wind or fire or even sheer *silence*) are a metaphor for the theophany of God: how God's presence is experienced by humans. This occurs on Mount Sinai (Numbers 16:31–34) and is frequently the case in the Psalms. Earthquakes are also described as the "earth's trembling response to the power of God's presence" (or appearance). This is not the same as the use of earthquakes as an expression of divine wrath—an idea that is alive and well in our times! The book of Revelation is filled with references to violent earthquakes that sometimes kill thousands of people, which is part of an overall apocalyptic vision of the judgment of God upon the wicked. There are hints of this in the "little apocalypses" of Matthew and Luke, including references to earthquakes.

Sometimes just the power and force of the divine, without any particularly negative associations, are viewed as the cause of earthquakes, or earthquakes are interpreted as being motivated by a particular event that has angered God or as signs of God's total, *generic* anger at human beings.

Biblical earthquake theologies don't end here, however; it is even more complicated than that. Earthquakes also seem to play a role in *events related to divine intervention* or that support the divine plan. In one case, an earthquake accompanies Jonathan's (a gay man's?) victory over the Philistines, increasing the "panic in their camp" (1 Samuel chapter 14–15.) In the New Testament, in Matthew's Gospel only, earthquakes accompany both the crucifixion and the resurrection of Jesus. In the account of the resurrection (Matthew 28:2), it is an earthquake that actually rolls the stone away from Jesus' tomb! The *elemental forces* of the universe are called to play a part in this cosmic drama of the death and resurrection of God's anointed. One may wonder if earthquakes were very frequent in those years or if those particular earthquakes would provide dating corroboration for the events. Was this earthquake simply inserted as a literary device meant to heighten the drama of the events or to connect them theologically to God's theophany, God's anger, or to the apocalyptic view of Jesus' life and ministry? Are the mention of earthquakes incidental to those events, or do they carry more meaning than most scholars have been willing to explore? Are they a part of the backdrop or a component of the events themselves?

Earthquakes as Spiritual Opportunity for Liberation

Perhaps my favorite earthquake story in the Bible is in Acts 16, the story of Paul and Silas and the jailer.

The book of Acts is the story of the preaching and practicing of the "unhindered Gospel" (Acts 28:31) and the increasing self-discovery of this new movement, which was hardly a church yet. Those early followers of the Way were adventurous, and totally committed to sharing the life-giving, healing grace of God in Jesus Christ. They lived and died to do this.

An earthquake figures in one story of the sharing of the Gospel. Paul and Silas are in Philippi, where they have met Lydia (the seller of purple, you will recall), the women in her prayer group, and, apparently, also some men who are now a part of the church in Lydia's house (Acts 16).

Inevitably, Paul and Silas run into some legal trouble. A slave woman, who the Scriptures say was possessed of a "spirit of divination," was harassing them. Almost offhandedly, Paul, who it says was "very much annoyed" (Acts 16:18), confronts the spirit, and the slave woman is released and in her right mind.

The men who profited from her spiritual or mental illness are not amused. She was a source of income, as people threw coins at this raving psychic. In this story, Christ's messengers align themselves on the side of health and are opposed to those who oppress, dominate, and exploit this slave woman. Paul's and Silas's gift from Jesus of healing is politically and economically *dangerous*. They have rocked the boat. So the merchants have Paul and Silas thrown into jail (without really knowing who they were or that Paul, for instance, is a Roman citizen and should have been exempt from such treatment). The story begins this way:

> About midnight Paul and Silas were praying and singing hymns to
> God, and the prisoners were listening to them. Suddenly there was
> an earthquake, so violent that the foundations of the prison were
> shaken; and immediately all the doors were opened and everyone's
> chains were unfastened. When the jailer woke up and saw the
> prison doors wide open, he drew his sword and was about to kill
> himself, since he supposed that the prisoners had escaped. But
> Paul shouted in a loud voice, "Do not harm yourself, for we are all
> here." The jailer called for lights, and rushing in, he fell down
> trembling before Paul and Silas. Then he brought them outside
> and said, "Sirs, what must I do to be saved?" They answered,

"Believe on the Lord Jesus, and you will be saved, you and your household." And the same hour of the night he took them and washed their wounds; then he and his entire family were baptized without delay. He brought them up into the house and set food before them; and he and his entire household rejoiced that he had become a believer in God.

(ACTS 16:25–34)

Later in the story, the magistrates discover that Paul and Silas are citizens and try to cover up their error. But Paul decides to rub their noses in it a bit. After stopping by Lydia's place to encourage the folks there, they head off again to share the Gospel.

There are some fascinating aspects to this story and to how we might use it to understand its relationship to the issues of sexuality and the church today.

Paul and Silas are singing hymns in jail. The other prisoners, it says, are listening to them. To these two *nuts*, perhaps. Or to some they represent a tremendous sense of hope, strength, and peace that emanates from them. Paul and Silas are no strangers to suffering for the sake of the Gospel. There was joy in enduring suffering for the sake of Jesus, for the sake of a slave girl, now free and in her right mind.

That same spirit I have seen among the South African political detainees, those who were tortured and illegally detained for years in prison for the sake of Jesus. I have seen it in those arrested in AIDS demonstrations, in those arrested in the early days of the civil rights movements, in antiwar protests. The joy of suffering for righteousness's sake.

The earthquake was sudden and violent so that the foundations were shaken. In this case, the earthquake, though it is not explicitly stated, functions as an instrument of divine providence. In doing so, the action is sudden and violent. *Shaking the foundations of the prison*—a powerful metaphor for the liberator God. God's action through Christ in these disciples continues to be the same: shaking the foundations of oppression or injustice, of the prisons in which we find ourselves.

One can only imagine how frightening that earthquake was nearly two thousand years ago—no radio, no Kate Hutton from Cal Tech, no retrofitting. As the quake subsides, there is shock, a stillness. No one moves apparently. We can wonder whether there is verbal communication among the prisoners, but apparently a decision was made. They decide not to use the earthquake as a reason to run away, to escape.

I wonder why not. Might it not seem logical to Paul and Silas that God had provided the earthquake as a means of escape to foil the enemies of God? Instead, they seem to have made the decision to stay for the sake of the jailer. Perhaps there wasn't time for them to escape, or they were unsure if the way was really open.

In any case, the jailer, upon waking and realizing what has happened, simply assumes the worst—that his prisoners have escaped and that he will be killed for allowing them to do so. His fear of what his fate will be is so acute that he plans to kill himself. But from the dark, there is a voice. How unbelievable that must have seemed to the jailer. The voice of the gods themselves. The voice of hope, of mercy: *"Do not harm yourself, for we are all here."* The jailer is stunned, I presume, by this act of unmerited charity. The prisoners *free* the jailer from his death sentence! He gets his life back in those words, "Do not harm yourself, we are all here." We never actually hear about the other prisoners again. But somehow Paul has managed to be the designated spokesperson and leader. On what basis did he convince the others to stay, one wonders? Did the other prisoners associate the earthquake with the powerful presence of these hymn-singing religious folks? Better do what they tell you, and stay put!

The jailer's whole life and agenda get converted in this story. He no longer seems to care at all what the magistrates do with him. He takes Paul and Silas home with him, feeds them, washes their wounds, and is overjoyed to be associated with them through baptism in Christ. His whole life is turned upside down, and he is grateful! Now he is no longer a prisoner of his *old* life, but a free prisoner of Christ.

I wonder how Paul and Silas knew that the earthquake could be used either as a way to escape or as an opportunity to testify about the love and grace of God in Jesus Christ. What a profound alternative reading, an alternative *earthquake theology* this is! Their own safety, comfort, or vindication is not an issue for them! Everything is about the opportunity to love, to be free, to testify, to save (the jailer's life and career, this time). There were no guarantees. The jailer could have chosen to kill the prisoners since he could no longer restrain them. He had the only weapon.

In some ways, the prison recalls the tomb of Jesus. I think of the angel announcing to the shocked visitors, "He is not here, he is risen." In almost a play on that story, Paul says, "We are all here." Of course the angel meant Jesus is not here in the tomb. But the point was, Jesus was still *here* but in a new way.

The violent earthquake (crucifixion, disaster) becomes the occasion for new life (Christ's resurrection, this jailer's physical salvation and spiritual conversion).

If as the National Council of Churches of Christ says, it is true that the issue of homosexuality (sexuality, really) is a *huge seismic fault* that threatens to divide the Christian church at the end of the second millennium, I've been thinking about what a provocative image this is, after all. Is this particular earthquake a disaster, an opportunity, or both? I'm sure the visitors to the tomb that Easter morning at first saw the earthquake as perhaps *one more* disaster (on top of the crucifixion, perhaps another indicator of God's wrath). But instead, of course, it became the method by which the disciples came to know the miracle of the resurrection.

The church is having difficulty seeing the *opportunity* in this seismic debate on human and "homo" sexuality! In many ways, gay and lesbian Christians, imprisoned by the church's outdated and erroneous view about sexual morality, are like Paul and Silas. We might well be expected to use this "earthquake" (the conflict in the church over sexuality) to *escape*. To just pack up and leave. The foundations of the prison are shaking, for God's sake! Can the structures and theology of two thousand years of Christendom really survive? Do we really want to risk being in the rubble?

But gay and lesbian Christians, like Paul and Silas, know that many nonbelievers are *also* imprisoned by the false theology of the church. The whole culture is permeated with the images and beliefs of a sexually repressed and phobic Christianity. Those who imprisoned Paul and Silas and the others were not the jailer but other more powerful forces "out there." There really was not any escape except to trust God, through their faithfulness, to convert the *entire system* from top to bottom. That's what Paul and Silas thought they were doing, and it is what we need to do!

So, they start with the jailer, with the keeper of the tradition, the foot soldier of the power structure, who may have little power in the culture but who did what he was told. Who then are those good churchpeople who keep believing and passing on traditions of condemnation, who are *just doing their jobs*, enforcing the outdated laws of the church? We can only hope and pray that as we are faithful, like Paul and Silas, and *do not run away*, the experience of our testimony and our faith in God (not the church) will be enough to convert the "jailer." Because ultimately the "secret" will be discovered: that we, gay men and lesbians, are *citizens of the household of faith*. Just like the powers that have realized their error in treating the *citizens* Paul and Silas so rudely, someday the church will have to repent of its treatment of its gay and lesbian *citizens*.

There is also the fate of our *fellow prisoners* in the Christian moral theology jailhouse (tomb) that is both bankrupt *and* corrupt. Bankrupt because it ceases to bring hope, new life, or healing to men and women who suffer terribly not from their sexuality but from how the church *has made them feel or not feel about their embodied selves*. The *least* the church could do, one would hope, is to *do no harm*. But it does great, profound harm.

And I say corrupt. Many closeted gay and lesbian religious authorities harm others in order to protect themselves. They do so because they have what *they believe* to be "dirty secrets," shameful realities about their own sexual lives. Many in church leadership and hierarchies are sick with guilt, shame, and lying. Then they dump this on the rest of us. These are not *only* gays and lesbians but heterosexuals as well: all those who cannot tell the truth about their own sexual histories, lifestyles, or fantasies and who will persecute others who do!

Who are our "fellow prisoners"? They are people who say to me nearly every day, "I'm not religious." This statement is a virtual political necessity in the gay and lesbian community. It might be OK or "cool" to be *spiritual*. But it should be a private, highly individual thing, like it used to be! Or very New Age or avant-garde. Never *religious*. Certainly not Christian.

When Fr. Malcom Boyd, Rabbi Denise Eger, and Rev. LaPaula Turner and I were arrested during an AIDS protest in front of the Los Angeles County Board of Supervisors, we were taken to our respective county facilities. The men had a much worse time of it than we did. They were chained to benches and not permitted to go to the bathroom for hours on end.

LaPaula, Denise, and I arrived just in time for lunch, which they served us in the holding cell. I think LaPaula and I were both aware that Denise was a little more of a novice at this than we were. I'd been in jail and had visited lots of people in this particular jail before. We sang songs for her and for ourselves (like Paul and Silas, I guess, though I didn't think of it at the time).

The guards were quiet and low-key, almost not seeing us. We were fingerprinted and kept in the smaller of the holding tanks. Across the aisle, separated by bars and glass, was the holding tank full of women, many of whom looked (to me) to be lesbian. I noticed all of them pointed at

196 | OUR TRIBE

LaPaula, Denise, and me. They saw my clergy collar. They were laughing, thinking this was cool: a bunch of preachers busted—for what?

I tried to communicate using the little sign language I knew. I smiled and joked, thinking they knew I was a lesbian. I was able to let them know we were there for an AIDS demonstration. They were all poking each other. They kept laughing until I looked at them and signed something like "I'll pray for you." One woman's face just clouded up, all angry. "Don't pray for me," she signed, folding her arms defiantly. Suddenly I realized that she thought I meant *praying for her because she was a sinner, a bad person, not like me.* This grieved and hurt me. No, no, I signed. "I'm a lesbian, like you." (I did look around before I said this to make sure no guards would see me.) "Really?" came the response, "No shit!" She was all smiles again. "Then you *can* pray for me," she signed. Collar or no collar, I was a *sinner,* just like her.

We at MCC Los Angeles also found this story of Paul and Silas useful, especially in the face of hostile fundamentalist earthquake theologizing about the loss of our building. It became possible to see ourselves as those who could say, "We are still here," after the earthquake! We are *not* going anywhere; we are still being the people of God in Los Angeles, especially for the gay, lesbian, and bisexual communities, for people with AIDS. For *anyone* who feels judged or excluded from the people of God, especially because of their sexuality. We are still here. Not arson, or persecution, or vandalism, or earthquakes can stop those who know the *real* truth: that we *are* citizens of God's wonderful realm whose ethic is one of unconditional love. We are still here, testifying to jailers, judges, magistrates, and our fellow prisoners. We do not experience things like earthquakes as God's special judgment *or* favor on anyone. But simply as one more marvelous opportunity to share the good news of God's love and to practice that Way in our own city and neighborhood.

PARABLES OF "HARD-LIVING" GAYS AND LESBIANS ON THE STREETS AND IN PRISONS

When I first joined MCC in 1972 I was very impressed by the fact that MCC from its earliest days had reached out to gays and lesbians in jails and prisons: "hard-living" people. [14]

In those days (the late sixtiess, early seventies), homosexuals did not have the more middle/upperclass urban image we sometimes have today.

We were still considered mostly pretty unmentionable and sleazy. There-fore, it was a little easier, perhaps, for us to identify with other social out-casts and misfits.

We had felt the terrible sting of rejection and the pain of inhospitality, and we were determined, with every breath, not to exclude anyone. We were going to welcome all people into our churches and hearts (sometimes, even if it killed us!). We who had been called "sodomites" had been *sodomized* by the church and the culture, and we couldn't bear to do it to anyone else.

In taking this stand, we found ourselves tackling the "sodomite" ten-dencies of some of the largest institutions in the country: the army, the prisons, the churches, the hospitals. Places others were trying to get out of, we were trying to get into! We were searching for our people.

As a *class* of people, we gays and lesbians have more familiarity than most with jails and prisons. They form a part of our history. I remember making my first visit to a lesbian bar in the "combat zone" (a street that contained a row of porno theaters, strip joints, and notorious bars) in downtown Boston in the early 1970s and having to run out the back door because a police raid was happening. Every now and then the police would just rush in the front door of a gay bar and begin rounding everyone up, busting the heads of those who resisted (and the heads of some who didn't). It was during just such a raid that someone said to Troy Perry (in 1968) that surely God *couldn't* love us. It was this statement that propelled Troy into actually holding the first MCC service.[15]

I pastored an MCC church in Worcester, Massachusetts, in the 1970s. After raids at the one gay bar in town (the Ports O' Call on South Main Street), my partner and I would rush to the police station. At the desk there was a TV monitor, where we watched the police beating young adults, even kids in their teens, while dragging them to their cells. We had to keep our mouths shut while we watched or risk getting beaten and jailed ourselves. If that happened, there would have been no one to come for us. So we watched, took badge numbers, times, and dates, while desk sergeants grumbled about our presence. Sometimes if there was a scuffle at the bar or a problem in the making, we would receive a call and race down to the bar trying to intervene before the police arrived. More often than not the police would just show up for a "surprise visit," and the very sight of them would set off a chain reaction that resulted in arrests and beatings. We then reported these beatings to the Human Rights Commis-sion, who listened empathetically, sometimes even held hearings, and usually did nothing.

While I was pastor of MCC Detroit, we formed a prison ministry team. This included a group of people (mostly lesbians) who began corresponding with inmates in Jackson State Prison, eighty miles from Detroit. Early on in the correspondence we learned of a lesbian prison inmate in DEHOCO (Detroit House of Correction, a women's state facility that I believe no longer exists) who wanted contact with MCC. I let that information sit on my desk for a few weeks, then finally got around to writing to her. The envelope came back several weeks later, stamped DECEASED. I remember how devastated I felt, holding that unopened envelope in my hands. They had a *pre-printed stamp* saying "DECEASED"! This gave me a clue about how often this had to be communicated to the family and friends of those in prison. I was never able to establish another contact with lesbians in jail or prison while I lived in Detroit.

In 1982, in Los Angeles, a group of women in MCC churches in the area formed a women's prison ministry. We knew no women in prison, although a few members of MCC Los Angeles had actually joined MCC while they were in prison in the 1970s through a jail ministry at Sybil Brand (the Los Angeles women's county jail, which also houses federal prisoners). That ministry and its leaders were no longer around.

Three of us prayed for some kind of opportunity. Two weeks later the lover of a friend of mine ended up in jail at Sybil Brand. My friend was not amused that I saw this as an answer to prayer! She was much too frightened to have me visit (and thus be identified as a lesbian), but she met a woman who was willing. I think I first visited her the way that family and friends do, standing in line outside sometimes for hours until they call your person's number. Later I would go through the process of certifying my credentials with the county so that I could visit these women as their pastor, meaning I could bypass the line and meet more privately in the "attorney room."

The word spread, and several of us on the team began visiting women on a regular basis, to the dismay of the fundamentalist women's chaplain at Sybil Brand.

We also learned a great deal from the woman who was the president of the group called Friends Outside, an advocacy organization for women in prison: Joyce Ride, mother of Sally Ride. (Her business card actually says, "Mother of the First Woman Astronaut.") Joyce knew all the ins and outs of these places and how to help us deal with an institution that didn't want us to be there.

One of my first encounters was with Yvonne. In her midthirties, Yvonne, a fairly butch Latina lesbian, had spent most of her adult life bouncing between jail, short stays in prison, and "tours" at Norwalk State Hospital. ("Jail" usually refers to a city or county facility, "prison" to a state or federal institution.) She was an alcoholic, without the possibility of decent long-term treatment.

Yvonne was in jail this time because she was awaiting trial and had no bail money. Yvonne drank at gay bars mostly, but she'd drink at a straight bar if she had to. One night she did that and went to the trailer park of the man who had been buying her drinks. The trip to his place of residence sobered her up enough so that she realized where she was and what the price was for these drinks. She tried to leave the trailer and he prevented her (she was about five feet four inches, average size; he was over six feet tall and huge— I saw him myself in court later on). He then tried to rape her, and in the process, she grabbed a knife from his kitchen and stabbed him.

He lived, but it was awfully close. She was so drunk she remembered nothing of the stabbing or the aftermath.

When I met her she was in jail, being prosecuted for defending herself. He was out of the hospital and certainly not in jail for attempted rape.

I saw this over and over again: women who were in jail for defending themselves or for harming, even killing, someone who chronically, systematically abused and endangered them.

We bailed Yvonne out and tried to get her into a decent alcoholic treatment program. I failed at the latter. She was not committed enough, probably did not have enough self-esteem to recover, and the opportunity was *not there*. She drank and used. The temporary housing situation I arranged for her disintegrated, of course. One or two nights she actually slept in my office. One night, after being released from the Glendale City Jail, with her consent, both of us crying, I took her back to Sybil Brand. I felt utterly defeated and enraged. It was the only way I could be sure she would live to testify at the trial. She did live and was sentenced to at least five years in prison.

I visited her in prison but noticed a rapid decline in Yvonne's general and mental health. Years of psychotropic drugs, shock treatments, prescribed medication, alcoholism, and despair had taken their toll. She died before she was forty, before she could complete her sentence. She died of cancer, said the rumor mill. But that's not what killed her.

Eventually our women's prison ministry established a weekly worship service and chaplaincy program at the California Institute for Women.

There I learned the very disturbing fact that for many of the two thousand women or so warehoused there (in a facility built for eight hundred), prison is the *safest* and in some ways the best place they have ever lived. And it is not a safe or comfortable place. It is prison.

In prison, these women have food and a bed (sometimes in the gymnasium without enough toilets). They have the same substandard medical care afforded to all people who are poor in the United States, only their choices are more limited.

I remember the stories of "Doctor No-Touch." He was the only physician who would actually come into one of the state facilities we visited on a regular basis. He was their primary-care physician. Apparently, some time earlier in his illustrious career, this doctor had been accused of improperly touching the women prisoners. His solution (or the state's?) was for him *never to touch the women*. In fact, he stood at least three feet away from them while he spoke to or *examined(!)* them.

Prison doctors come in only two types: those who really also want to be social workers, who are idealistic, and who generally don't last long; and the other kind—the incompetent, negligent, and sadistic. The same can often be said of prison chaplains. As hard as the regimentation is and the various forms of humiliation, there is a kind of community in many of these prisons, especially where women have long stays. Women may be able to form actual friendships. They are not controlled, abused, or exploited by their male family members, lovers, friends, or pimps. Lesbians in particular often find themselves in positions of leadership, excelling in an all-female community, not competing with men or having to combat as much homophobia. I saw lesbians who for the first time in their lives felt some self-esteem, some sense of success (in work, schools, or just socially) in prison in ways they could not feel successful *outside*.

This, of course, is a major cause of recidivism. I met women who committed crimes in order to get back into prison to be with lovers or friends. Who, when they left prison, were leaving the only home they had ever known to be anything remotely like a home, where there was some safety from violence (not totally, by any means), lots of rules (boundaries), a pretty clear system of rewards and punishments, and the possibility of intimacy. For most of these women, leaving was like trying to catch a speeding train, like leaving home without a safe place to go. One solution would be to make prison more unattractive, less safe, as many have suggested. How *bad* would it have to be, I wonder, to be less safe than the *outside*?

It was really hard for me to take in this lesson: that prison, with the boredom, the regimentation, the arbitrariness of the discipline at times, the negligent medical care, the bad food, the limited opportunities (women get much less of the percentage of funds for job training, rehabilitation, and education in the California prison system than do men), the overcrowding, the shame attached, the fact that they often lost their children—even with all this, prison was an *improvement* in their lives! For some it was the only positive attention and support they ever got from *anyone* in authority; the only real education that they got.

Over and over again, as we prepared to welcome women and to be a part of their "program" as they tried to reestablish a life outside of prison and outside of the environment that had led them to prison in the first place, we ran into this. They were lonely and afraid, and it took money and volunteers to help them make it on the outside. Some had babies or children to care for as soon as they got out, had no place to live, and only two hundred dollars. Usually, if they made it past the first two weeks, I began to have a little hope. I watched them try, and try hard, and then give up and go back. They'd go back exhausted and defeated.

The lesbian lifers always fascinated me. The ones I met, of course, were a select group—those who were motivated to come and be part of a lesbian-identified church in the place they might very well spend the rest of their lives. These women did not come primarily because I could help them when they got out. They were there to make life better on the inside for themselves and others. There was a kind of freedom among the lifers. Somehow, this boundary of time and space helped them relax. They had a place finally to be who they were, in a fundamental sense. This final, very hard reality of lifelong imprisonment freed them in a way. They were the ones who gave MCC inside the walls the name "Free-Spirit MCC."

Some of these women were very admired by the others and given affectionate nicknames. They were available for spiritual and emotional support to the other women. They oriented them. They were the ones the others looked to, to see if they thought we from MCC on the outside were OK. We had to prove ourselves to these women first. They also always displayed to me this tremendous kindness and openness.

Who Preaches in Prisons?

Protestant religious ministries in jails and prisons do tend to be dominated by fundamentalists. They are our primary "competition" for the women's hearts and minds. This, I believe, is true for several reasons. For the most part, mainline Protestants have simply written off people in jail or prison—for class reasons primarily and because their racial group (white) is underrepresented among prison populations. More poor and working-class people and people of color (even if they now have jobs and money) have relatives or friends who are or have been in jail or prison. Therefore, the churches that reach out to and serve those ethnic groups and classes will tend to be involved in jail and prison work.

This became especially apparent to me after I began pastoring at MCC Los Angeles. Our church is about 40 percent people of color. On an average of at least once a week I hear about family members or close friends who get shot, stabbed, raped, sent to jail or prison, who are returning from jail or prison, getting out of the hospital from a gang fight, or who get killed in a drive-by shooting. I would guess that 95 *percent* of the time it is people of color who tell me these stories.

Members of our congregation who love each other and try to work together, especially in the gay community, *live* and sometimes *work* in different worlds, with different dangers and pressures. Sometimes it's like we live in different cities that only occasionally (like during the riots or earthquakes) get to touch or see each other.

Because political conservatism or an "apolitical" stance (the same thing!) makes these religious groups less threatening to the status quo of the criminal justice system (especially jails and prisons), fundamentalists are much more welcome in such institutions by the authorities. They are less likely to question either the prison's rules or the officials themselves, and, in a sense, are seen as working hand in hand with the institution to control the prisoners.

Finally, fundamentalist theology is also well suited to this purpose. It works entirely on an individualistic framework. The focus is on the individual's sinfulness and the need for salvation. It feeds on guilt and shame and seeks to help the person control themselves, using the fear of eternal punishment and the desire for eternal reward. It is well suited to the prison context and philosophy. It has simple, straightforward answers for someone whose life is in ruins, who feels desperate, lost, and hopeless. It also helps them to stop focusing on the frustrations of this life, of their present circumstances, or on their experiences of injustice or oppression. It's all their fault, and God will forgive them (if they behave from now on and keep quiet), and things will improve in the *next* life. Nothing else is important.

What happens to gays and lesbians in jail or prison is that they are not only losers in this life but in the next life as well! They are often harangued from the pulpits of these institutions as the worst of sinners. The fundamentalists (and Catholics, secondarily) are practically given a franchise on prison ministries and are free to preach their homophobic gospel without interference from the government, which builds and maintains these institutions with our tax money (including gay and lesbian tax money). Some of the ministries are privately funded, but there are state-funded chaplaincies that are sometimes extremely homophobic.

One major exception to this practice has been the presence of a paid (by the state) MCC chaplain at Vacaville, California — because they have so many prisoners with AIDS and HIV, and MCC clergy have more experience with AIDS than anyone else. Our presence at Vacaville is a profound breakthrough.

Every time MCC goes into a prison, we have had a fight on our hands. If it does not come from the institution itself (only because we have already fought them in court and won), we face harassment and opposition from the fundamentalist chaplains who work there and who cooperate with prison officials. They want no one visiting prisoners who are going to inform them of their rights, to challenge the institution's rules, policies, or practices in any way, or to challenge their homophobic theology and biblical interpretation. In all fairness to the front-line prison officials and guards, it is sometimes not too hard to understand why. Underfunding of basic services and overcrowding create a constant state of emergency that is dangerous and difficult for everyone. When people like us come along, all they can see is trouble.

At one institution, the sequence was as follows: a group of women wrote to me saying they wanted UFMCC services at a state women's prison. I contacted the chaplain and had a conference with him. I reminded him of the fact that we had sued the state of California some ten years before and had won the right to visit our parishioners and hold worship services for them in state prisons, like any other church. He then tried to debate with me about homosexuality and the Bible. I gave him our materials and said it really wasn't important to me whether or not he agreed with us, but we wanted to hold these services.

He agreed and gave us Thursday nights twice a month. We went and met these women for the first time. The crowd was a little smaller than anticipated, and then I realized that they were "letting" us use the administration room, which required that everyone attending had to sign a register before entering this part of the facility! This meant *coming out* in writing to the institution. Nevertheless, some women braved this and came anyway. This took remarkable courage. I felt embarrassed that they were forced to go through this just to meet with us for the first time. In subsequent weeks, the numbers grew. Gradually, the women became less afraid.

We were clear that all women (not just lesbians) were welcome, and some straight friends came as well. Then we ran into other problems. We would arrive, and they would say that there had been a "problem" inside, they were doing a *count* (of prison population) and we would not be able to get in until 8:00 in the evening (we were usually there at 6:30 and the prison was an eighty-mile drive from the church).

So we would say, "Fine, we'll be back at 8:00." We knew they expected us just to leave. But we didn't. We went away and came back. This meant that we would not leave until nearly 10:00, and still had to drive eighty miles home. When we did return, often only a few women were there to greet us. They weren't sure whether we had just not shown up, or had been delayed, or if we had been there, whether we were coming back. It took a long time for them really to trust that we'd be that committed. Sometimes it was obvious that they had been waiting for us *all that time*—that we had been lied to. Other times we almost got the feeling the prison official had scheduled this extra count just to interfere with our program. This happened nearly every other time we came, and it was meant to discourage us and the women inside. Instead, it made us more determined.

Finally we were able to get out of the administration building into a classroom on the inside, where no one had to sign in and go through security to come to our services. Then they changed the prison recreation schedule and made Thursday night softball practice and shopping night! Women worked together to shop for each other so they could take turns coming to church, but "competition" with the softball practice was too hard for us to overcome, and our attendance suffered again. We petitioned for another night or even a weekend time but were turned down.

Only when the fundamentalist chaplain was hospitalized for an extended time did we get a break. The Catholic chaplain was more relaxed and empathetic. We asked him for a weekly meeting time on the weekend with the ability to use the chapel, and we got it all. Six years later we are still meeting every Saturday in that chapel.

But the harassment didn't stop. Many times our ministers and volunteers would arrive at the prison to find that their names had not been left at the desk and "cleared," even though we had sent the officials a list in writing and had called and double-checked during the week. When we would arrive at the desk, as we did every week, and try to get in, we would be denied. There was no avenue for appeal, and many times women would be waiting for us at the chapel and we could not get in. Meeting with prison officials and chaplains would clear the problem for a month or two, and then it would start all over again.

But the women still came, and they waited for us. They waited for women who were lesbians like them, who preached about a God of compassion and justice, who understood their sorrows, their feelings, their goals, their hopes and fears. They wanted to hear about a God who had not forgotten them and who was not judging them for being who they were. A God who wanted them to know they were loved just the way they were. What we hoped to accomplish was that in meeting MCC clergy-women and lay volunteers, the women would have *enough* of an experience of MCC that when they got out they could come to an MCC service and feel at home, feel a connection that could help them make the transition to the outside.

Sometimes we even arranged it so that one or two UFMCC lesbians or friends would be right there to greet the women as they were released and bring them to a Sunday morning service right from the prison itself. (We even encouraged them to petition for Sunday morning release, even if that meant staying an extra day or two.) They would then see the clergy and lesbian volunteers they had come to know and trust just a little bit. We then often had to help with the difficult issues of temporary housing, job search, child care, readjustment. Sometimes we would actually be successful, and there are women who have been able to leave prison behind permanently. Finally, it was *not* the best place they'd ever been.

Kenneth was seventeen when he entered Jackson State Prison in Michigan, a poor, biracial, effeminate gay man (adolescent). He had killed someone in a drug- and gang-related context. He was still in the first few years of his life sentence when I met him. He was the first gay prisoner who ever wrote to me. Somehow he had gotten hold of a regional gay publication that had mentioned me and MCC Detroit.

I knew Kenneth for nine years. Then they moved him to another prison and I lost track of him, I'm sorry to say.

It was so hard to believe. This bright, engaging, spiritual young man, his life trashed so early by a tragic series of events. Not that Kenneth ever *pretended* to be innocent or anything other than who and what he was. He was refreshingly honest. Almost instantly, he grasped the message of UFMCC, *a church for all people with a special outreach to the gay and lesbian community.* Behind the stale walls of Jackson State Prison, he breathed us in, our willingness to know him, to love him and his friends. He knew his cellmates and fellow gay prisoners needed a nonjudgmental, inclusive, compassionate perspective on the Bible and homosexuality, on God and the church of Jesus Christ. He was a leader, handsome, energetic and passionate about what he believed.

Kenneth always talked nonstop when we met. He was an organizer, and the prison hated that. But he was smart and overly polite; sometimes he reminded me of a black drag queen version of Eddie Haskell, from the 1950s television show *Leave It to Beaver*. He *really* irritated the authorities and entertained us! He knew how to get things done. He got as many as eighty or ninety prisoners to sign a petition to have MCC come inside the walls of Jackson State Prison. He didn't discriminate either—he talked his Muslim friends into signing as well! We would coach Kenneth at our bimonthly meetings, fitting in lessons about homosexuality and the Bible, teaching about UFMCC, our beliefs. He would take these back inside and weekly send us more names of people to visit while we were there. Our trip to Jackson got more involved; four or five of us would go and spend a whole Saturday visiting these gay men. Mostly lesbians went on these excursions. There we were, four or five white lesbians visiting mostly men of color who were also gay.

That confused the authorities at the prison terribly. *They couldn't figure it out.* What was this all about? Why were we visiting these men? What were our perverted or sinister motives? Somehow they just didn't buy the church thing. We must be on some kind of weird sex trip. They could never believe that we believed we had anything in common with these guys—many of them "dangerous criminals."

They could never believe that to us these men were brothers—brothers in Christ and gay brothers. We saw ourselves in them. We saw in their prisons our own prisons, we saw their real and coming freedom as our freedom too. We had a common foe as well—a ruthless symbol of the racism and homophobia that kill and ruin so many lives: Jackson State Prison, which prides itself on being the "largest walled prison in the world."

Every week we were fighting the officials, the fundamentalist chaplains, the guards, and the terrible self-images of these men, their despair, their grief, their fears. We touched them when permitted, we prayed for them, we even eventually found homes for some of them who made it out. Mostly, we told them over and over again that God did not hate them or us for being gay and that their lives had meaning, purpose, and value to us and to God. Sometimes I think we should have prayed for an earthquake!

They petitioned to hold worship services in the prison, and the request was denied. Having won a similar suit in the state of California just two years before, we felt very excited about our prospects. Meanwhile, we kept up our visitation schedule and correspondence with these men. We also petitioned for the right to serve them Holy Communion, and were again denied.

We spent nine years and thousands of dollars in state and federal court while the state stuck to its story that we couldn't hold these services because the inmates who wanted to attend would be endangered. The state did not think it should be required to *prove* that abridging their constitutional right to freedom of religion was necessitated for security reasons. None of the eighty or so gay men who asked for those services believed that the other men would attempt to hurt them if they went to MCC services. But the state insisted that the reason it wanted to keep us out was for the safety of the prisoners, gay or straight, who wanted to attend MCC. We even argued that if they thought there would be a problem, why didn't they put on a few extra guards and just test out their theory for a few weeks?

We lost our final appeal in federal court, which supported the prison's claim that the anticipated "violence" that would occur if MCC held services there was enough of a reason to keep us out. Violence that none of the petitioners anticipated or were afraid of facing.

By the time the last appeal was heard nine years later, I had left MCC Detroit and was working for MCC in California. The appeals court did rule that we could serve communion, under close scrutiny, to five prisoners at a time in a small office just off the visiting room. The last time I saw Kenneth was in that room. For the first and only time in Jackson State Prison, I consecrated communion with these men, and we shared communion MCC style. Two of the men had never received communion in their lives. Kenneth had been Catholic, and the other man was Baptist. So I explained communion first, then consecrated. I asked Kenneth to serve me, and that was almost too much for him. I remember how his voice broke and his hands shook as he served me. Nine years he had devoted to this moment, this small victory, this holiest of communions. I left to catch my plane to California, but I will always feel like I left a part of my heart in that room.

Kenneth would hold small meetings of MCC on the yard, in the dining area, wherever the men could congregate and converse unmolested. He read the MCC bylaws carefully and noticed that we ask each church to take an offering each Sunday and forward 10 percent to the headquarters. Kenneth took this obligation very seriously and was deeply troubled because the men were not permitted to carry cash on their person or to send cash anywhere. So we worked out a compromise that he suggested. A lot of the men whom Kenneth evangelized were drag queens, only some of whom could manage to buy or get hold of makeup (I have *no* idea how). And for the "butch" guys, cigarettes were always in demand. So, Kenneth took up collections of makeup and cigarettes, which he distributed to the less fortunate among them and even managed to get to those who were in solitary confinement. Sometimes the collections were so generous he hardly had space in his cell to hide it all! He was still bothered occasionally by the dilemma of how to tithe 10 percent to headquarters, but we just kept telling him that he was doing the right thing and that they were a wonderful example. Theirs was a powerful new twist on Jesus' story of the "widow's mite": two cigarettes and half a used lipstick—a powerful illustration of the doxology sung in so many churches every Sunday: "We give Thee but Thine own, what e'er the gift may be. All that we have is Thine alone, a trust, O Lord, from Thee."

6

Equal to Angels

Throughout history and in many places in the world today, gay and lesbian people have been demonized. As documented in previous chapters, the concept of homosexuality (and homosexuals) represents for many people the often unconscious collective sexual fears and fantasies of the heterosexual majority. We have been lied about, projected onto, and made to bear the burden of a sexually phobic and sexually obsessed culture.

It is particularly the radical religious right (in various religions, not only Christianity) that has demonized us. And of course gay and lesbian people have had to struggle to overcome both the internal and external effects of this process.

Just recently my lover, her mother, and I were driving to visit friends in Los Angeles. Paula's mother was relating the latest homophobic comment she had heard in her small Michigan hometown. One of Paula's now ancient elementary school teachers is a member of Paula's mother's church. Somehow the subject of *those people* came up, and "Mrs. Smith" (not her real name!) said, "Well, they're all heathens, you know!" "Heathens." Paula's mother said it made her speechless. Her daughter a *heathen*? What does this term mean in the late twentieth century? What images does that evoke? Words like *heathen* and *pagan* evoke racist, sexist images—white, male, oppressive Christian missionary stereotypes. This is more than ignorance; it's more mean-spirited than that. Gays and lesbians are sort of the ultimate *other* lurking heathenishly by schoolyards, or in public rest rooms, or sleazy bars, or . . . You can fill in the blank.

So, our demonized public image made me think again about the possibility of gay and lesbian angels.

The passage in Matthew 19 about marriage, divorce, and eunuchs that was examined in chapter 4 is related to another passage, Mark 12:18–27, in which Sadducees are trying to trick Jesus (again) with a question about marriage. I do wonder why he got asked a *lot* about marriage — because he was, presumably, single? Their question asks Jesus to comment on our future marital "states" in heaven. Jesus says people won't marry in heaven but will be *isangelos*, a Greek word meaning "equal to angels" (Mark 12:25). It sounds almost as if once again, Jesus is not putting much spiritual significance on heterosexual marriage. Almost as if by *not* being married anymore we are *more* like angels. (Those who marry are contrasted to *eunuchs* in Matthew 19; then those who marry are contrasted to *angels* in Mark 12.) Were those who did not marry in this life *more* angelic to Jesus? Was he implying that angels are nonsexual or nongendered or that nonsexuality is *more* spiritual? This has been the prevailing interpretation — one that may have supported the idea of a celibate clergy and their spiritual "superiority."

Another possible interpretation might involve the fact that eunuchs and barren women were devalued in Jesus' culture (and other cultures). They were seen as "disabled," and this was a sign of God's disfavor. Marriage and children were the ticket to immortality, a sign of God's *favor*. Not to participate was to be "cut off." In another story Jesus *also* questions the traditional view of physical disability as a sign of God's disfavor (the man born blind, John 9:1–34). I wonder if the connection between Mark 12 and Matthew 19 is that in both these passages, Jesus was challenging the devaluing and even demonization of those who did not have a heterosexual marriage and/or did not reproduce. Was Jesus indicating that being "married with children" was *not* the only way to please God? Was he covertly, subtly, validating the lives of those who did not fit neatly into that mold, and comparing them to angels?

It is useful here to remember a few other things. Jesus lived in a sex-segregated culture, where nonrelated men and women did not converse or socialize — a rule that he flagrantly violated. Jesus traveled with women, stayed in nonrelated, unmarried women's homes, taught and touched and conversed with women, including Gentile women. Friendship and even romance in this culture was largely a same-sex (if not erotic) activity. Romantic heterosexual love was the exception, not the rule. In that context, when Jesus spoke positively about heterosexual marriage and negatively about divorce, he did this in a way that honored *women's* needs and points of view.

Therefore, it is not so farfetched to see in these passages a critique of "eunuchs-barrness bashing." Another way to look at the role played by eunuchs in the Bible is to compare it to the role played by angels. Eunuchs appear and disappear in scenes from the lives of major and minor biblical characters—especially prophets and kings. They are mysterious, androgynous figures who have specific functions: rescuing the prophets, carrying messages, shifting the balance of power, helping the underdog to win the day. This role sounds remarkably like the role of a *guardian angel.*

I also have wondered if the angels who appear in Bible stories seem *gay* in any way. What about the pair of angels who stopped to see Abraham on the way to Sodom and Gomorrah? Were they male angels or just male *appearing*? What if we were willing to view them as two *male* angels, a same-sex (or nonsexed?) pair that arrived at Lot's home and were subsequently threatened with rape?

What a difference it would make to see the *only potentially gay characters in the Sodom and Gomorrah story as the angels and not the wicked Sodomites!*

This would seem like an almost unbelievable reversal, especially with a demonized view of gays and lesbians. But in prisons in the United States and other countries today, for instance, it is *not* the lust-starved homosexuals who prey on poor heterosexual men and "sodomize" (violently anally rape) them. It is *heterosexual* men who prey on homosexual men or on smaller, younger, or weaker men (gay or straight), using them as a substitute sex object in prison. All prison officials know this, and police records substantiate it. In Los Angeles they segregate gay men and transvestites into a separate city jail not because they are likely to be *predators* but *because they are likely to be victims* in the jail. I remember when I first learned of the segregation; I felt outraged. Then I learned from the inmates that segregation saved them a lot of suffering. In fact, some straight men *pretend* to be gay when entering the Los Angeles County jail system in order to do what they call "gay time" in the safer, homosexual jail. This becomes a problem for county jail officials, who once asked if MCC clergy would help them identify the *real* gays. Somehow they thought our gaydar (gay radar) would be foolproof. We know it never is. We declined to help.

Therefore, an alternative biblical interpretation of Genesis 19 might be that two *gay* male angels were the potential victims of anal rape, and this interpretation actually *fits* with the sociological data about who is likely to be the victim or predator of gay rape! There are gay men who have raped other gay men. But far more heterosexual men rape homosexual men than vice versa.

The two angels in Genesis 19 are performing a function that is consistent with that of both angels and eunuchs in the Bible: they are messengers of God, attempting to protect God's people (Abraham and his family, especially Lot), shifting the balance of power, rescuing the faithful.

These angels are coming to warn God's people and anyone who will listen about God's *rage*: God's rage at the violence, cruelty, indifference, and wickedness of these communities. The angels, in fact, just by their presence *provoke* and *expose* the very violence they have come to condemn. Gay and lesbian people do this all the time in our culture. These angels were nearly the victims of a gay bashing!

While being themselves, fulfilling the purpose for which they had been created, minding their own business, they are nearly raped and killed by an angel-phobic, perhaps homophobic, crowd. Many gay and lesbian people are victims of violence every day just for minding their own business and going about their lives in the way God intended them to do.

I want to make it clear that I am not saying that all gay and lesbian people are angels or angelic. What I am trying to suggest is that there are powerful biblical correctives to the demonized view of gay men and lesbians. (One of which, ironically, is Sodom and Gomorrah!)

We gay, lesbian, and bisexual people need to see ourselves and be seen as *fully human*, neither as angels nor demons. I remember when we asked the World Council of Churches on behalf of MCC to *consider* including gay and lesbian people (who are executed and tortured in many countries just for being *suspected* of being gay) in their human rights agenda. We weren't asking them to support *civil rights* for gays and lesbians, or religious validation. Just *human* rights: meaning the right not to be imprisoned, tortured, exiled, or murdered simply for being homosexual. When they hesitated, hemming and hawing, whining that this was "bad timing" for the WCC (never mind the "bad timing" for those being abused and murdered!), I realized the depth of the problem once again: they're not sure we're human! Human rights seemed to them to be an unreasonable request *at this time*. It made me remember that many people still see us as a "behavior" or an "issue" to debate, not as beings in need of safety or inclusion. Talking about human rights *and* gay and lesbian people in the same sentence was *difficult* for them to tolerate.

Recently a lesbian I know was a participant in a support group for women of her culture and race who were surviving with breast cancer. She was very out of the closet in her personal and professional life, but in the few weeks she'd been attending, the subject of sexuality or partners had not come up. Two days before Janice's surgery, a woman in the group challenged Janice about the fact that she is lesbian and said, "I can't support you in this group if you are a lesbian." Janice was hurt, speechless, never dreaming that this would be a problem. She never returned to the support group. Being a woman of color and trying to stay alive with breast cancer was *not enough* to bring solidarity, to overcome homophobia! It was OK with this woman to turn Janice out, to cause her stress two days before surgery, for her to live *or* die without human support from other *sisters*. How do we unmask this kind of violence?

In some ways the concepts of "angels" and "demons" are constructions of a perceived split in the human moral and spiritual self—the good and bad in all of us. On the other hand, the Bible and a lot of Christian (and non-Christian) theology have posited *actual beings* in a spiritual realm, know as demons or angels. There has been a virtual fad in recent years of speculating about the existence of such angelic beings. (Possibly a sign of millennial fever . . .)

We probably get more of our ideas about angels from popular culture (Clarence the bumbling angel in *It's a Wonderful Life*, for instance) than from the Bible. In the Bible angels are often fierce, frightening, or so well disguised that they are able to pose as ordinary humans (like the angels in Genesis 19).

What I am interested in is the process of *suggestion* and *association*, not necessarily a thoroughgoing theology of angels. In Los Angeles (the city of angels) one of the AIDS service agencies, the one that provides lunches to housebound people with AIDS, is called Project Angel Food. To those who are lying in beds of pain and weakness (sometimes with no one to visit or stay with them during the day), a person appearing at their door with a smile and a hot meal *is* an angel.

Gay men and lesbians were the ones who started most of the AIDS agencies in the United States during the first decade of the AIDS epidemic. Those organizations were built and are currently sustained by hundreds of thousands of volunteers and volunteer hours. One of the sociological realities that has made this possible is that proportionately fewer gays and lesbians are encumbered with the demands of child care and raising children. But even those who *are* have been swept into the tremendous community efforts that have cared for hundreds of thousands of ill and dying friends, lovers, neighbors, and strangers. Armies of lesbian and gay angels, gay and lesbian Mother Teresas, feed, clothe, bathe, nurse, hold, hug, touch, carry, and love the sick and dying men, women, and children who have AIDS. It's not that straight people have not also been there, done it— but *we've* done *most* of it. And we've also done the praying, the memorials and funerals (sometimes when no one else would do them), and the comforting. We've done this in the face of the virulent, religiously motivated homophobia and AIDS phobia that communicate to the world, "AIDS is God's gift to the gay community."

The need has become overwhelming, and many gay and lesbian persons with any leisure time or disposable income have been pressed into service or extra giving in some way for some period of time. For those of us in UFMCC, AIDS has dominated our local church pastoral care services and our community outreach programs for over a decade.

Everyone who serves selflessly in our culture is deemed an "angel" in the popular mind. The term *angel,* as in "be an angel," has come simply to mean someone who will serve another not for selfish gain and who does it cheerfully, without being expected to be paid back. Somehow deeds of kindness and charity are beyond what we think we can reasonably expect of other humans. Somehow, "be a human" doesn't conjure up the same warm, openhearted, giving image!

In fact, "I'm only human" is the great excuse for letting ourselves and others down. It is the all-encompassing excuse for screwing up. What a definition of humanness!

Sometimes the concept of angels is linked to those who have died, as a description of their afterlife role. I have not found a particular biblical justification for this point of view. Mostly the Bible seems to view angels as a separate category of existence. Angels are a special species of spiritual beings, independent of humans: they are messengers from God who communicate with us from time to time but who mostly seem busy keeping God company in heaven.

Nevertheless, this popular version of the afterlife has humans living a quasi-angelic existence and sometimes includes the assumption that after death we get transformed (or recycled) as angels. It's not clear to me if this includes all people, even ordinary people (like the inept Clarence from *It's a Wonderful Life*), or only *really, really* good people. Also, the relationship of angelic existence to what the church has called the "communion of saints" is not very clear. However, popular theology does not worry itself about theological *correctness*!

The concept of the communion of saints in Christian theology is the belief that those who die *in Christ* commune together eternally before the throne of God and that, from time to time, the church experiences their collective witness and presence (Hebrews 12). We might say that this is the way in which Westerners incorporate the ancient (and, in indigenous cultures, nearly pervasive) practice of venerating (or worshiping or honoring) one's ancestors.

In fact, I remember the story of a young man in Germany who was the lover of the German-born pastor of UFMCC Hamburg. This young man had been a "boat person," a refugee from Vietnam. At age eleven he was rescued by Australians and eventually sent by churchpeople to Germany where he was placed in a foster home. John was gay. A Vietnamese gay man, he was now a German immigrant. His religion of origin was a Vietnamese native religion that was based on ancestor worship. He attended one of his first Christian worship services ever in London at an MCC European conference. There, at an AIDS vigil, he heard people calling out the names of those who had died of AIDS, praying for them and their families and friends, naming and mourning the losses. John, for whom English is a third language, was not sure what was happening. He whispered to his lover, a former Baptist pastor, "Are they calling on their ancestors?" It was a very logical and reasonable assumption! Also, there was *truth* in that question. Hebrews 11 speaks of our "ancestors in faith" and what it means to remember those who die in faith as part of a heavenly community. Many of those who have died of AIDS are our *spiritual ancestors*, our particular communion of saints.

One of the things that has happened to lesbians and gay men because of AIDS and because of the virtual epidemic of breast cancer among women in the United States and among lesbians is that we have had to experience the death of dozens or even hundreds or thousands of people we have known personally or have known of, who were often our own ages, more or less. We are experiencing this *selective holocaust* while the rest of the world goes on with business as usual (meaning the usual, expected, and also horrific losses — car accidents, other illnesses, etc.). There are times when I have greeted my friends and colleagues at UFMCC meetings, and we have spent the first five minutes saying, in small talk, not "How are you?" but a litany of "Did you hear? Did you know that James died, that Ginny is in the hospital, that Al is not expected to live the week?" People whose deaths would have had a big impact on my life ten years ago sometimes—terribly, tragically—become a footnote in my day, as in "By the way, Bob died (yesterday, last week, did I forget to tell you?)."

In December 1993 we had a very long staff meeting at MCC Los Angeles. At the end of the meeting, we were making prayer requests. I asked for prayers for our young assistant pastor, Dan Mahoney, who was dying of AIDS, and for a young colleague, a student clergy, Doug, who had been in a class I had taught. I mentioned that I was going to visit Doug in the hospital the next morning. My associate pastor, Lori, turned to me, put her hand on my arm, and said quietly, "Doug died this morning." I remember the shock wave—like a little electrical jolt—that went through me. She thought I knew already. I didn't. Now I did. And there was the *terrible* thought that was *partially* a relief: one less hospital visit to make—then guilt. I was too late: he had left without my visit. How is his lover Bruce doing? I filed those questions in my mind and went home.

The next day I went to the Veterans Administration Hospital business office with my assistant pastor's lover, Patrick, trying to cut through red tape to get Dan into a hospice. This took nearly three hours. While I was at the hospital, my father died. I flew into my office as usual, and a volunteer said, "Your mother has called twice; she's holding on line one for you now." My mother *never* calls me at my office. I knew before I answered the phone.

While I was in New York at my father's funeral, Dan Mahoney died. He had been my assistant pastor *and* dear friend for many years. At his funeral, I learned of the death of two other people whom I knew and of the critical illness of another. Sometime later that month, I realized that Doug's funeral had been held the same day as my dad's. It seemed finally to have happened to me—what had happened to so many of us: the body count got too high, the pile too deep. I had lost track, I couldn't keep up, I kept meaning to call Doug's lover; I think I left a message on his machine; I'm not sure I ever did. Three months later I managed to go over to him and hug him at the funeral of a mutual friend's father. The circle closed for a moment—but only for a moment.

The lines between life and death blur in this process. The less-than-totally reliable rumor mill sometimes has people dead and buried before they're hospitalized! Or it leaves others behind, pitifully long dead before anyone has time to notice. Sometimes when people get ill they shut out their friends and church family. The hardest days for some of us are finally getting through to someone who tells us, "Santiago died three months ago; didn't you know?"

Lloyd was an angel, I'm sure of it. I met him through fellow angel Lew. Lew ended up at a different hospital than he usually went to, and afterward I would come to believe that it was so I could meet Lloyd.

On the AIDS ward that day at this hospital, there were a number of patients in need. Also, as usual, I was already running behind schedule, which meant I was not feeling as relaxed and attentive as I would like to be while visiting people in the hospital. I finally got *out of there* and was rushing through the lobby to the parking lot when a woman stopped me.

I must digress for a moment. Being a clergywoman and wearing a clerical collar in public is always an interesting experience—especially in lobbies, on lines, or in elevators, where someone feels compelled to make conversation. Once, in an elevator at the Veterans Administration Hospital, a young, tall, pleasant-looking man said, "Are you a minister?" (That, by the way, is the most common question. I'm not sure that any clergy*man* in a clerical collar has ever been asked that question.) Over the years I've tried to think of clever comebacks, but none of them quite matches the strangeness of the question. I think I always want to ask them why they think anyone would wear this silly outfit if she or he were *not* a clergyperson? What is it they imagine I'm doing in this shirt if I'm *not* a clergyperson? Anyway, sometimes, "Are you a minister/priest/clergyperson?" is the whole of the matter. But this day it also included "*because* . . . " (uh-oh, here we go!). At this point the young man looked furtively around in the empty elevator while also assessing just how many floors we had left in which to continue this conversation: ". . . because the doctors want me to give them a sperm sample to take a test, and they want me to, you know, touch myself to get the sample. I thought maybe there was *another way to get it*."

Now, as a frequent victim of people's sexual projections and unique and interesting forms of sexual harassment, I can pretty much tell *which* kinds of conversations are going in *what* directions with *what* motives. Even though I might have *preferred* this question to be the garden-variety sexual come-on or harassment (a new variation on an old theme), I had the sinking feeling that he was absolutely sincere. It is strange to think that I might have preferred it to be harassment—but that's probably because then I could have just confronted it or brushed it off. I also recognized that he was developmentally disabled in some way, though this was not immediately apparent. I replied, "So, you were taught that masturbation is a sin, and the problem is that these doctors are asking you to do something you were taught was wrong?" "Yes," he said, relieved that I had understood him and said some words he couldn't quite say. Somehow, in the next few seconds, I was able to ask him if this test was really necessary and important. He said, "Yes." I asked him to consider whether he could let himself think about how God had created and loved him. Could he perhaps think that God would make an exception in this case because of his health and that God would not be angry at him if he masturbated for a really good reason? At this he broke into a smile and said, "Yes, ma'am, thank you!" and ran off the elevator.

Sadly there was no time to talk to him about God and guilt and sexuality and all that good stuff of contemporary sexual and ethical discourse! And I didn't want to give him just *my* answer. But he needed permission to think of God (and his own body) differently for the moment and to *try on* an alternative answer. It was a strange momentary dilemma for me. At that moment, to him, I had the authority to speak for God, as a clergyperson (perhaps a lesser type of angel) to whom he could ask a very private, vulnerable question in the confines of our temporary elevator/confessional. He related to me with a touching, childlike innocence and trust, not worrying that I would be offended, or shocked, or put off, and I guess I wasn't. I took him seriously, at his word. And I knew he simply needed to be released from a false sexual guilt, from a terrible legalistic burden: forced to choose between health and God's approval.

I've had hundreds of encounters like these, some even more "high risk." Being female and lesbian, I've probably had more than most. Women are great, wonderful, when they see me in my collar: they get excited and curious. On one airplane trip, a Baptist flight attendant couldn't stop looking at me or talking to me. She wouldn't let me get back to reading my book. Women who have always wanted a woman pastor but have never seen one before often want to confide in me or to touch me, take me home with them, replace their male pastor with me.

Ralph was an HIV-positive member of my church. His seventy-year-old mother, a gospel singer in ministry with her husband for *fifty years,* was getting divorced. (The husband had run off with a younger female choir member.) She was devastated, and her church family shunned her, and her male pastor *blamed* her. Divorce is always the woman's fault. Her shame and rage were overwhelming her, as well as her vulnerability— ashamed and divorced at age seventy, with a son who was vulnerable, too. We talked for hours. She was embarrassed that she had always teased Ralph about going to *that Church!* (meaning that awful gay church.) She loved being able to talk to a woman pastor, *forgetting* that I was a lesbian from *that Church*!

While attending a Roman Catholic seminary, I took a class with a group of older Catholic sisters, none of whom had ever even had a chance to go to college. The course was on prayer and included self-esteem as part of the subject matter discussed. Sister Dorothy complained that all these years in the convent she was supposed to *obliterate* any thoughts of self, and now she was expected to account for her level of self-esteem! I fell in love with these women. And they doted on me, which simply increased my infatuation. They were *so* excited that I was a clergywoman. They wanted to know about my sermons, what I wore, they touched me before and after every class.

Then they invited me to lunch after class one day. They wanted to hear *all* about my church and ministry. All my internalized homophobia got stimulated. Somehow, in some corner of *my* self-esteem, I had come to rely on these women, their approval, their support. Would it continue if they knew I was a lesbian? But I couldn't dodge them or their questions anymore. So, I told them first about UFMCC (then later about me!). When I told them of our gay and lesbian outreach, Sister Elisabeth got quiet and said to Sister Dorothy, "But we were always taught that homosexuality was *wrong*, Sister!" Sister Dorothy rushed to my defense, "Listen, they lied to us about a lot of things, Sister: remember that self-esteem business?" Right on, Sister Dorothy. They *did* lie to us a lot, especially about our bodies, about being female or gay. The night the sisters came and visited me at MCC Detroit was a special treat, a memory to treasure. The Catholics at MCC Detroit that night were a little traumatized at first to see eight nuns—in their habits—troop into the second row of pews in our sanctuary: they thought they were having a horrible *lapsed-Catholic nightmare*. But by the end of the evening everyone had calmed down. As an extra bonus, seeing Sister Dorothy take communion from *me* healed a lot of doubt in a lot of formerly Catholic MCCers that night.

Back to Lloyd's story. I was in the lobby, rushing as usual, dressed in my suit and clergy collar, when Lloyd's sister stopped me. Now when I am in a hurry, you have to be very quick and determined to stop me, and she was. She grabbed my arm, in fact, and said "What kind of clergy are you? I mean," she amended, "what kind of church are you from?"

Well, I looked at her. It was just possible that she was a lesbian. She had spotted me. So I cut to the chase; "I'm with MCC."

She grinned, "I thought so! My brother is upstairs having surgery right now. He has AIDS, and he's having a hard time. Will you see him?" I said yes, got the details, and went back the next day. (My friend Lew, by the way, was then transferred to another hospital or went home that day, his angelic mission accomplished!)

Lloyd was a little guy, strawberry blond (just like his lesbian sister—my gaydar had been right!), with a sweet Southern Illinois/Kentucky country accent. He poured out his heart about dying, about all his worries (ex-lovers and family members, gay and straight, leaned on him a lot). And his business (a West Hollywood drugstore) was really like a ministry to Lloyd. He loved his customers: they were more like clients or parishioners. He felt too needed, too responsible, to die.

Something happened to me when I met Lloyd. For about two years previously I had been nearly unable to cry at all. I might tear up a little, but I could not cry and certainly could not weep, even by myself. I was shut down, with all the compounded grief and anger. The part that could just spontaneously weep or tear up (which had never ever been easy for me anyway) was totally locked away. As I sat with Lloyd, this gentle, little stranger, I held his hand. He began to sob quietly, and the sight of him (I was identifying with his hyperresponsibility) made me cry. The pleasure of those tears (fogging my glasses, wetting my cheeks) was enormous. My crying did not disturb him: it seemed to help him feel not so alone. Together we cried for so many things, including ourselves.

Every time Lloyd went into the hospital, I would see him. And I would hear a little more about this man's life. After crying with him, I cried every day that week, in my car, at home. It became natural and easy to tear up in my office, at hospices and hospitals, even when I spoke or preached. I felt like I had been healed of a disability. Lloyd had helped me in that moment to reopen to my own tears.

We held his memorial service at the juice bar next door to his drugstore. The place was packed with family, friends, and customers. A big poster-size picture of Lloyd in a happier, healthier time dominated the room. Over and over people testified to Lloyd's kindness and generosity. How much he gave and gave away. How he saved their lives, their dignity. How he was more than a druggist—he was a friend, healer, and a brother.

Lloyd is a part of my own communion of saints. Sometimes, having lost count a long time ago, I wonder if I know more people who have died than I know ones who are *presently alive*. Sometimes the line between the world of the living and the alive and the world of the dying and the dead is very blurred for me—as if I, like so many in my community now, live in that strange borderland between the living and the dead, where people are continually crossing over. It is a mysterious and awesome place to live. You learn how true it is that death is not a moment but a series of moments, a process. And everyone does it their own way. I have sat by the dead bodies of young dear friends, women and men, held their still-warm, gradually cooling hands. Watched their strained and pain-lined faces relax. Miraculously, tenderly they have seemed to grow younger in that twilight moment of release.

It is a great privilege to accompany them to their border crossing. It is also not what I expected to be doing in the fourth and fifth decades of my life. And I'm so enraged and overwhelmed at times that I want to find *someone* to blame: I want revenge, I want someone to pay for all this needless suffering, including, I guess, my own. Who pays for all this stolen life and stolen time, including my life and time? And then I think of the arrogance of that thought, that complaint. Who guaranteed or guarantees anyone one minute of life? Where do I get off feeling *ripped off*—especially when I've had the privilege of loving and serving the dying?

I'm not the only one, I've discovered, who has been profoundly, eternally impacted by the untimely death of dozens, even hundreds of friends, colleagues, and acquaintances. Other friends and colleagues report seeing people in public who they are sure, for an instant or longer, are friends who have long since died. Now and then I will have a powerful sensory memory of someone and then check the date: it's their birthday or the anniversary of their death.

Jean Foye was a very *human* angel. A lifelong alcoholic with "bouts" of sobriety, she knew everyone, especially Hollywood old-timers. One day she wandered sullenly into the church. She was a raging, lifelong confirmed skeptic and a poet. You can almost automatically have my heart for two reasons: make me laugh, or be an artist, any kind of artist. Jean was an artist—*and* could make me laugh! And as an alcoholic she was also a consummate *bullshit artist*. But she was also the other kind of artist, a crafter of words.

Jean took whatever art was in my preaching and let it inspire her poetry. When she died of cancer at seventy-two she left behind a wonderful legacy of poetry—except it was not organized.

The day I sold my car was a particularly difficult day for me. As I hurriedly emptied the glove box, a poem of Jean's fell out (she'd been dead a year already). "How did this get in here?" Then I remembered: when she stayed for the Sunday evening services or came on an occasional Wednesday night to church, I would sometimes drop her off on my way home. Almost in lieu of carfare she would often shove a poem scrawled on an envelope or church bulletin into my hand, such as this one about the story of Jonah and the whale:

RELUCTANT PROPHET

*Both were dwellers
in deep places (one
in the dark Bowels
of ships and great fish
and wounded pride.
the other
in the silvery belly
of the seas.) Both
heard God saying
"GO!"
but the whale
did as he was told.*[1]

The poem left in my glove box was one I had forgotten to "cash!"— left unopened, uncashed for almost a year. There it was, lovely, fresh, right on time with what I needed. She was dead a whole year but still dazzling me with her gifts.

Jean was a beloved if somewhat less than stellar graduate of the Alcoholism Center for Women, which is more a movement and community than a "center." But in her last few years, Jean found a faith and relationship with God that matched the passion hidden in her religious skepticism. She found her church in her community. It was just irreverent enough, just real enough, and just open enough to art and irony so that she could tolerate it.

When she was dying, I was in Mexico. But the day that she died, a lay minister in our church, Woody, showed up at the hospital. Other people from church began to arrive, and the nurses were irritated and skeptical: "Who are these people?" Woody simply announced unequivocally that they were all members of Jean's family. An African-American gay man, an Asian gay man, another white lesbian, and Woody. Family?! She died surrounded by those who would happily claim her as family. You *bet* they were her family. You couldn't have asked for a finer family, if a little unusual. Now from time to time, gracefully, Jean's poems pop up in all sorts of odd places—in a pile of papers, in my car, in my heart and mind—like this one:

BUT NOT FORGOTTEN

Whether or not I find the missing thing
It will always be
More than my thought of it.
Silvery-heavy, somewhere it winks
In its own small privacy
Playing
The waiting game with me

The real treasures do not vanish.
The precious loses no value
in the spending.
A piece of hope spins out
bright, along the dark, and is not
Lost in space;
Verity is a burning boomerang;
Love is out orbiting and will
Come home.[2]

"SEND THEM"

The days prior to Christmas are always very busy in any church, and that is no less true for those of us at Metropolitan Community Church. Advent is often a frenzied time, as we try to add a dimension of piety, reflection, and *centeredness* to the cultural holiday bombardment. Since the industrial revolution in the West and especially in the United States Christian pastors seem doomed to fight this battle against commercialism, *putting Christ back into Christmas*, sometimes guilt-tripping our people as they try to walk their own tightropes of overspending, overeating, overdrinking, and other holiday compulsions.

Not only that. But holidays are a time when Americans are most vulnerable to suicide, in overt or more subtle forms. Pastors get more late-night phone calls: there are more strangers calling for help than usual—for emotional, financial or spiritual help. More folks end up in hospitals and emergency rooms. Funerals are twice as traumatic at holiday time.

This is even more true in *minority* communities. And it is much more stressful in the gay and lesbian community. Alienation from family and traditional support structures (church of origin, for example) are felt much more deeply during holiday times. Some gay and lesbian people are simply not "out" to their families, and they go home having to be very vague about their personal lives. This brings on feelings of guilt and shame and reinforces a sense of isolation. Also, it may mean that lesbians and gays feel compelled to lie about their relational life, friendships, and social, religious, or political activities. ("What did you say was the name of *that church* you're attending?") Some just avoid contact with their families. Or perhaps Mom and Dad know but ask you, beg you, *please* don't tell Grandma, it will kill her! Or don't come out to your fundamentalist brother-in-law. "Let's not argue at Christmas!"

Some people who come out to their families are told not to return home for the holidays—or at any time. Other gay and lesbian couples, patiently trying to give their families space and time to "adjust," go their separate ways for the holidays, stealing a minute or two on an upstairs phone to wish their beloved "Merry Christmas," out of earshot for the family's sake.

Increasingly, there are gay and lesbian couples or individuals who *finally* get to deal with just the usual family and in-law issues during holiday season! What a red-letter day it is for a lesbian when she realizes that her mother has the same kinds of issues with her brothers' wives or sisters' husbands that she has with her lover! It is such an ironic sign of acceptance—when this lesbian can deal with ordinary family dynamics that are not primarily about homophobia! We need a family "graduation" ceremony at that point. Ordinary, garden-variety in-law conflicts are such a welcome relief to gay and lesbian couples.

For single gays and lesbians, holidays may be a time when they are pressured to date or marry heterosexually. Another good reason to come out!

Holiday times are a special challenge in our church. In addition to the usual Advent services and midmonth church and staff Christmas parties, we hold workshops designed to help people "beat the holiday blues." We go Christmas caroling at gay bars, in hospices, and we try to provide alternative family events, helping people deal with their present status vis-à-vis their families and providing extra support. Some people leave for home for the holidays and let us know they plan to come out to their families. Sometimes that's out of a strength of conviction or a need to be honest. Sometimes it occurs in the midst of coming out about HIV or AIDS. In any case, we send people off with promises of prayer, support, and hugs.

We also always offer a Christmas Day Open House. We realized that many times people from MCC would go home after a Christmas Eve service to a long, lonely Christmas Day. Some people need an excuse to leave uncomfortable family scenes ("I'm needed at my church today, Mom!") or a place to hang out, with food and friendly faces.

Ben Rodermond loved food. At special church occasions, he would always bring a treat, something sweet and fattening. His blue eyes twinkled with mischief, his ruddy complexion partially hidden by a Vandyke beard and a waxed, old-fashioned, handlebar mustache. Soft-spoken and a little shy, he retained his distinct Dutch accent. Ben was a large, tall man who rode a motorcycle, but you instantly sensed he was a gentle, kind person.

Ben loved all kinds of good food, including Indonesian food. He went to Indonesia after World War II. Then he came to the United States, where gradually in the fifties and sixties he began to find other gay people. Ben was there in the earliest days of MCC, feeling a strong, passionate connection to the social Gospel preached by Troy Perry. Even though Ben was not a citizen at the time and was risking more than most people, he stood openly with Troy at the first demonstrations for gay rights in Los Angeles.

Ben also loved food because he knew what it was to be hungry. Ben and his sister Henny and other members of their family had hidden Jews in their home in Holland during the Nazi occupation.

To avoid being conscripted into the Nazi army, Ben went underground for many years as a teenager. Part of the time he hid in a small attic crawl space, while his sister brought him what little food they had, along with news from the BBC. Part of the time he roamed the streets and nearly starved to death there. But he survived. He survived and eventually found friends, gay and lesbian brothers and sisters, and a spiritual home at Metropolitan Community Church of Los Angeles. He had no patience for injustice, for bigotry of any kind. And he had a permanent sweet tooth. Back to my story.

I try to schedule very little during Christmas week, just to leave room for the unexpected and to be able (while choirs are rehearsing, deacons are decorating the church, logistical problems are being resolved!) to be free to reach out beyond our church walls a little to those who are more marginalized, especially in this season.

So that was how I happened to meet Michael on Christmas Eve, 1992.

We had three Christmas Eve services scheduled for that evening, two in English and one in Spanish. The bulletins were done. The church on Washington Boulevard was filled with evergreens. We prayed that it would not be too cold (as it can get in the L.A. desert climate), as our inadequate heater seemed only to *taunt* us with the hope that it might actually heat up the sanctuary.

My sermons were also done: one for the earlier crowd that included more seniors and people with young children, and one for the more lively "midnight mass" group, on their way to or from Christmas parties or family gatherings. This was one of the occasions in the year when people brought straight parents, children, and family members or gay and lesbian friends who wouldn't be caught dead in church on an ordinary Sunday but for whom it was *cool* to show up on Christmas Eve.

So I had the entire day *free* on Christmas Eve, which is what I had planned. There were no last-minute emergencies and only one person in the hospital (which would be my last stop before getting to the church office later that evening).

I decided to stop by three hospices on my way into town. I have always been told by hospice and hospital staff that churches and groups visit patients (especially those without families) all during the weeks up to Christmas but that the visits come to a halt on Christmas Eve and Christmas Day. Most people, including clergy, are simply too busy on those days with their own families and church business. So it felt like my unplanned Christmas Eve and Day visits were more needed and possibly more timely. I set out to visit with a kind of quiet hopefulness, not knowing what would await me.

The first place I went was a hospice I had visited a great many times. At least half a dozen of our members had died of AIDS in this hospice. I knew many of the staff, some of whom were members of UFMCC or who had associations with us over the years. So they didn't look too surprised to see me.

It was a foggy day. The hospice was nestled in a wooded area near a park in downtown L.A. It is a small facility, with a comfortable living room and a devoted staff. This Christmas Eve, it was quiet in a kind of eerie way. When I arrived everything seemed so still. All the holiday hubbub was over before it had begun. There were no family members hanging around as there often are. No music was playing.

I asked the staff if there was anyone who needed a visit from me today. Two staff members looked at each other and communicated non-verbally. Then the nursing coordinator, a man, said, "Well, there's Michael—he's having a hard time." They related to me that they had had a Christmas party the day before. Michael was too upset and maybe too angry and ill to come out of his room. They said that Michael was physically very near death, ready to die, but he seemed anxious and afraid. They knew nothing about his religious issues. But they said, "He just can't let go." They told me he was twenty-five years old and had a sister.

With that little bit of information, I knocked on Michael's door and entered. Even with all the death and dying I had seen, I wasn't quite prepared for this one.

Michael was young. And maybe of average height, but he weighed only about seventy-five pounds. For some reason (unusual in a hospice) he had a nasal-gastric tube and tubes coming out of his mouth and abdomen. He looked a little alarmed when I entered the room. I sat down, told him I was a minister. (I thought my clerical collar might have alarmed him, as in "A clergyperson I don't recognize has come to see me—the end must be near!")

He had a notebook by his head, and he lay facing me on his left side. With his right hand he held a pencil, and I noticed a lot of scrawls on the notebook. Michael was communicating by means of this notebook, since he could not talk with the tubes in his nose and throat. His face was filled with pain and fear. He struggled to position himself so he could write on the notebook. It took quite some time for that to happen. I also realized that he was so weak that he could barely press hard enough to make a recognizable mark on the pad.

I panicked. What the hell was I doing here? I thought to myself. How are we going to communicate? Maybe I'm just frightening him *more*. I felt guilty for feeling uncomfortable. I wanted to flee from the room. I knew that only Michael, God, and I would know the truth if I just left. Whose big idea was it to come here on Christmas Eve, anyway? No normal person would have chosen to be here! Was I trying to be heroic? Brave? A glutton for punishment? And now I was making this kid's suffering worse!

As I thought these thoughts, Michael had finally gotten pencil in hand. "Help," he wrote. That took two minutes to write. Help. "Killing me," he wrote. Then he pulled on his gastric tube, writhing in pain. Perhaps he thinks the members of the staff here are trying to kill him. Does he have dementia? Or is he just angry, exhausted, a little disoriented with his weakness and the medication? There was no way to know for certain. So I spoke, "Michael, I know you are in terrible pain. No one is trying to kill you, Michael." I touched his head with my hand. "You are dying, and they are trying to help you have less pain and discomfort." At that point, a tear came down his cheek. Michael struggled again to write, with agonizing slowness. He wrote again, "Help me."

I wanted to run. I have never wanted to leave a room so much in my life. Obviously I wasn't getting through, and I was frustrating him. But I touched his head again and said, "Michael, I don't know if I can help you or not. All I can do is pray for you. Do you want me to?" He seemed to nod, I wasn't sure. So I gambled and went for it. I placed both my hands on him and prayed about his fear. I prayed that he could trust God a little more. I prayed for the pain to decrease and cease, for him to be able to relax and trust God, who loved him. As I prayed, I could feel his tears on my hands. Then I felt my own tears.

We opened our eyes. He wanted to write again. This time, the writing came swiftly, mercifully. In a flourish he wrote, "This is a hospice. Christmas Eve. What are you doing here?"

Great question! I had asked it myself about twenty minutes ago. I laughed a little and said, "Well, right now, Michael, I'm crying with you." Then I noticed the Bible underneath his notebook.

"What church?" he wrote.

"Metropolitan Community Church." He showed no sign of recognition. Imagine that—someone in Los Angeles who had never heard of UFMCC! So, as succinctly as I could, I told him *the* story. I had to assume at this point that it was likely that Michael *was* gay. I told him I was gay and about Troy Perry and UFMCC. I could see he had never heard of our ministry or about the fact that one could be gay and Christian. His eyes brimmed with tears, he even seemed to smile just a little, in between what looked like *electrical* jolts of pain. I talked a mile a minute, flooding the room with every reassurance I could manage to speak with confidence.

When I took a breath, he wrote, "Angels?" I said yes, I believed in angels and that he had the name of the greatest angel, the archangel Michael. Then he wrote, "Gay angels?"

"Gay angels?" It all came clear. Michael did not want to go anywhere he would not be welcome, including heaven (maybe especially). But if gay angels would accompany him, there was hope! Suddenly I remembered Ben Rodermond from Holland, who had died only three months before in the room next door to Michael's. Ben was an angel, in life and in death. I could see Ben's face suddenly, I could see him coming for Michael, bringing his little gay brother to the throne of grace, holding his hand, healing his fear. "Yes, Michael, there are gay angels: one of them died a few months ago in the next room," I said. Gay angels, what a wonderful thought; the room seemed to be filled with them. "Thank you, God," I kept saying in my heart.

Then Michael wrote again: "Send them."

"Send them." He was ready now, and somehow he thought I had the ability, the authority to send the gay angels for him. So I prayed again for that very thing. Michael seemed calmer. His eyelids rested a little. Gently I touched his face and hands and kissed him good-bye.

That night at the Christmas Eve service, in our very cold sanctuary, we prayed for Michael. I called the hospice the next morning; Michael had died in the wee hours of that Christmas morning, led to his Maker, I'm sure, by Ben and his fellow gay angels.

7

A Queer Theology of Sexuality

If we were really about to propose a "queer millennium,"
part of what might characterize this new era would be a
new theology of sexuality.

Many of us in the gay and lesbian religious community have talked
about this for a long time. We have struggled to understand how feminist
critique and gay and lesbian experience might not just *add to* a theology
of sexuality but might be able to reframe the discussion. This has been difficult because for the most part, we have seen our theological agenda as
trying to "normalize" gay sexuality for the public, struggling for our
human rights, wanting simply to be included in the panorama of human
life and lifestyle. We've been bogged down by the necessity to do biblical
or theological *apologetics*. But what if we actually claimed a role in
reshaping the basic questions concerning God and human sexuality?

Every time mainline denominations in the United States try to
"study" the issue of homosexuality, the study group always realizes that it
cannot study homosexuality in isolation. The issue of human sexuality is
the locus of most of our real, deep conflicts, and this is the reason we cannot seem to talk about homosexuality rationally or with a sense of ease or
comfort.

A National Council of Churches of Christ staff member noticed
that when she was assigned to one of the three or four dialogue committees on UFMCC or on homosexuality that were commissioned by the
NCC over a ten-year period, she suddenly found herself becoming the de
facto "sex expert and counselor" at the office. Everyone began consciously
or unconsciously to assume that she had skills or expertise (or a sense of

openness and compassion) that she was not sure she could honestly claim for herself. She said, "When conversations at the water fountain became incredibly interesting, complicated, and intimate, the single contributing factor to their changed perception of me was my staff connection to our study group!"

This is where the stories of Sodom and Gomorrah and Gibeah become very useful again. If the sin of Sodom is *not* gay or lesbian sexuality, if it really is about violence and particularly sexualized violence, then we have a new place to begin. The sins of Sodom and Gibeah were about the violent uses of sexuality, the punishment of the "other," those who are different for reasons of race, gender, sexuality, or culture (or religion, perhaps). It is the hatred of the other, acted out in violence and sexual abuse. It is certainly much too euphemistic to call this behavior *inhospitality*.

However, we can turn this around and ask the question, What is the nature of godly, healthy sexual contact, and is it possible to use the concept of hospitality as a positive model for theological reflection about sexuality? Could the concept of *bodily hospitality* be useful in beginning to construct a new theology of sexuality and sexual relating that is somewhat free from old sexual rules and roles? Could it be a first step that would inform and undergird a new and healthier sexual ethic?

PROMISCUOUS HOSPITALITY AS A "QUEER" GIFT

Hospitality, as I have stated earlier, is a spiritual gift that has decidedly "queer" connections. There are profound differences among lesbians and gay men in this regard, but I think this idea works for both communities. One stereotype of gay men is that they are *fabulous* cooks and hosts of great parties. Perhaps this connection of hospitality and gays is as simple as the notion of a "queer sensibility": the love of gay men for elegance, for hospitality as an *art form*. Certainly there are gay men who are slobs or who can't cook or decorate or set a gorgeous table, but it does seem like there are a disproportionate number of them who do have a *flair* for hospitality of this kind. This has cultural and historical roots, which Judy Grahn has traced, calling us "transpeople," people of the world between genders. Our job is partly to be cultural go-betweens. Eunuchs of old, we recall, were "court officials"; many were gay and responsible for *palace hospitality*.

In England recently, I spoke with a gay man who had been the butler to a high-ranking member of Parliament. He told me that the royal family preferred gay men as palace servants because they were the *best* at providing hospitality of all kinds. Why has this queer stereotype persisted for thousands of years? Saying all this always means walking a narrow tightrope: speaking of gayness in essentialist terms can simply reinforce stereotypes. Even *neutral* or *positive* stereotypes can be used in politically dangerous ways.

When I think of lesbians and lesbian culture, I think of potlucks and an easy flow of work, preparation, food and home, sex and friends. For lesbians, hospitality is hardly ever *formal*. It is fluid, communal, and easy, with everyone pitching in and not a lot of ownership of the "product." Also, it may be characterized by permeable boundaries that include parents and children and other family members, as well as bisexuals and men.

Perhaps the experience of having been left out or put out of our homes and families (even if we later reconcile with them and heal the rift) makes us more willing and open to inviting and accepting each other into our homes and living rooms and kitchens and, sometimes, bedrooms. Perhaps our neediness or loneliness has made us almost "promiscuous" in our desire to provide hospitality. Being shut out has made us want to *include* with a vengeance.

I have a collection of particular holiday memories from the first few years after Paula and I arrived in California. In the early eighties, the second year we were here, we rented a fairly large house, which we could afford because we had a roommate at the time. It was Thanksgiving, the year of the U.S. Cuban refugee resettlement. UFMCC churches got involved with resettling hundreds of gay and lesbian Cuban refugees. One of Paula's former students was stationed nearby in the marines and was too far from home to go back for the holiday. We invited ten or so friends, the student, my cousin Linton, the UFMCC pastor who was the chaplain for the refugees, about five refugees, and some others whom I've forgotten. Most of these folks were gay or lesbian but not all. Every day of the week before, Paula and I would find out that we had each separately invited someone else. I think there were thirty-five or so people there. We actually managed to seat everyone in two rooms and at tables outside (this is Thanksgiving in California). I cooked the turkeys and basic vegetables, others brought their own dishes. The Cubans (mostly drag queens and one lesbian) experienced their first traditional (hah!) U.S. Thanksgiving, which included stuffed artichokes, Mexican lasagna, a California fruit salad, a few Asian dishes, turkey, and dressing.

Other years we'd have family members of the people I had pastored who had died of AIDS. For most holidays over the last eight or ten years, someone with AIDS or HIV or who was recently bereaved (that's most of us) has been at our table. It's just a fact of life.

Each holiday has produced its own one-time-only extended family du jour. This is not a *hobby*. It is a way of living and being. It is an adventure, and it has a lot to do with being lesbian. It has everything to do with how we view life and relationship, with our own emerging values. It has to do with our own (for better or worse) family histories, how we both react in opposition to them, and how we sometimes unconsciously recreate them. It has to do with a belief that our home, our time, our table, our resources, our skills, our affection and capacity to live are to be *shared*. The sharing should support, nourish, and enrich others and ourselves, maybe for a day or maybe for years.

Many lesbians and gay men consciously create environments of hospitality in their homes or organizations. They do this as a gift, a way of life. And I don't mean that straight people don't do this. But there is something, perhaps, about being "unhinged" from the conventional family constructs that opens up the opportunities, the desire both to deconstruct and to reconstruct this aspect of our lives. In fact, these days, as straight people have to deal with in-laws from more than one marriage, or divorced parents have to develop a holiday "schedule" with their kids—in other words, as predominantly heterosexual families get more complicated, they begin to resemble gay and lesbian families more and more!

BODILY HOSPITALITY

The Bible itself speaks of the human body as the "temple" of the spirit. Our bodies are our *home*. Our body/self is the home, the locus, of our identity.

In *People of the Deer*, Farley Mowatt describes his own learning experience with Native Canadians who hunt the vanishing caribou. He lived with them for a time and at first felt very critical of the shelters that they built.[1] These were nomadic people. To Mowatt their shelters seemed flimsy and inadequate. He could think of many ways to improve them!

Gradually it dawned on him that the shelters were built this way because they were not these people's actual *homes*. The shelters only served to cut down on the extreme winds and the snow or rain, but the Native Canadians' true *shelters* or homes were their own *bodies*, covered by the skins of the caribou. Their clothing was carefully made and was all the shelter they needed. Their bodies had been honed, toughened, and adapted to their primary need for warmth and protection. They carried their homes with them *on* and *in* their own bodies in a way that made our view of home (as a building) superfluous.

Some of us, particularly nonnative people, have difficulty identifying with our bodies or understanding our bodies as our homes. We are terribly disconnected from our bodies, as if our bodies are a *thing* to be dealt with—as if we are *not* our bodies or at least not *in* our bodies.[2]

Dwelling in Our Bodies/Homes

But our bodies are *home*. I think of that when I think of the purpose and importance of our skin, for instance. Our skin serves a number of simultaneous functions: it is the first element in our body's immune system—keeping out germs, disease, infection. It is simultaneously the *organ* through which we experience one of our five senses—the sense of touch. Our skin is also an important participant in our sexual response system. It is the means through which we touch and experience the touch of others. We are constantly having to interpret with our minds and hearts the meaning of the ways in which we are touching and being touched. Our skin is the locus of erogenous zones that are mysteriously and powerfully connected to our sexuality. Our skin is also the primary identifying characteristic of race. Along with the marks of our gender, it becomes the most highly politicized component of our body.

Our skin, therefore, symbolizes and embodies both our *immunity* and our *vulnerability* (physically *and* politically).

I have seen this poignantly illustrated in the experience of people with AIDS. When persons with AIDS experience an opening in their skin through a cut or sore, they do not heal as well because their immune system is not functioning properly. At the same time, the skin itself is a part of the immune system. So the effect is compounded. As the skin breaks down, it acts very much like a home whose roof or walls or floors have holes. The rupturing of this protective layer creates a *new* kind of vulnerability. Many persons with AIDS, like burn victims, have lost the outer layer of their defense system against disease because of severe skin disease. Suddenly the skin, rather than being an organ of safety or defense, is itself the *enemy*. It becomes the cause of suffering, pain, intrusion, even death.

People with AIDS respond in various ways to this experience. For some, it opens them up and helps them become more emotionally vulnerable. For others, it necessitates doubling their emotional defenses.

My friend Rick was a very handsome, effeminate gay man who loved to clown around. He was an artist and had gorgeous, prematurely gray hair (he was in his early thirties), full lips, and bright blue eyes. When Rick got AIDS, he was infected with something called psoriatic arthritis, a painful and disfiguring joint disease that also erupted in psoriasis all over his body. When I hadn't seen him at work in a few weeks (he worked across the hall from an office I frequented), I called him at home; I knew he must be very sick. When I went to see him, his feet were triple their normal size and almost black. He had psoriasis on nearly 75 percent of his body. He could barely hobble to the bathroom and hadn't eaten in days. The psoriasis was in his hair and eyebrows, in what was left of his full beard and mustache, inside his mouth and under his eyelids, inside his ears. In his bed and on the floor were layers of his skin that he had shed. I could have filled a wastebasket with the shed skin. He cried and I cried. I told him he had to go to the hospital. He didn't want to go. I told him if he didn't go voluntarily, I would have to call an ambulance (I wasn't even sure they would take him). I told him if he didn't go, he was going to lose his feet, although I didn't really think they could save them at this point. Finally he agreed to go. I talked three members of our AIDS ministry team into taking him to the hospital. They carried him down the stairs while he alternately joked and cried. They had to leave all the windows in the car open because the stench was so bad. He was literally rotting from the outside in.

Rick lived almost another six months. They never had to amputate his feet, but neither his feet nor the psoriasis got much better. In the last weeks of his life he could not be touched almost at all because of the excruciating pain and because of the danger to others of the gangrenous infection that covered so much of his body. Yet just before Christmas, Rick was still able to joke and laugh and relate. I will never know how.

The last time I went to see him, they would not let me in the room, though his mother was able to be with him off and on. The doctors were with him at the time, and it was just too stressful for him to see anyone else. I sat out in the hospice dining room and kept hearing this high-pitched scream. It was weeks before I could really allow myself to know that *that sound* had come from Rick. He was so exhausted, his strength so depleted, that he could only cry out in a high-pitched wail that sounded like a child. Now and then, unfortunately, I can still recall it.

He died New Year's Eve, not wanting, I'm sure, to enter another year with such unrelenting pain and suffering.

I remember that for weeks after that, I would look at and touch my own skin and think of how the smallest cut or blemish can annoy or embarrass me. I wondered at the health of my own skin, at how even with my aging process, it is still relatively smooth and healthy and resilient, and at how I take my own skin for granted. I wondered at the mystery of skin in different places on my own body—the calloused parts, the tender parts, how it loosens with age. How the *accidents* of gender and race and genetics and disease bring such incredible power and meaning to the color and texture of our skin. I wonder still at the politics of my skin, which is the living "wall" of my body/home. How does the outer relate to the inner? The colors and texture of our *walls* and *floors* and *roof*?

An acupuncturist friend of mine told me that in Chinese medicine and philosophy the skin is primarily related to the lungs and to breathing. This is why, she said, people with respiratory problems also often have skin problems. Recent diagnostic descriptions of asthma, for instance, include skin problems as a symptom of the disease. Our lungs, necessary for breathing, for life itself, can also be the pathway of infection and disease, a way in which we can take in toxins, allergens, germs.

Sexuality, too, especially in the age of AIDS, contains this paradox. Sexuality can be the means of tremendous self-expression, power, desire, and fulfillment of the urge to connect with others. It can also be the way in which we experience shame and abuse, disappointment, isolation, obsession, violence.

This is the physical, graphic way in which we know the paradox of living: to live is to risk, often even to risk life itself! Jesus said paradoxical stuff like this all the time: to save your life, lose it! By dying, we Christians believe, Christ gave us the gift of eternal life. Jesus (I once heard someone say in a very oversimplified explanation of the incarnation) is God with *skin on*. God risking God's self in human flesh and vulnerability.

The Jesus who said he wanted to be identified with "the least of these" today has AIDS, including Kaposi's sarcoma and life-threatening psoriasis in the skin that *contains* divinity.

Bodily Differences: The Politics of Ownership

It is interesting to compare the differences in our bodies with the differences in our homes.

Some of us own our own homes. We have a sense that we can control them—decorate, remodel, improve, neglect, or furnish our homes in any way we please. Similarly, some of us have a consciousness about our bodies, an intentionality. We believe we can or should control our weight, hairstyle, shape, and so on.

Others of us do not believe that our bodies are our own. Many children, maybe even most children, have a sense that they are not ultimately in control of their own bodies. Parents, or guardians, or sometimes even older children or other adults may seem to "possess" a child or his or her body. Sometimes this is done out of seemingly good motives—to protect, for instance. In other cases, it may be in order to exploit the child. Many children have to *struggle* for privacy, for a sense of boundaries, for even a clear idea that their own body is really their own body and not the "property" of someone else.

Many parents believe that in a sense, they *own* their children, just as they think they own the bodies of their pets or plants (also a primarily-Western modern idea). This goes on long after the natural developmental process of separation and individuation has occurred or *should* have occurred. Many women feel as if their fathers or husbands own their bodies, as if they cannot make independent choices about their own bodies. For some this lack of ownership is less obvious. It is framed simply as a desire to *please* another—a spouse or lover. This desire is reflected in the belief that one should shape or decorate or clothe one's body in a way that pleases the other, without thinking about what pleases *oneself*. Men also do this, although to a lesser extent.

People sometimes "lease" their bodies, rent them out. There are women who lease their bodies for the purpose of procreation, as in surrogate parenting. There are others who less formally lease or rent out their bodies but do so nevertheless—who exchange their bodies for shelter, food, clothing, for warmth, affection, addictions, money.

If you are in prison, you soon learn that you do not own your own body. "They" get to control a lot of things about your body: what you eat, what you wear, when and where you sleep, your health, where you spend your time. They can control your contact with those to whom you speak, touch, communicate. There is no right to privacy, no matter what they promise.

This happens to people in other institutions, even to those who are supposedly *not* being punished. Certainly it happens to people in hospitals, nursing homes, and shelters.

The reality of the politics of how much control we have over our own bodies and under what circumstances is staggering. Some of us *say* we own our home—but the truth is, the bank or mortgage company really owns it! We're *working* toward owning it. We may actually get to own it before we die, if we don't sell it or remortgage it! Very few people who say they own their homes actually own them "free and clear."

Free and clear. What a concept! I remember how I felt in high school when I knew I wanted to get out of the suburban town I lived in and never come back. I knew the way to do this was to go to college, for which I had no money. Going away to college seemed to be the method of getting free and clear. I knew I couldn't bear to stay home and go to a local college. I didn't even really know why—I just wanted out. Something about growing up in the era I did, where I did, I never quite felt like my body, or time, or life was really my own. I always felt like I owed somebody something. I'm sure my parents also felt that way growing up. It wasn't that I lacked what I needed or didn't feel loved. It was something other than that, a system of assumptions in which I lived. So I went to work in an electronics factory and began to save up to go to college. My mother also got a job in anticipation of having three children who would probably all move away and go to college.

All through high school and during summers and vacations from college, I worked in that factory. I hated it. The pay was lousy, but I could work overtime. The only thing that kept me from going crazy was the knowledge that I was doing this so that I would never have to do this again. I was literally selling my hours, my time, my body/self so that I could leave, so that I could have more choices about how to spend my time. I remember feeling angry that because I was a young female with few marketable skills that suited the opportunities available in that industrial park, my time and my body/self were worth so little. I felt the grief of lost hours, days, even years, sold to make fuel boxes for airplanes so I could get out of there.

As children, adolescents, then young adults, we struggle to have a sense of identity and independence vis-à-vis our body/selves—physically, mentally, emotionally, even spiritually. What does it mean for us really to have a sense of control over our own bodies? Women have special issues about this related to the fact that we can potentially "share" our bodies in the process of conception and birth. The whole abortion debate is centered around a woman's right to determine whether or not her body will or will not be used to house the embryonic life of another human being. Being pregnant is a very powerful and unique experience of *bodily hospitality*. What does it mean to share the inside of your body, your food and blood and energy and every single minute of every single day for about nine months with someone you don't even know yet? How does this change your view of your own body, the whole concept of hospitality?

How does our sense of being at home or not being at home in our own bodies affect how well we are able to share our bodies when we want or need to do so?

I think of women who are addicted to drugs or alcohol or who smoke, and get pregnant. How does it feel to them no longer to have the freedom to risk abusing their bodies in certain ways, because another person's life and health are at stake and have intruded in their lives? And if many of those with such addictions have problems with self-esteem and loving their own body/self, how can they possibly love this unknown other more than they love themselves? Some women with little support and resources, money, family, friends, or hope are *tremendously* courageous as they attempt to take care of their bodies in new ways—unfortunately *not* because they love themselves but because they are trying to be a better "host" to a new life.

It also takes courage for some women to face the fact that they are not equipped to share their body with another at a particular time. That saying an honest "no" now may mean a more healthy and wise "yes" later.

In the early days of gay and lesbian liberation, I came out in the city of Boston. In 1972 there was only one lesbian bar in Boston, and it was located in the "combat zone," an area of several blocks in downtown Boston that used to house porno theaters, nightclubs, strip joints, leather bars, and gay bars. My friend Julie says it was called the combat zone because MPs patrolled the area during World War II to protect GIs on weekend passes.

There was a constant turf war among the city, police, various Mafia interests, and "legitimate" business interests. But the weapons of the war were sex and drugs. And the *victims* were the patrons and providers, the sexual outlaws, the young and restless, the old and frustrated, the lost and lonely, the adventurous.

Jacques's was a notorious place that had a heterosexual prostitute bar in front, with a "lesbian room" with a pool table in the back, and a leather bar in the basement. I was twenty-two, just out of the closet, and had only been to one other gay bar in my life. (I'd been to Forty-second Street in New York, but only in the daytime!) I was in seminary at the time and had just barely found UFMCC. I was curious about this lesbian bar. So I went there, twice.

I remember trying not to dress too much like a tourist or college student. I felt shy and totally out of place walking by the older women prostitutes perched on bar stools in the front corridor. I remember wanting to look at them and wanting to avoid looking at them all at the same time. Both times I was too afraid to descend to the leather bar downstairs. I didn't really understand what that "scene" was about. The first time my experience in the lesbian "area" at Jacques's was OK, no big deal. Tough-looking middle-aged lesbians competed good-naturedly at the pool table. I nursed a beer for about an hour and went home grateful to have gone unnoticed.

The next time I went, about half an hour into my sojourn, beer bottles started flying across the room, and the next thing I knew we could hear sirens and police entering the front door, where the prostitutes perched. There was a mad dash for the back door as women vaulted over the pool table and knocked over furniture to get out. As we were trying to leave, we literally ran into guys in leather, as well as some drag queens, who were rushing up and out of the basement. Jacques's was closed down soon after.

Years later I would sit with the older lesbians at the new lesbian-owned, non-Mafia bar called the Saints. These older dykes loved to entertain us with stories about the "good old days" at Jacques's and other combat-zone clubs. They wore their scars like badges of courage! They told how the cops came to know them by name after a while, sometimes letting them crawl voluntarily into the paddy wagons without the customary beatings on backs, legs, and heads. Sometimes they were so drunk and disorderly they reasoned that they kind of *deserved* the treatment they got. They loved to play "top this," about their experiences of danger and violence, how they *got away* with flipping the finger at life, the cops, and God. Defiantly queer, they recounted rituals of cross-dressing, drinking, posturing, raids and cops and jail—all lived within the parameters of having to go to work or being in the closet to some degree. Secrets, danger, defiance, shame, and submission—all the elements of queer life, pre-Stonewall.

Twenty years later I would meet a heterosexual woman who knew some women *I* had known at combat-zone strip joints in Boston, clubs like the Two O'clock Club and the Mouse Trap. Most of these bars were owned by organized crime. All sorts of illegal activities went on there (drugs, gambling, prostitution). They paid off the police not to shut them down. The police had to raid these clubs every once in a while just to make it look good to the citizenry. The gay bars were the easiest to raid because the queers wouldn't object. They were used to it; they expected it. No one would stand up for them.

Julie grew up in the suburbs of Boston, in what she describes as a "nice Jewish home." But she struggled very hard to have a sense of herself, her body/self. At about age nineteen, after a brief failed marriage that included a stint of rural "living on the land," Julie came home to her parents' house. One day she started dancing in the living room when they were not at home. She described this experience of loving to dance as an experience of loving her own body, of enjoying looking at herself in the mirror as she danced. She got this idea in her head that she could be a go-go dancer in one of "those clubs" she had heard about in downtown Boston (like the 1970s TV show *Hullabaloo*, she thought).

Julie was very naive. She did not know what these clubs were really about. But she found them, found out, and decided to become a dancer there anyway. She was young (most of the strippers in these clubs were well into their lifelong careers!) and a great dancer with a beautiful body. Julie learned quickly and well and loved to perform, to be watched, to dance. Somehow she managed to escape hard-core drug addiction, although she used drugs (setting a boundary at not shooting up). She participated in extensive sexual experimentation, but she never yielded to the pressure to participate in the prostitution business that boomed in these clubs. Julie was already amazed by the money she made stripping, but she could have more than tripled that amount by just turning a few tricks.

She told me her story with a mix of enjoyment and sadness, sharing this secret of her past and how exotic and adventurous it seemed. She hinted at all the pain and the stresses and confusion inherent in such a life. For instance, two weeks after starting her dancing career, her parents found out and threw her out of the house. They called her names worse than those she heard in the clubs. Her brother came after her with a knife.

In some strange way, there was some healing for Julie in telling *me* her story. I'd been to some of those clubs and others just like them. I'd been there as a clergyperson trying to find "my people" and as a patron shyly trying to discover something about myself and my own sexuality. Like Julie, I'd grown up very sheltered about sexuality and my options, with no sense of being at home in my own body.

I also had to chuckle because I vaguely recognized Julie's description of how she felt looking in the mirror and being a performer. As a person who gets up in front of crowds a few times a week, I, too, am a performer. Preaching is, or can be, performance art. Especially in this television age. I have to use my whole body/self when I preach. In order to keep people's attention (people who are used to looking at television or lots of action), I have to work at it. Part of my preaching task is to help people who are often numbed by oppression or by the competing messages and pressures of the world to *feel*. I have to help them feel so that they can also think about and find a relationship to their *own* spirituality and a relationship to God.

And there is something interesting about comparing preaching as a performance art to stripping! Sometimes I do have to strip down. I have to be real. I have to share not just my thoughts but my heart, my fears, my struggles. Sometimes I have to *bare my soul*. My preacher friend Judy Dahl describes one experience of getting up to preach on Sunday at her church and just confessing, "I have no business being up here today, but we preachers often preach what we need to hear ourselves."

What Julie and other women who worked in those places did was to provide several "services." The strip shows were entertainment, but they were much more. Sometimes, they were the only sexual stimulation and experience some people had. For others, they were a form of sex education. They occurred in a sleazy environment, but they were still education—education that was *not* happening, by the way, in the wider society of this sexually repressed and obsessed culture.

Also, these places were offering a kind of hospitality. Hospitality to the fantasies, the repressed longings for sexual contact—or for contact of any kind, perhaps. Lonely, desperate people who felt unfulfilled, suppressed, or that somehow their own sexual needs and desires were unacceptable anywhere else felt welcomed and, to some degree, acceptable in these places. Women like Julie—young, beautiful, enjoying their own bodies and putting on a show—invited those who watched to feel and to fantasize. In the combat zone, those "anything goes" zones, there was ironically a profound sense of safety and permission, partly made possible by anonymity. There were also sometimes profound shame and guilt. There were danger and crime. There was risk of arrest or punishment (unless you were really rich and famous and could buy everyone off). So, this hospitality was very costly. It was costly also to many of those women, who having entered this "glamorous" life often never got off the merry-go-round of drugs and prostitution. Many of them died of overdoses or of being beaten to death by pimps, boyfriends, or tricks.

When Julie and I talked, she really warmed to the story. Because I'd been there, too, she didn't feel *judged*. We knew some of the same people. We were struggling to understand our early adulthood experiences of trying to feel at home in our own bodies and what it meant to share out body/selves with those who needed *hospitality*.

The first stripper I ever met, I met at church. Her stage name was "Frosty Winters." She was a headliner at the Two O'clock Club. Her name came from her act. Apparently in a certain lighting her skin had a somewhat green-gray-mint tinge. She built her act around this physical "special effect." And she was a lesbian. Lots of these women were bisexuals or lesbians. (Julie was shocked when I told her this.) Women who stripped for men, for money, some of whom also turned tricks for money, were also lesbians. They had a private life *on the side*, usually with a butch who often resented like hell that their "fem" stripped for men or turned tricks.

Frosty and her lover, Claire, found MCC Boston in the first few weeks of our existence there in 1972. They had first heard of UFMCC while living in Florida (a lot of strippers worked Florida clubs in the winter). Claire, though butch by most standards, had also been heterosexually married, had five older kids (none of whom were with her) and a brand-new baby boy. Claire contacted the church because she wanted Eric to be baptized. She was the first lesbian mother I ever met.

I visited Frosty and Claire in their little apartment in the South End of Boston. I have to admit, I was fascinated by Frosty and her career, and this was probably the reason I checked out the combat zone in the first place. I was also doing "missionary work," dropping off church ads and cards in the clubs and in the gay section of the porno shops. (There were no gay newspapers or organizations or coffeehouses to take them to!)

Frosty and Claire were warm and hospitable to me. I never told anyone how old I was in those days because I thought I was probably too young to be pastoring. I worried about my credibility. I suspect they knew anyway, but they were sweet to me and treated me just like I was an adult and a *real* pastor!

Eric was my first infant baptism. He was an adorable six-month-old, a blond, healthy baby. It thrilled me to touch him with the water, to hold him in my arms, to welcome him to the people of God who called themselves MCC Boston, meeting at the Arlington Street Unitarian Church.

Two weeks later, I got a late-night call from Claire. She was hysterical. She sounded drunk. Frosty was *moving out*, leaving her. Could I come over now? I put on my clerical collar and took the bus to the South End, enduring the stares of all who had never seen a woman in a collar. (Well, a collar *and* a blue jean jacket.) When I got there, it was quite a scene. Frosty, as it turned out, had an expensive heroin habit, and Claire was tired of it. Frosty didn't want to be lectured or controlled. Claire was worried about Frosty's dealer and the danger to themselves and the baby. Frosty, wearing dark glasses, and looking like hell, was leaving with her bags; she gave me a "Sorry, kid" look as she exited.

Claire was crying (as was the baby), and I finally noticed the gun. Claire was threatening to kill herself with it, and she raced out of the house. I followed her. I grabbed her and spun her around, and she pointed the gun at my stomach and said, "If you try to stop me, I'll blow you away."

Now, I had never seen a real handgun. I'd seen my Grandpa's rifles, mostly sitting high up on a rack at the farm. But I'd never seen anything but a *toy* handgun.

This was one of those "pastoral moments" that neither the Religion Department at Allegheny College nor my six weeks of seminary had prepared me for. There was no time for "theological reflection" (unless you count the prayer that went something like "Oh, shit!"). There was no time really to consider the options. I think I did believe that if I let her go, she would shoot herself. For some strange reason (maybe because I knew she'd been a Catholic), I didn't believe she would really shoot me. Of course, this could simply have been denial! No time to sort that out, however . . . I mustered up all the "priestly authority" I could manage and said sternly and, I hoped, convincingly, "Give me that gun!"

She did. She just handed me the gun. Now, I'd never *held* a real gun either, and when its heaviness landed in the palm of my hand, so did the realization of what had just happened or nearly happened. My knees got wobbly. Claire must have sensed this, and she proceeded to help me into the house. She was also starting to enter the weepy phase of her drunkenness. So we sat in the apartment, the gun underneath my jacket next to me on the couch, as I held Claire while she cried. And the baby was crying, too.

There was no manual for this. I left my home address and phone number on the kitchen table, covered the sleeping Claire with a blanket, took the gun, Eric, a few diapers, and a bottle, and caught the bus home.

Claire got sober for a while, but eventually drank again and lost Eric to the foster care system. Years later Claire caught up with me, when she got sober again, and she told me that Eric had graduated from high school and was in touch with her again.

A lot of my ministry, and the ministry of UFMCC over the years has been to gay/lesbian/bisexual families in distress. Sometimes, just like in all families, adults who can hardly manage to take care of themselves are trying to raise and take care of children. UFMCC churches often function as all large extended families do—they help celebrate victories and bail each other out in crises. The crises of gay and lesbian families are often exacerbated by all the self-esteem challenges associated with coming out; and with trying to become whole and healthy, in our lesbian and gay bodies, minds, and spirits.

HOSPITALITY AS A CENTRAL BIBLICAL ETHIC

Hospitality was essential in a desert culture, especially a nomadic one. In biblical times if you traveled anywhere in the Near East, you had to depend on the kindness of strangers and acquaintances alike. You had to treat the sojourner well because you might need to depend on someone yourself in the future. There was a common appreciation of the true vulnerability, the fragility of life in a desert climate. *It was not a moral choice to be inhospitable.* To do so was to violate the deepest commitment to being human and in community.

This is one of the reasons the stories of Sodom and Gibeah are recorded in the Bible. These are stories about the abuse of strangers who required hospitality.

Sexual abuse of anyone—stranger, friend, or family member—is the grossest kind of inhospitality. Unfortunately, in our day sexual abuse is rampant. It is a sign of the deterioration of ethical human community. It is *not* primarily a "homosexual problem." It is a human problem. It results from the alienation from our own bodies and from the bodies of others.

Jesus came from a heritage of desert hospitality. As a person who during his ministry was without a permanent home of his own, he depended on the hospitality of others to survive.

Jesus knew what it was to give and receive hospitality. He knew how to be a guest. People were always inviting him to dinner! He almost never cooked; maybe that wasn't his gift, and he knew it. Perhaps others cooked for him because he knew how to appreciate good cooking. Also, he was probably a wonderful conversationalist. He brought interesting people with him to dinner and ate in all kinds of elaborate and humble settings. Dinner and table fellowship were always an excuse to talk about his passion—the nature of God and God's love, the way to live in harmony with neighbors.

He was vulnerable as a guest, dependent on the kindness of others for food and drink and presumably often a place to sleep, if not actually a bed. He probably had to deal with eating food that wasn't at its best and with accommodations that were less than adequate. He had to put up with attitudes—those who didn't like the men and women he chose to spend time with.

Sometimes he had a hard time setting boundaries. The dependence on others for food and drink and a place to sleep sometimes meant these people thought they could impose on him. How does someone without a room of his own ever have privacy? The Bible says Jesus went off to the mountains to pray or sometimes had friends or disciples row him across the lake. But even there he was often intruded upon.

But Jesus was not only a guest. He also provided his own kind of hospitality. He opened himself, his heart, his body. He invited people to question him, to touch him. And they did. He invited them to test him, to see if his words were matched by his deeds. He even invited them to challenge and criticize him. Which they did.

The Last Supper is the only dinner where it appears to me as if Jesus is really the host. He makes arrangements for this dinner with his friends and disciples. We have to assume that others actually cooked the food and served it, but Jesus has somehow arranged for this meal to occur. And the reinterpretation of the meal is a very powerful experience of bodily hospitality.

Jesus reinterprets Passover for the disciples at this meal he is hosting. Jesus linked the story of the deliverance of the Jews from slavery to his own life and ministry and death. Jesus proposed a way for this new beloved community of Jews and Gentiles, slave and free, male and female, to embody freedom together, for the healing of the world. Furthermore, they are the guests of the savior. He is feeding them literally, as he has been feeding them spiritually all along. And he uses food and a meal to symbolize his relationship to them now and in the future. In fact, he asks them to think of him in the future whenever they share a meal together, whenever they eat bread and drink wine. Jesus' choice of symbols for himself are very provocative, sensual, and imbued with the images of hospitality.

Jesus asks his guests to ingest him, the reality of his life and death and teachings and being. To ingest his healing presence. This is a very risky image.

It certainly risks, at that time and at any time, being associated with cannibalism. But we do not feed on the dead body of Jesus at communion. We are invited to take him into ourselves, not as a dead martyr but as a risen, victorious savior. We are invited to eat and drink from the endless supply of the energy of God that was and is incarnated in the Body of Christ. This imagery is also very sexual, in a nonsexual context. It is sexual in a positive sense — it is about Jesus' own bodily hospitality toward us. The giving of himself physically, spiritually, and emotionally is connected to sexuality in the broadest sense of the word.

The fact that it has always been taboo to see *anything* in Jesus' life as sexual is a product of our distorted view of sexuality. If sexuality is a gift, then it is a gift Jesus had and experienced and shared. The longer I live and the more I heal from the sex phobia and sex obsession of our culture and religious culture, the more I see a desexed Jesus as a tragedy (sometimes a comic tragedy), if not a heresy. To imagine Jesus living to age thirty-three as a virgin with no sexual desires, longings, or experiences is utterly dehumanizing. I know and have been close to people who have chosen to be celibate. None of those persons has ever claimed that he or she had no sexual feelings, desires, or experiences.

It is as if sex is the *only* human experience we insist on denying Jesus — as if the "fullness of God" and human sexuality cannot cohabit in the person of Jesus or in any of us. As if we dare not explore that "enigmatic border" of the connection *in* Jesus of sexuality and spirituality. And this would explain why Christians, at least, dare not explore that connection in ourselves.

Only a Jesus vulnerable enough to be taken could give authentically. I think Jesus shared the gift of human sexuality in a poignant, sweet, metaphysical way at the Last Supper. He invited his followers into a permanent union with him, through bodily symbols of giving and taking. He was preparing for an ultimate act of hospitality—his own suffering and death for their sake, for God's sake, for the sake of the integrity of the mission. He was willing to open up his body and spirit to suffering and pain, to sacrifice, and to the possibilities of resurrection.

SEXUALITY, STRANGERS, AND BODILY HOSPITALITY

If my body is my home, then my decision to share my body with another person is a lot like my decision to share my home. The process includes developing a strong sense of what it means to have responsibility for my home. I have to work on developing a sense of my identity as a body/self, including a sense of having *ownership* and responsibility for my own body.

Some of us need to heal a great deal from the ways in which we were alienated from our bodies—or from what we went through just in order to *gain* a sense of independence for our body/self.

I believe that to share ourselves sexually is to give and receive bodily hospitality. Hospitality, to me, can function as a helpful metaphor for ethical sexual relating, which honors the self and the other.

To share sexually with someone is literally to *make room* for them in our body and in the space surrounding our bodies. Quite literally, in most forms of sexual intimacy, we enter each other's bodies in some fashion. Whether through kissing, especially deep kissing, various forms of penetration, or holding and stroking playfully or passionately, we have entered the most physically private and protected areas of each other's body/self. And to use the AIDS phrase that has so *clinicized* the nature of sexual activity, we often "exchange bodily fluids." Those are fluids produced from within us, that we manufacture, and they constitute another way in which we have contact with each other's bodies.

I do a good deal of couples counseling, mostly for lesbians and gay men. It seems to me that sometimes people who are married to each other or who are in a long-term committed relationship hardly know each other. They are long-term strangers.

I remember one couple I counseled for a holy union many years ago. They had been together nine years and had *never had a fight*. Not even an argument or a cross word. It was hard to stay in the room with all that buried rage. I tried to tell them that it would probably be a good idea if they learned how to trust each other enough to fight, because otherwise when they finally did have a fight, it was going to be too big to put back together again. Several months later their first fight nearly killed one of them, and it ended the relationship *and* the friendship.

And not all "anonymous" sex is really all that *anonymous*. I want to be careful not to romanticize here. I have had very little experience in my own life with sex with strangers. The few experiences I've had were almost all (with two exceptions) pretty disastrous as far as the sex was concerned, and I may be mostly to blame for that! One of the experiences was enjoyable sexually but was terrifying for other reasons, as should become apparent.

My first year of being out of the closet was full of new and dramatic experiences. I fell in love and had sex with someone for the first time in my life. And like most lesbians, I thought that meant we were married— for life! I moved to Boston, found UFMCC, and started pastoring while going to seminary full time and working nights in a hospital as a nurse's aid. I worked with dying patients, never imagining that years later I would need to recall all that learning. I became a public queer and was temporarily alienated from my parents and family. I cut my hair. I wore a clerical collar for the first time, and people called me "Pastor."

When I went home for a few days at Easter in 1973 to try to talk to my parents (or while they tried to talk to me), my lover had an affair with a young lesbian choir director at MCC Boston. (We were all young in our early 20's) She moved out of our apartment. I was beside myself. I was emotionally dependent on her. I also was terrified of being single or even thinking about dating. I felt like a failure—like I was a rotten lover or partner. I hated being dumped. I begged to be taken back. I threw myself into schoolwork and church with a vengeance.

One night I thought I'd better try to go out and at least meet some lesbians. So I went to a mixed bar on Boylston Street. I had two drinks, which was one too many for me. I was feeling lonely, desperate, and very angry. And who should appear but the choir director who, by the way, had dumped my now ex-lover after two weeks! (My ex, however, had not failed to mention that those were two weeks of *great* sex.)

Melanie, the choir director (not her real name), approached me all drunk and flirty. A fantasy of revenge concocted itself in my vulnerable state. I'll show her (meaning my ex)! Rules about pastors or assistant pastors sleeping with volunteer music directors were nonexistent in our new world order at that time. But I really did know better. Nevertheless, I was so hurt, needy, curious, flattered, and angry that I followed her to her car and to her bed.

Melanie was the second person I'd ever had sex with, and I'm pretty sure she didn't know that. She was in control, and it was hot, vigorous, adventurous sex. It was as if my sexual imagination had been hermetically sealed until that moment! It excited, frightened, overwhelmed, and exhausted me. In later years, I would come to associate the frenetic, almost insatiable quality of her sexual energy with women who were incest survivors—there was no relaxing or ebb and flow of energy.

Suddenly, at six in the morning Melanie startled me awake and pushed me out of the bed. As it turned out, her *lover* was about to come home from work. Her lover, who, it seemed, was the owner of the new lesbian bar and the most notorious butch in Boston. I knew that if Maggie found me in *her* bed (it was *her* bed, her house) with Melanie she would kill me and *then* ask questions. I threw on only *some* of my clothes and ran sneaking out the back door of Maggie's house, praying I would not run into her on her way home and my way back to the train station. Some revenge! I was terrified for years after that anytime I ran into Maggie, who became a very prominent lesbian activist in her time.

I remember talking to a very young hustler named Bobby years ago, who worked "the block" of a major city. He was trying to explain to me what sex meant to him, especially with these strangers who circled the block mornings and evenings looking for sex from male prostitutes. There were the occasional one-time customers but mostly several "regulars," he explained. He told me a very poignant story about one regular. He was a middle-aged man who was quite seriously deformed, so much so that he had special hand controls with which he drove his car. Bobby knew the exact day and time this man would always arrive. When he first met this fellow, he was a little frightened and even turned off by his disability.

The "customer" had explained to Bobby that no "normal" person would voluntarily want to have sex with him, so this was the only way he believed he could have sex with another human being—to pay for it, under circumstances in which he could be endangered or exploited but which had the benefits of certain controls. No danger of emotional pain, for instance—a simple transaction: money for sex. However, with his special needs and circumstances, he preferred to find a hustler he could count on to show up. It was very important that he be able to pay for sex. The man did not believe that anyone would enjoy having sex with him, so paying was the only way to ensure that he kept the balance of power. The man was very afraid of being pitied.

Bobby learned a lot from this man. About people with disabilities, about courage and dignity. He began to like him. They talked about stuff, stuff other than sex. And they always had sex. Bobby never thought much about the sex when it was going on—with any of his customers. Sometimes he enjoyed the physical sensation, sometimes he didn't. He didn't have to. He did it for the money. Actually he thought he was straight, and he was just doing this so he could eventually move to California.

But something else began to happen. Because of this man's disability, they had to be a little creative sexually. That unhinged something in Bobby. More than any other customer, Bobby looked forward to seeing him. There was something playful and intimate about their exchange. At one point, Bobby felt bad—like he was enjoying this as much or more than the customer. He felt like he shouldn't be getting paid. One day he ventured to say that to the man. The man felt enraged, humiliated; he felt somehow that Bobby didn't want him to pay because he felt sorry for him. Bobby tried to tell him that wasn't it. Bobby finally told me that he kind of loved that guy. He was having a lot of feelings. He wondered how this man spent his days and nights. He wished they could go to a movie or have a meal. But Bobby's expression of his feelings frightened the man, who never again returned to the block.

I think of this story as a parable. Jesus might have told it if he lived in our culture. How do we "pay" to get our needs met? How do we sell ourselves? And how do our fears of lack of control or fears of giving and receiving love and intimacy disable us as lovers and friends?

The Fear of Strangers

We live in a culture that is riddled with the fear of strangers. And for good reason. Unlike in Jesus' culture, we do not feel we have any obligation to strangers. Strangers are not potential neighbors. They are potential murderers, robbers, rapists. We do not see *ourselves* as strangers, even when we are. Strangers are a nuisance, are dangerous.

I remember my father telling the story of seeing a car broken down by the side of the road. A woman was alone in the car, which was disabled by a flat tire. It was winter. My father spoke to her through her closed window and offered to fix her tire if she would let him in the trunk. She was obviously afraid of him. She opened her window just a crack and put the keys through (apparently not realizing that he could then have opened her door with those very keys if he had wanted to!). He fixed her tire, patiently pushed her keys through the crack in the window, and sent her on her way. Then his own car wouldn't start. No one stopped to help him, and he had to walk to the nearest gas station to *get help*. He always laughed at the irony of this story, but he never said that he would not stop to help someone again.

My goddaughter Rechal has always been a great teacher. I remember when she was about four and in preschool. They were learning about not talking to strangers. She was with me in the grocery store, perched in the little seat in the grocery cart. She was trying to figure out this *"stranger" business*. As we passed people in the grocery store, she would say, "Are you a stranger?" People would laugh and usually respond by saying, "Yes." Some would add, "But maybe the next time we meet we won't be." Everyone seemed conscious of what she was struggling with. We established that the pharmacist, whom we had seen for a few years, was probably *not* a stranger.

So, we think we *can* trust some strangers in certain roles, and maybe they are not total strangers. To children, especially very young ones, nearly *everyone* is a stranger. When a mother holds her infant in her arms for the first time, are they strangers? In one sense, they have known each other for at least several months (depending on how long the pregnancy was, how long the mother knew she was pregnant, and so on). In another sense, they are meeting each other for the first time.

We come into the world, spending our first nine months inside another's body. Dependent on another's hospitality. Is our sexuality really partially a longing to renew that kind of intimate interdependence, that first experience of living inside another, safe and welcomed (perhaps)? How does that experience shape our sexuality, and in what way?

But all children arrive as strangers. These are strangers that we are mostly *not* afraid of because they are so small. But some new parents are *very* afraid of the demands, the needs, the reality of this new, strange little life. We do have to get to know our children. They have their own personalities, their own uniqueness. We cannot *assume* we know them.

How confusing it must be for children to learn of our distrust of strangers when they are themselves so new, so unknown to us, and when there are so few people known to them. But we learn. We learn to ignore strangers, not to see them. Especially if they are unusual, physically different, or needy in any way. Adults can walk by and not hear people begging, or see people with deformities or unusual clothes. Children, on the other hand, have to be taught not to notice. We adults are often embarrassed when children just say what they see, talk about what they notice. First we stop saying. Then we stop noticing. The "stranger" business that did not make sense to Rechal that day does not make sense to me and never has.

Rechal knew that to get along in school, she had to meet strangers and get to know them. Every new teacher was a stranger. *I* think about the message we teach in church and Sunday school: The only way any church can really grow is by seeking out and inviting and welcoming strangers! All week long, strangers call our church for information, direction, counseling, and help. The most powerful experiences that people often have are coming to the church and being welcomed even though they are strangers. I remember two young men who called, desperate, because a friend had died. A "community church" (not UFMCC) up the street in a very gay neighborhood was cold to them and said they didn't let *strangers use their church.* We not only let them use our church but we let them use it for free. We helped them set up and clean up and provided greeters to assist them. This became the beginning of an important relationship with those two men.

UFMCC pastors have to struggle with these issues. We have to be sensible, but we often have to take chances in meeting strangers. I've gone to the homes of many people who are dying; sometimes I've gone alone, sometimes with other church members. I almost never think about my *safety.* I think about how to help without being intrusive, what it means to enter someone's home for the first time because they or their lover or friend or son is dying.

I also meet strangers who come to us because they're in love and want to be married or have a commitment ceremony or to have a baby baptized or dedicated.

Inviting strangers into our circles of friendship and love and acceptance is what a healthy, open church experience is about. Yet this is so counter to everything that our culture is teaching us about the fear of strangers.

The process of creating friends from strangers is one of the most fundamental human experiences. Jesus talked again and again about how we might find ourselves in need someday, and wouldn't we want the stranger to behave as if they were our neighbor (the Good Samaritan—Luke 10:29–37). Jesus spent his life and ministry touching and being touched by strangers, some of whom loved him, followed him, cared for him, fed him, anointed him, touched him deeply. Others of whom also betrayed and denied him, beat and crucified him. Some strangers refused his invitation, including one stranger whom it says Jesus *loved*. It is a strange thing to say that one *loves* a stranger, but it says that of Jesus. What did he love about that person? This was someone who had everything but was unsatisfied, longing for a deeper relationship with God. Did Jesus identify with this young man's search, his longing? Was it some mysterious sense of connection or communion in the moment?

I've been attracted to some strangers in my life. For various reasons, perhaps, Jesus was attracted to something in this man and called it love. But I've also even felt sometimes that I loved strangers. Sometimes when people come to communion at UFMCC, I have that experience. People whom I've *never* seen before, whose names I do not know, come to me for Holy Communion, to share the Body and Blood of Christ—the most intimate of all Christian sacraments. I don't know a thing about them or what draws them to the table or to this ritual.

Most of the time, if I don't recognize the people who come to communion, I'll ask them their names. I started doing this early on at MCC. I thought it was important, especially for gay and lesbian people, to hear their names at the communion rail. As they received the Body of Christ, to know that it was for *them* and that God and I wanted to know them. To know at least their names. Sometimes someone may look especially troubled or needy, and I have asked them if they need a special prayer for some reason.

People come to the communion rail very vulnerable, emotionally and spiritually. They automatically trust that the persons serving are trustable, know what they are doing, and will not only not harm them but will minister to them. Sometimes they get more than they asked for; sometimes, I'm sure, they get less.

Communion with strangers is a very important part of our Sunday worship and daily church experience. I think about what it means for me to pray for strangers, to touch them, to feed them, sometimes to hug them, to say their names. And more often than not, I find myself loving them with a love that is more than me. I know it is God's love loving them through me. This is a humbling and wonderful experience, as is having a stranger willing to accept that love from me.

It is also very sensual if not sexual, in the most innocent and nonexploitative way. We exchange bodily fluids at our communion rail—tears, sometimes perspiration, and the Blood of Christ. I have jokes with my congregation sometimes about how my vestments get a lot of wear and tear. By the end of the day, my vestments and sometimes my shirts and jackets have accumulated tears (and sometimes a little snot for good measure), sweat, makeup—as people have cried with me, laughed, touched, hugged, and kissed me, especially all day Sunday. Add to that the sticky fingers of children and, if we have a class, chalk dust, and I go home with a pile of laundry needing to be done. The experience is at once very holy, very tactile, and very demanding. It is a way in which I can provide bodily hospitality to strangers and friends, colleagues and family alike. It is a way in which I sometimes feel a profound solidarity with Jesus and with these strangers as well.

And sometimes the strangers themselves are angels. People show up all the time at the church who are probably mentally ill, lost, needy, not even caring what *kind* of church we are. Some of them are hard to deal with; very few are ever really dangerous. Some of them occasionally bring great gifts of all sorts. I've been prayed for in unbelievable ways by them. Some offer just a smile, or a perspective, or a joke. Sometimes I feel like they are themselves a test for me—especially when they show up on a bad day. Sometimes I feel like they are wasting my time and energy. But when I really think about it, they are *not* the ones who have really wasted my time and energy.

Isn't the fear of strangers really the basis of racism and homophobia? They are based on fear of those who are different from us in some way. And, if we all start out as strangers, isn't the fear of strangers really the fear of intimacy, of getting close, of being vulnerable? Is this why we have had to find ways to separate sexuality and intimacy? Are we so afraid of our own longings and desires for connection, for closeness, that we have developed a whole culture of fear for strangers? I believe that the unhindered gospel that Jesus embodied calls us to overcome those fears.

JESUS, SEXUALITY, AND THE SABBATH

If it is true that the issues of human sexuality constitute a "seismic fault" that is threatening to divide Christians and the Christian church, how are Jesus' life, ministry, and teachings useful to us in either easing the tension along the fault or practicing "earthquake preparedness?"

I believe that it is extremely difficult for modern people to understand how controversial Jesus was in his time and why. Two thousand years of Christian teaching have put us to sleep with a "Jesus meek and mild" so that we appear to be worshiping a *nice guy who finished last*. The sharp and shocking message and practice that Jesus instituted are lost in the layers of sentimentality. He has been co-opted and normalized, especially by the majority and those in power.

It is useful to compare Jesus' Sabbath controversy with our controversy about human sexuality. This analogy I *believe* will help us understand Jesus' purpose and our dilemma.

What Exactly Was the Sabbath?

Many scholars have tried to discover ancient antecedents to the Hebrew Sabbath. Essentially, the Sabbath was a weekly festival in which Israel's relationship to God was honored and remembered. The Sabbath was about rest. Tradition said that God had created the world in six days and rested on the seventh. It was a celebration of creation itself. Israel was to *imitate* God and honor God by resting on the Sabbath. It was a time for worship and recreation.

The Sabbath was also connected to the experience of the Exodus. Israel *could* rest because they were no longer slaves. Slaves had to work seven days a week. But they had been delivered by a God who did not believe they should be slaves to anything, including work. They were to rest on the Sabbath as a sign of their freedom, as well as a sign of their partnership with God in creation.

Over the centuries, the Sabbath grew in its significance. It began to have political as well as religious meaning. "Keeping the Sabbath" became a primary sign of being a Jew. It was a sign of national identity. Other nations were aware of this peculiar custom among the Jews. Nations sometimes, in fact, used this information to gain an advantage over them. There are many stories in the Bible and the Apocrypha of Israel being attacked on the Sabbath. In some of these stories, God comes to their rescue. In other stories, Jews are martyred for their observation of the Sabbath. This becomes, by Jesus' time, a considerable historical legacy.

There were many in Jesus' time whose ancestors had died rather than defile the Sabbath. Keeping the Sabbath was an essential part of showing that you were a loyal Jew, that you were proud of your heritage, that you loved God, that you were in touch with your history and your people. In addition, the Sabbath was already being mystified, as in the concept of the "Sabbath bride." In Jewish Sabbath worship, the Sabbath is welcomed into the synagogue as a bride into the bridal chamber. It is a lovely, embodied, holy, and sensuous image. The Sabbath is the bride of Israel, much as the church is the "bride of Christ" in the New Testament. There was a sense of a mystical union between the concept of the Sabbath and the concept of Jewishness.

Sabbath preparations could be simple or elaborate, as they may be today. The preparation and the celebration were a part of the holistic understanding of faith: faith includes one's heart, mind, body, and spirit. The Sabbath observance required participation of all of these in study, prayers, food, rest, family, home.

The Sabbath provided a wonderful weekly reminder of the important things in a person's life. In our contemporary secularized culture, both the Jewish Sabbath and the Christian Sabbath are fading fast from the scene. We live in times of excesses, of twenty-four-hour stores and restaurants, of workaholism, of slavery to work and profit, of the disappearance of leisure time. The days of regular mealtimes for families, of weekly play and recreation times, or of worshiping together are disappearing. Life's rhythms are very frenetic. For many people there is no Sabbath, no rest, no holy time of stopping to pray or relax, make love, or take time over a meal with friends.

Our modern Sabbath-free life is the nightmare the ancient rabbis feared. A society without rest is one without God, without health, without balance.

The Sabbath was also the means of expression of identity. Not to keep the Sabbath is to forget who you are. Cultural and religious identity are located in the celebration of feasts, of holidays.

We experience this with the Latin ministry at Metropolitan Community Church Los Angeles. Even though many of the participants in our Spanish-language service at ten in the morning also speak English, it is so comforting and identity-building for many people to worship in an MCC *in the Spanish language*. It gives the lie to the claim that gays and lesbians are primarily white, Anglo, and not Catholic. Also, Latin ministry leaders have struggled to preserve the varied Latin American cultures in our life as a community. For instance, Protestants and Catholics celebrate Holy Week differently and with different intensities. This is compounded by the fact that in many Latin countries, from Holy Thursday at noon through Easter, no one works. It is a prolonged Sabbath. Many Latin people feel very alienated when life goes on as usual during Holy Week in the United States, even if the church has services every evening or all day Sunday.

Also, we had the *palms* issue. Most Protestants in the U.S. hand out palms on Palm Sunday, and they are pitiful little things, little strips of palm leaves, that Sunday school children would fold into the shape of a cross and pin on their clothing. That, for us, is Palm Sunday.

The first Palm Sunday that the Latin ministry held a service, they were dumbfounded. Palms for Palm Sunday in their experience were huge palm branches that the church members waved as they processed with them into the sanctuary. The next year we had to order two different kinds of palms.

And sometimes, it is a matter of food or how one throws a party. All of these factors contribute to a sense of tradition, peoplehood, identity, comfort, home.

In our church we have two "layers" of tradition. The first is what we bring with us from our ethnic or denominational background. What we want to preserve, especially if it helps others feel more at home and welcome at MCC. Some people, still dealing with severe internalized homophobia, wonder if we are a "real" church. They look for signs, some of which are as simple as *Does this experience look, sound, smell, feel like church* (meaning churches they attended, grew up in)? We have to preach frequently about helping people let go of *some* of these associations in order to free them from negative aspects of their past religious experience or to make room for others. The second layer, that I'll deal with in a little bit, is the tradition we create.

Ethnic signs and signals are another matter, also complicated. We're not a melting pot, we're more like a tossed salad in that regard. But we have to negotiate frequently about how "user friendly" we are in a cultural sense, for many kinds of people and cultures.

Marlene came to MCC Los Angeles one Pentecost Sunday in May. I had met her nearly eighteen months before and had been waiting for her to show up. I had spoken at a group on coming out, and she had been a participant. We had connected, and I knew she was filled with religious conflicts. She wanted to come to church but might have a hard time getting there.

It was a gorgeous day, and I was waiting in the small vestibule at Crescent Heights Methodist Church (we were meeting there during the early days of renovation of our church property). I smiled and said, "Good morning, Marlene." She was shocked that I remembered her or her name. But I had remembered. I remembered the intensity, the need. I had prayed for her, and I smiled at her and at the satisfaction of answered prayer.

It was nearly six months before we discovered the importance of Marlene's arrival at MCC on Pentecost. She did not know it was Pentecost. But later on she told me how as a little Portuguese Catholic child, her most precious *religious* memories were of an annual Portuguese religious festival. There were always parties, wonderful food, and a big parade through the small northern California immigrant town. Each year a little girl was chosen to be the *queen of this parade*, honoring the Virgin Mary. The festival was a religious and cultural one, in which Marlene took pride. Her fondest memory was of the year she had been chosen to be the queen of the parade, at about age ten. With all the negative and oppressive memories of church and childhood, this festival and her *one* moment of glory stood out in contrast. It was something precious that she had kept alive in her heart. A precious Sabbath experience.

Later, she would feel as though that joyful loved feeling she remembered from the festival connected to her experience of God at MCC Los Angeles. She came home to herself in a gay and lesbian church experience that accepted all of who she was—lesbian, Catholic, and Portuguese.

I remember the moment that she was able to tell me that the Portuguese festival was on the feast of *Pentecost*. I reminded her that her first Sunday at MCC Los Angeles (and her first really adult experience of going to church, at age forty) was also Pentecost. It was as if her mind and body and spirit knew exactly when to return to church. She returned on the very Sabbath day that represented the most affirming, powerful, positive experience of God she had ever had.

This experience, this *coincidence* was an important part of Marlene's spiritual journey. She had an agenda and a timetable. Marlene had cancer. She came to the church seeking physical and spiritual healing.

A little over two years after that Pentecost, Marlene died of breast cancer. She always expressed her hope for both kinds of healings but rejoiced that she lived long enough to experience a healed, renewed, and joy-filled relationship to God. She learned how to pray, she bought her own Bible and became a virtual "church mouse," present nearly every time the doors were open. And when she felt well enough to come. She basked in the freedom to think and feel and pray to the God of her own heart and understanding, like a child welcomed home after a glorious parade. The memory of her still blesses us at Pentecost and throughout the year.

We have lots of homegrown traditions. Often we do something once, and the next year it becomes a "tradition." We invent these customs and celebrate yearly events because they provide a sense of linkage, connection, and reliability in a very unreliable world. Also because for us, many of the old traditions have such painful associations that we need at least to redefine them, if not reinvent them, for ourselves. Plus, we express ourselves, our own culture, our own history through these new traditions. This is one way in which we get to tell the stories again and again of how we have survived and triumphed. Truthfully I have a lot of respect for those who have valued *keeping the Sabbath.*

As much as my own ministry and UFMCC have been iconoclastic, we have also been about conceiving and creating culture, community, and traditions. And we do find that the hunger for *roots,* for tradition is so great even the very *new* practices get formalized quickly, and people get very attached very quickly to them. So I have great sympathy for the rabbis and others who were alarmed by Jesus' Sabbath challenges.

Part of the problem in Jesus' time was a typical human problem. Sometimes those to whom we give authority go too far. Over the centuries, this had become the case with the Sabbath. Because the Sabbath was so important, many people were anxious to "do it right." So they asked the authorities to tell them in detail, over many centuries, what was the proper way to observe the Sabbath. What was the definition of "work"? How could I know for sure if I engaged in some activity that it was or was not work? As often happens with human beings, ordinary people gave away their own power and capacity to interpret for themselves the laws and word of God. And the religious experts and authorities, who love to spend time, energy, and breath debating the fine points of the tradition, had a great time with this.

Of course, what was a fascinating philosophical debate for scholars, rabbis, and others became difficult, confusing, and overwhelming to laypeople who either went to extremes to be obedient or who began ignoring the experts (while sometimes feeling guilty). I want to say clearly that it is wrong, it is anti-Semitic, to see this as a Jewish issue. All humans in our religious and social traditions struggle with this tendency. Humans give away power to experts. Experts like to complicate things (that's sort of what they get paid for). Then the system gets too clogged and cumbersome, and there are rebellion and possibly reform. The idea that these struggles with the law are a uniquely Jewish issue is a mostly Christian slander of Judaism.

The idea that Judaism is about *law* and Christianity is about *grace* is a total misreading of the Torah and of the New Testament as well. The Exodus *is* about grace. The Hebrew prophets preached grace, and many modern Christians are so law-bound that they have, it seems, no connection to the divine grace that was Jesus' heritage and his passionate mission.

The other factor that affected observance of the Sabbath was that Israel had changed sociologically. The earliest memory of Sabbath observation happened among nomadic and then rural agricultural peoples. Urbanization and political factors created a more complicated society in Jesus' time. People lived and worked differently from each other. There was a more complicated class structure. Some could afford to and did participate in all aspects of Jewish religious and cultural life. But there was also now a significant underclass, called "sinners," people who were no longer part of the mainstream. This underclass was created in part by years of urbanization and foreign domination. Alternative economics and foreign influence contributed to the erosion of national pride and identity and increased horizontal violence among Jews who had been conquered by the Romans. All these factors contributed to a sense that the Sabbath and Jewish traditions and life were really made only for *some*. For *good* people, for good Jews.

In addition, the reality that Jewish ancestors had died rather than violate Sabbath laws had had a certain kind of effect on the meaning of Sabbath observance. It became much more serious. It had become a litmus test of loyalty and "correctness." Its connection to joy, rest, recreation, leisure, and freedom from slavery was less important than its connection to loyalty to the law and national identity. The Sabbath, perhaps, had become weighted down, overloaded.

Into this picture steps Jesus, whom the Bible says "went to the synagogue on the Sabbath day, as was his custom" (Luke 4:16). Jesus had grown up hearing all the stories about the Sabbath and had observed the Sabbath all his life. Presumably, keeping the Sabbath was as much of an assumption in his household as in anyone else's. He himself was not a part of that growing underclass of people identified as "sinners" who no longer observed the Sabbath. He might have had ancestors in his own family who had died rather than defile the Sabbath of the Lord. Jesus never questioned the need for a Sabbath.

But what he did do was to flaunt his violation of specific Sabbath laws. I use the word *flaunt* deliberately. "Flaunt" is a very gay-connected word. When gays and lesbians are public in any way, even in the most modest and subtle ways, we are accustomed to being told that we are *flaunting* our sexuality. It is definitely an accusation with negative connotations. I'd like to redeem the concept and look at flaunting as a method of activism. Jesus did *act up*. He was protesting "Sabbath abuse," I believe. Jesus violated the Sabbath laws in a *public* way. He did not violate the Sabbath laws quietly, behind the scenes, discreetly, just because he thought they were unnecessary. He publicly and flagrantly violated them in ways that brought attention to himself, to his disciples, and to his teaching and ministry.

Also, Jesus violated the Sabbath laws not only to save lives or heal or for some *great cause*. He sometimes violated them casually, as in the story in Matthew 12:1–8. The disciples were walking through a grainfield with Jesus and were plucking the ears of grain and eating them as they walked. They were observed doing this by the religious authorities. This was a clear violation of the Sabbath laws, and Jesus knew it. It was not an emergency. Every Jew knew that you were not to harvest on the Sabbath. Most reasonable, thoughtful Jews prepared their Sabbath food ahead of time, carrying it with them (they weren't allowed to walk too far either).

Obviously, Jesus and his followers had not bothered to prepare for the Sabbath. At this point, they were already perhaps "on the road," with no home base from which to prepare for the Sabbath. In any case, lack of preparation or consideration of Sabbath restrictions was like desecrating the memory of your ancestors. All this for a snack in the field? And if they had simply acknowledged their error, stopped what they were doing, all would have been forgiven. After all, it was a *minor* infraction, really. It was nitpicking just a little. The problem was, Jesus was *not* sorry.

He *argues* about it. Even though he acknowledges that he is technically in the wrong, he argues (Matthew 12:3–8). He uses King David as an excuse, talking about how David ate the Bread of Presence in the sanctuary when he was being hunted down by the high priest and was starving and in danger. David thought that the preservation of life was, in that sense, above the law.

But Jesus was not starving, and for the moment anyway, he was not in danger. In a way, I think he was being a smart-ass. He was in their faces about knowing the Scriptures as well as they did. He didn't buy that they had any more authority to decide what was proper on the Sabbath than he or his disciples did. This is what pisses them off. He talked back to them. He flaunted breaking the tradition that their ancestors had died for. He acted like he had more authority than they did.

Jesus doesn't stop there. He claims to be *Lord of the Sabbath*. Jesus acted like he thought he was God walking through that field with his disciples—embodying the love and rage of God. And along come the religious police. They encounter one who claims to be the Lord of the Sabbath, who is outraged because the Sabbath was supposed to be a gift.

It was a *gift of God to humanity*. It was not meant to be a burden, a drag. Maybe people were not *supposed* to die for it (oh, terrible blasphemy!). Jesus perhaps was in a situation similar to the one Americans faced about our participation in the Vietnam War. The more questionable our participation, the more strident the defense. When people questioned the authorities about the politics, the purpose, and the ethics of the war, they were labeled "traitors."

The Sabbath was a gift. It was created so that human beings would not be crazed with work, would not enslave themselves to one another or to work or profit or business or even to good deeds. It was created so that they would remember that they, as a part of creation, were good, and that pleasure, joy, rest, health, relationships, and relaxation were all part of what it means to live happily in union with God. God never intended for "religious police" to patrol the streets or grainfields in order to capture and punish the Sabbath violators. The *human* authorities were the ones who were violating the Sabbath with their tight-assed rigidity, anxiety, and narrow views of Sabbath.

A sane, healthy institution of the Sabbath would not require intervention by religious police. The authorities were involved because something was not right with the institution. Wise, healthy Sabbath celebration was not so fragile an idea that it needed propping up by police. It would continue on its own merits, because it was a pleasure, because people looked forward to it. Jesus was, in that moment, the righteous fury of God. *God* was violating the human version of the Sabbath laws in and through Jesus and the disciples that day. It was a divine conspiracy.

And Jesus was touching and getting to know "those people." Those "sinners" who were not decent enough to follow the laws, to keep the Sabbath. They sought him out. He broke other laws by eating and drinking with them, by talking with them, by touching them.

They were his Sabbath. With them, Jesus was at ease. They provided rest from the weariness of the battle. They were his joy, the balance in his days and nights. They were real, and open, and loved to hear (not debate) about the God Jesus thought he knew about. They converted him every day with their need, their desire. The Sabbath was meant to be a *time-out* for everyone. The time when we took a breath, when we revisited who we are and why we do what we do. A time-out from the games we play. Jesus' universalism went against his culture, as it does against most cultures when absolutized.

Jesus also went against the grain in his interpretation that the Sabbath was made for humanity. By Jesus' time, some were insisting that the Sabbath was only for Jews and that Gentiles who celebrated the Sabbath ought not to live.[3] Of course, other rabbis in the past had stated in the Talmud that "a Gentile who read the Torah was like a high priest." Jesus was definitely on their side. For many Jews the Sabbath was a *national* symbol, a matter of cultural identity and integrity. A Sabbath for all seemed to violate that understanding. In a culture that was under fire, that was experiencing persecution at the hands of Gentiles, it must have seemed like betrayal for anyone to suggest that *all* people, including Gentiles, were eligible for the blessings of the Sabbath. In fact, Jesus' first sermon on the Sabbath in Nazareth, as recorded in Luke 4:16–30, starts out OK, but then Jesus manages to infuriate his listeners. They get so angry they chase him out of the synagogue and to the edge of a cliff. He has to sneak out of town and barely escapes. He got in trouble for telling them that some of the Gentiles listened to the prophets better than the Jews did. He said this to people who were sick and tired of having to be nice to Gentiles who were oppressing them, taking their land and money, running their government. They didn't want to hear it, not from a local upstart who thought he knew everything. What did *he* know from Gentiles?

The Sabbath was also meant to be an equalizer, but instead it had been co-opted into the service of class distinctions. It was meant to be an equalizer when everyone, rich or poor, could rest and remember that for all of them, freedom was costly and should be valued and cherished. It was also a *free* gift of grace, available to all, not just to some who could afford to "do it right." The Sabbath was also meant to be God's way of getting our attention. Instead, of course, people were paying attention to the rules about the Sabbath. I remember someone asking the question, "Which would you rather go to—heaven, or a film and lecture about heaven?" People were choosing the latter. Not the Sabbath but lectures and manuals about the Sabbath. The Sabbath was a taste of eternity, of life with the Creator. It was a holy time and space. It was meant to be a time of joy, pleasure, and restoration.

Jesus did not violate the laws of the Sabbath because he had more important things to do and the laws were in the way. He publicly flaunted the laws because restoration of the Sabbath was a *part* of his mission. If for Jesus the Sabbath was to be an *occasion of grace*, a means by which the people of God could regularly renew their covenant relationship, then for the "religious police" the Sabbath was the great litmus test of *sin*, of loyalty to nation and religious authority.

It is through this view of the Sabbath controversy that I want to begin to make my case for the connection between the Sabbath and sexuality.

Sexuality Was Made for Humanity, Not Humanity for Sexuality

Just suppose that like the Sabbath, sexuality is a gift from God! There are lots of churches today that say this is the basis of their theological understanding of sexuality. They say "sexuality," but they mean heterosexuality, or as I have heard it labeled, *heteronormativity*.[4] Let's face it: for much of the history of Christian thought and practice, sexuality has not been preached about, or taught about as if it were a gift at all. Historically, sexuality was seen, at best, as a necessary evil—something humankind *has to do* if it is going to continue to exist. But it has also been seen as something degrading and base, appealing to negative attributes of humanness. The church, marriage, and Christian life were supposed to function like a *net* or *restraint* around human sexuality. Sexuality was to be controlled, policed (like the Sabbath). It was dangerous. Women embodied sexual lust, and men could easily become "prey" to its temptations. Sexism particularly poisoned our view of sexuality. Repression and obsession became the pattern we are still stuck with today.

I can imagine God's fury about this. God's fury at the way the story of Adam and Eve was distorted to mean that sex and the Fall are synonymous. The Sabbath, a gift of God, became a primary way Jews could break the law, sin. That is very similar to the way in which sexuality is rarely seen, in a Christian context, as a means of grace but as the primary occasion for sin.

We've ruined sexuality just like we ruined the Sabbath. We've become obsessed with "doing it right." Which does not mean relating sexually in ways that are mutually pleasurable, fulfilling, healthy, balanced. "Doing it right" has often meant minimizing pleasure, an obsession with *what goes where*, seeing sexuality as a duty, as not being worthy in itself but *only* justified for the sake of reproduction, for example. "Doing it right" has meant creating and obeying rules about when, with whom, how, how often, and what you were supposed to feel or not when you have sex. Religious police have haunted the bedrooms of Christians for two thousand years.

"Doing it right" has certainly meant, just as it meant for the Sabbath in Jesus' time, taking the *fun* out of it. Maybe it isn't sex that aggravates the religious police—maybe it's fun. Like the Sabbath, sexuality was intended for our mutual joy and pleasure. Either as the means for procreation or as the most intimate, powerful human expression of connection and intimacy, *sexuality is about our being made in the image of God*, who is the Creator, and who is still creating. Insofar as we are in touch with our sexuality, we are connected to our passions, to our love for life, to joy, pleasure, and to the work of creation. The gift of sexuality is the gift of the means of *creative relationship*, of a God who loves joy, fun, and pleasure. What a thought!

Instead, of course, we have chosen to view and act as if our sexuality is a terrible burden. A curse, not a blessing. As a characteristic of humanness that needs to be controlled and legislated and about which we need to create endless rules and then enforce them with guilt and shame, with fines and jail sentences.

We have succeeded in so distorting human sexuality that healthy, whole, Godly human sexuality seems terribly remote, out of reach, the exception to the rule.

Sex has become something we both yearn for and dread. For many in our culture, dependency itself has become eroticized—so that sexual pleasure is derived primarily from the domination of others. Our sexual appetites and cues have been shaped and distorted by cultures that are sexist, racist, and homophobic and that abuse or hate children. Sexuality is seen as a *commodity*, something that is bought and sold, not shared. It is reduced by some to an addiction, masking the deeper hungers for intimacy, connection, love, and friendship.

We are a mess about sex, and the churches have helped create this mess—and they have not only *not* helped us to heal but they continue to hurt. I think of Jimmy Swaggert, pathetically confessing how he has "sinned," playing the part of the repentant sexual pervert, acting out the religious repression-obsession merry-go-round that characterizes so much of our sexual culture. All his ranting and raving, preaching about sexual sins all those years were simply the flip side of a sick pattern of acting out dangerous and "kinky" sexual situations. For me the startling truth is that his *preaching was as sick as his sexual adventures*, only less honest perhaps. The preaching, the condemnation, simply fueled his lust and certainly the lust of others. His was a twisted lust that was about a lack of deep, embodied sexual connectedness in his everyday life, a lack of normal, healthy sexual pleasure.

I saw this at work in Jerry Falwell's recent TV commercial. He was advertising Part 2 of *The Gay Agenda*, a video that features footage from the 1993 gay and lesbian march on Washington. Jerry goes on and on titillating the audience about what is in this video. "It's so [disgusting] that you can't show it to children," he says several times as he smirks. He gives a few "sneak previews" of the footage they have, some of which, of course, features the more campy and outrageous participants in the gay march. But the whole *tone* of his commercial is as though he is hawking a form of *fundamentalist porn*! As if he is saying, "Buy this disgusting video and see their filthy perversion for yourself!" (In the privacy of your home, your bedroom??) "Show it to your pastor," he says, "but don't let the children see this." (Read that as: it's *really really* dirty!!) His eyes glisten. He is so excited about this video, you can almost see the drool on his chin.

Who, I wondered, would buy this film? Probably people who have unnamed, unexpressed curiosity, including sexual curiosity, but no acceptable way to have it satisfied. People who go to church or watch religious TV, who would never go into the porno section of a video store! People whose sexual imaginations have been crippled since childhood—or gays, lesbians, or bisexuals who are deeply in the closet. People who may not even consciously realize they are gay. Or some who do, who know they are homosexual, watch the video, get aroused, feel guilty, watch

Falwell, repent, and repeat the cycle all over again. Perhaps they masturbate as they watch it. Feel twice as guilty. They then send a donation to Jerry Falwell or vote for the religious right's candidate for the school board. The cycle will repeat itself until they get caught (often sexually acting out in a high-risk situation), are publicly shamed, and either kill themselves or find their way to UFMCC or someplace where they can heal.

Sex, Like the Sabbath, Is an Equalizer

For many fundamentalists, the orgy of confessing and repenting, the fanaticism, the rhetoric are all either a *defense* against unacceptable sexual feelings, or they actually provide a *substitute experience* for them. For Catholics, I see a tremendous polarity here. The vast majority ignore the Catholic church's teaching on birth control that is contained in endless books, pamphlets, and Vatican pronouncements. Most Catholics see the religious police in this issue as irrelevant and give them no power. In Mexico I found that contraceptives were more visible in grocery stores than even in drugstores in the United States. Most Catholics do *not* believe what the church says God wants from them vis-à-vis birth control. But the church still has a lot of power to shame the divorced, homosexuals, or anyone who doesn't conform to other rules that the church claims are God's laws.

On the Sabbath, the divine and the earthly were not to be polarized, but were to come together, to be married, to be in harmony. The Sabbath was the bride of Israel. Our sexuality is a gift from God. It is not meant to be something about which we are tormented and tortured, or with which we torture and torment others. It was meant to be one of the primary ways in which we experience connection with God and God's purpose in creation. Our sexuality, rightly lived and celebrated, is to draw us closer to God, not to drive us away from Eden. Millennialist theology claims that in a renewed Eden, sexual happiness will be our portion. Sexuality is to be a joyful component of Eden, not what drives us away.

At one point in our stormy relationship, I teased the National Council of Churches of Christ in the U.S.A. I said, "Do you know where I see the greatest unhappiness about sexuality in the world today? Not in the gay and lesbian community. Not in the prisons or hospitals I visit. Not even in the streets. The greatest unhappiness about sexuality I see is at *meetings of the National Council of Churches.*"[5] And by that I meant that sometimes I felt as if MCC should have a counseling room at the meetings. Often we did, but it was my hotel room or the hotel rooms of other UFMCC visitors at the NCC. Sometimes we counseled in hallways or doorways. People would seek us out to talk about their gay son or daughter, their child with AIDS, men who were gay but couldn't tell their wives. A heterosexually married staff person's lover died of AIDS, but he could tell no one. He sobbed in my arms in the corner of a meeting room. Men and women whose marriages were troubled for other reasons would choose *us* to talk to. I held governing board members in my arms who cried about their divorces or the struggles of being widowed. Some harbored shameful secrets or sought us out with painful questions. Some came to me wanting to know if I thought that so-and-so was gay.

Others knocked on our doors late at night hoping to God no one saw them. Some people would never be caught *dead* talking to me, not realizing that that in itself was a dead giveaway.

I could always tell who the gay or lesbian or bisexual people were at a conference with the "pamphlet test." We would put out our pamphlets on a table with other literature. People would glance at them, some would pick them up to peruse them, some would take copies. But if the person saw our literature and *then looked furtively* over his or her shoulder ("Were any religious police lurking nearby?") before putting it down *or* taking it, I knew he or she was struggling with shame or guilt, I knew he or she was probably gay or lesbian.

Some people were cruel and judgmental and asked inappropriate and prying questions they would never ask of a heterosexual person or wish to be asked themselves. There were people who knocked on our doors late at night looking for sex. Others who came on to us at the dinner table, or *under* the dinner table, or sitting next to us on a bus on the way to an NCC event. Men who thought lesbian meant "hard to get" or that it meant we were bisexual or liked "three-ways" or that we were open to "kinky" sex. We who were supposed to be *worldly* and sophisticated about such matters found ourselves shocked at times, amused and sometimes not amused.

Some folks would proposition us for sex and then vote against us on the floor of National Council of Churches of Christ meetings. They were self-hating homosexuals, bisexuals, or heterosexuals experimenting while away from home. Sometimes the temptation to "out" these folks was nearly more than we could bear.

It also seemed to me that NCC meetings were, in general, very unsexy. They were dull, controlled, and often devoid of much passion. As youth, feminists, and social justice advocates faded from the scene, the meetings became even less "sexy."

I use the word *sexy* here literally (as in not many people acted like they were in touch with their own sexuality in a joyous way) and symbolically, as in *interesting* or *exciting*! It was as if *we* from UFMCC provided the "sexual energy" for the meeting. Late-night meetings, conferences at the hotel *bar* until two in the morning. Confessions, intrigue, negotiations, capitulations, attempts at co-opting (seduction!), rage, grief, feeling of any kind seemed mostly to happen in relationship to our presence. It was a way in which I sometimes personally felt exploited: It took years for me to understand this. We were their avenue for sexual projection and excitement. It was *not very good* for us, however!

Harassment aside, most of what we did at NCC meetings was to listen to people and to love them and try to keep our own boundaries, perspectives, and self-esteem. What sadness to witness all of this pain and struggle over the gift of sexuality! And then the National Council of Churches of Christ would continue to act terribly wounded that we were *forcing* them to deal with these controversial issues, as if it had nothing to do with them!

A group of Presbyterians, in the context of trying one more time to find a way to help the church work through its issues about gays and lesbians, suggested that the church needs a new basis for sexual ethics called *justice/love*.[6] The furor that this suggestion caused would make an excellent study in the sexual pathology of the church. But justice/love is exactly what Jesus was saying about the Sabbath. The Sabbath was made for us, not us for the Sabbath. Sexuality is a gift for us; we were not created to serve an outdated, oppressive, sick sexual ethic. How can we, in the spirit of Jesus, restore and reform sexuality, as he attempted to do with the Sabbath?

Sexuality, Sabbath, and Play

The Bible doesn't say a lot about the Sabbath and play. But part of resting is not just sleeping, it is about refreshment. It is about doing activity other than work. Paying attention to our children. And children cannot *not* play—not for long. Not unless they have been very hurt or damaged.

I think that sexuality is also ideally about play. The church—and most adults, I think—are too *deadly serious* about sexuality. Sex is supposed to be fun, I think. Sometimes it is romantic and about passion and great love and all that. But whether with a relative stranger or with some-one you've known and slept with for twenty years, sex should be fun, at least sometimes. It can be lighthearted, casual, play for play's sake. Not always goal oriented (whether the goal is children or orgasms). Just play-ing for play's sake.

Children play like that. Children who are overanxious about games, losing, or the rules have had their play controlled by adults too much. Children love to play (even *board games*) without a goal, without *points* or structure. Children love just to play for playing's sake. Adults have diffi-culty playing or making love this way. But we can *learn* to enjoy what our bodies do and what they want to do just because we *can!* Good sex can be one wonderful way that adults play. It costs less than lots of other forms of entertainment. And you can be naked while you do it!

If we are honest, something about being naked is in itself plenty of reason to be playful. When we are naked we are certainly vulnerable, and it probably makes us feel younger (as long as we don't look too closely). But even old people look like children in a way when they are naked. To be naked together when there is safety is to be free children together. Children love to take off their clothes—have you seen them? We laugh and think it is so cute when they do it. When we are undressing children to help them change clothes, they enjoy running from us, thrilled to be unencumbered, knowing somehow that doing this makes adults laugh and a little bit ner-vous. Children love to make us nervous and to make us laugh. They sense we have forgotten something, and they are determined to remind us.

Good sex is playful, at least part of the time. What if we could touch each other sexually the way children touch their own and other children's bodies with a sense of wonder and discovery and laughter and trust?

And, some of us need to rest up to play. We are so weary, so worn, so tired of adult living. We need to rest *before* we can play. So we need the Sabbath in order really to have positive, playful sexuality. What if the con-cepts of the Sabbath and sexuality together are what could really make for justice and peace?

What if the church of Jesus Christ really saw as its mission to provide the Sabbath—rest for weary adults who overwork, rest for single mothers, for workaholic fathers, overworked gays and lesbians? What if the church *stopped* overworking and really taught people to rest?

And what if the church was a place where people learned about play and the value of all kinds of recreation? What if we taught and practiced that sexuality is a form of adult play, whose boundaries and guidelines include justice and love? Maybe then our children would be happier to grow up.

Like sex, the Sabbath, at least in biblical times, and other times in history, was a great equalizer. *All* were to rest on the Sabbath, even the servants, the sojourners within one's gates; anyone who came under the shelter of one's household was eligible and invited and expected to keep the Sabbath. In a society that enjoyed self-rule, this was no problem. In a society where Gentiles ruled or non-Jews were one's employers, this did not work as well. Often poorer and more marginalized Jews under a system of foreign occupation were not in a position to bargain for the right to observe the Sabbath. In order to survive, to stay employed, they had to forgo this privilege. Meanwhile they were reminded by religious leaders (who were not in those circumstances) that their ancestors had sacrificed more than a job for the Sabbath—they had given their *lives*. They had done this, of course, not after generations of occupation but when the conquerors first came. And they had done it together. There was *not* that same sense of cultural solidarity in Jesus' time. Lots of Jews had "sold out" in various ways to the Romans—the tax collectors being the most notorious. Since the Romans were less oppressive than other foreign governments (they allowed Jews to worship in the Temple, for instance), this process of becoming more divided over Sabbath observance had occurred very gradually, over time. So the Sabbath that had been so unifying and universal in its origins, so available to everyone, celebrated at so little cost, had become a source of division, pain, and inequality.

Sometimes when churches study "human sexuality," this is just a euphemism for wanting to study *homosexuality*. Other times, the term "human sexuality" is a way to *avoid* talking about homosexuality—as if, of course, homosexuality were not human! When churches, for instance, proclaim that they really do believe that human sexuality is a gift from God, they *do not* also affirm that gay and lesbian sexuality is a gift from God. In the early days (the early 1980s) of our application to the National Council of Churches of Christ in the United States the most troubling UFMCC declaration was that homosexuality, as a component of human sexuality, is a gift from God.

Sexuality is, or should be, a great equalizer. "*Love* belongs to everyone because the best things in life are free" says the old song. Sex, of course, is not always free and it is not always, or perhaps even mostly, about love. It has become commodified and can be very costly. Unsafe sex, these days especially, is costing billions of dollars and may end up costing millions of lives before the century ends.

Sex tourism also compromises the ideal of sexuality as a great equalizer. Many Asian countries, in particular, have become economically dependent on the sex tourism trade to such a degree that they *cannot* safeguard the health of their people (especially women and children) or their blood supply without causing economic hardships. This is an extreme global example of the eroticization of dependency, and it is causing tremendous suffering, shame, loss, and death.

Because sexuality is a universal human experience, one would hope that it could be a bridge, a way in which we could begin to communicate across gender, racial, and class lines. But this is not so. It was particularly poignant to me in our "dialogues" with the National Council of Churches of Christ that certain churches were always reluctant to participate, or did so only grudgingly. Those churches labeled the "historic black churches" fell into this category. After a little while, it became abundantly obvious that they were not about to expose the sexual tensions, issues, and struggles that were emerging in the African-American community in the context of a white-dominated organization. The black churches are marginalized and patronized in the NCC. Their agendas are different, and the black churches participate mostly as a way of ensuring that when push comes to shove, at least there will be some white folks who with their influence, power, and money may be able to act in solidarity with black people in our country. But black leaders from those churches in the NCC are not naive or overly optimistic. And they do not want to expose their *internal* struggles around sexuality to people who might use this information negatively against them in some future context. All the debates about the "black family" in America that have been dominated by white voices always end up hurting the self-image and political realities of African-Americans. For African-Americans to find safe contexts in which to deal with these issues, where they will not be exploited by white people who want to blame black people for *everything*, is very challenging.

This was also true with the Orthodox churches in the council. Orthodox churches represent a community of people in the United States who are assimilated at a tremendous rate (alarming to Orthodox traditionalists). This fact creates tremendous anxiety about the future of Orthodox faith in America. The cultures from which most Orthodox people come are disappearing in the United States at the same time that the countries and cultures they represent are going through tremendous turmoil. Orthodox leaders, it seems to this outsider, put up with the ignorance about Orthodox spirituality and cultures and with their own internal conflicts about the nature of ecumenical fellowship with Protestants, in order to ensure support from the NCC on issues that are vital to their survival, or to the survival of the countries and cultures from which they come. It costs the black churches and the Orthodox more than most in terms of their identity and dignity to belong to an organization like the NCC. They are continuously having to evaluate whether or not it is worth it. Meanwhile, the NCC seems for the most part oblivious to the fact that it costs *these* groups more to affiliate with a culturally white, Protestant organization, than it costs *most* of the churches in the NCC. Instead, the leaders and white Protestant majority seem to whine a lot, mostly behind the scenes, about how much *trouble* these groups are. They keep them involved because it makes the council look more inclusive than its policies, practices, and agendas really are.

For several years now, the NCC, along with other church groups and denominations, has talked about what it would mean to provide a "safe space" in which to deal with the volatile issues that sexuality raises. The problem is, of course, that the church itself is *not* a safe space. And if the church has a hard time providing a safe space for free discussion and exploration around *less* volatile issues, how is it going to achieve this goal of safe discussions around sexuality? The concept of the Sabbath is in many ways related to the concept of sanctuary. It expresses in time what *sanctuary* communicates in terms of space. The church needs a Sabbath, a sanctuary, in some corner where it can rest, relax, and take all the time and space it needs to recover its integrity as a place of justice, love, and safety for all people.

Jesus healed on the Sabbath. Interestingly, he did not heal people on the Sabbath only as a matter of life and death. There was a provision for that in the laws (there were all kinds of emergency provisions). But Jesus wanted to *normalize* healing on the Sabbath and to point out that it should not have to be an emergency, a matter of life and death. Any good done on the Sabbath should enhance the meaning and purpose of the Sabbath. So, he healed a man with a withered hand, someone he could just as easily have healed the next day. He said in effect, "It's my Sabbath and I'll heal if I want to." If the purpose of the Sabbath was to provide wholeness, balance, joy, and connectedness to God as a standard feature of one's life and week, then how was healing someone ever a violation of that understanding?

How is the gift of sexuality connected to healing? We certainly know that touch itself is healing. What if our sexual ethic were based on what *good* or *harm* sex accomplished, not on what rules we followed? Touch that happens in massage or by being stroked or petted, or by stroking or petting another (including a pet, for instance!) actually lowers our blood pressure and increases our mental and physical health! We all learned in science classes about the infants who were deprived of touch (while they were well fed and clothed and otherwise cared for). Touch deprivation caused a *failure to thrive,* which meant that some of them died. People are dying emotionally and spiritually, if not also physically, because they are not touched. Some people have learned ways to trade sexual "favors" for touch. This is tragic, sick, and sad. People should be able to have their touch and sexual needs met, together or independently, without having to trade, sell, manipulate, or be deprived.

I know that coming out as a lesbian and a sexual person was one of the most *healing* events in my life. It seems to me that that is true for many, if not most, gay and lesbian people. Contrary to what some have said, I do not believe that most gays and lesbians would prefer to be straight; we would *all* prefer to have the stigma removed from our sexuality, but I can recall meeting only a *few* gay men (and no lesbians that I can recall) who have wished they were heterosexual.

For some people, it is only the guilt and shame that precedes their coming out that are so painful. For some, the first sexual experience of any kind is overwhelming, frightening, and mixed with pleasure and pain. For most gay people to whom I have talked, their first *homosexual* experiences were confirming and included a sense of great relief, of coming home to their body. To their true feelings and nature. Sometimes the first sexual experience also included coming home to a new community. The strange thing is that for many lesbians and gay men who came out without the benefit of UFMCC or good books to read or support networks, all the shame and guilt and secrets and even the hiding and lying were *worth it.* That amazing truth, in an awful way, attests to the power of authentic sexuality as healing.

My first sexual experience with another person was an experience of connecting the upper and lower halves of my body. Of connecting sight and sound and smell and healing and touch. Connecting my hands to my heart, to my mouth and legs. All of me with all of me and all of her. I can still recall the incredible joy of the *permission* to touch and feel and explore. I became willing to be plugged in and turned on, and I found that everything worked! I felt successful; I who had felt so *disembodied* was pretty good at this, even the first time out!

And, of course, the sky was bluer, food tasted better, the songs were sweeter, the parting at college graduation sadder.

Don't you think that on the Sabbath, when the cares and distractions of work are not intruding, that the sky is bluer, the food tastes better, the wine is sweeter, friendships are more tender, family is more precious? The Jewish Havdalah service has always been one of my favorite rituals. It is the service at the end of the Sabbath. Tradition says that you are to sniff from the spice box because if you do *not*, you might faint because of the trauma of the Sabbath's departure! Tradition also says we get an extra soul on the Sabbath and that its departure will cause us to feel bereft and faint. The image of the Sabbath as a doubling of our soul — as, in a sense, a soul-mate — is very sensual. The havdalah has the sweet, sad mood of saying good-bye to a lover. Our lover, the Sabbath bride.

As a lesbian who grew up feeling uncomfortable being viewed as a sex object for men, I had taken refuge in a self-image as a *somewhat butch* sort of nerd. Someone who didn't care very much about how she dressed (that wasn't really true, but I certainly didn't want to dress myself for men!) but who was really smart, verbal, able to take care of herself. This meant having to manage being invisible and visible at the same time, a kind of sleight-of-hand sexual identity. I was very self-contained, though I think I managed to be fairly affectionate, particularly with women friends.

Try as I would, I could never quite picture myself *enjoying sex* with men. I also never allowed myself, until I was twenty-one or so, to think about actually having sex with a woman. Sex with men, the only option I consciously considered for twenty years, seemed undignified and silly. Every time I thought of it, I thought that halfway through I would probably either start laughing or terminate the transaction in disgust. There were even men I knew who I thought were cute, or handsome, or quite likable. But every time I'd think of sex, it was all over. I just knew I'd be clumsy, and so would they! And somehow, other than the fact that it was expected and required if one was to have children, I didn't get *the point*. What was the big deal? I knew by then that pleasure and enjoyment were supposed to be the point. It just made no sense to me that any amount of sex with a man would achieve that.

Making love for the first time to a woman showed me and healed me of my perceived "disability." My body had so little practice at sex or pleasure, even on its own, prior to this event. But I remember the unparalleled pleasure of sexual arousal through the touch of another. How we trembled and groped at first, and yes, giggled, even laughed, and cried. But no disgust. Only joy beyond words, tender connections, passionate stretching, searching, *dancing lying down*. Generous exchanges of bodily fluids! And then exhaustion and blessed, blessed rest: Sabbath.

What would it look like for gay and lesbian people to experience the church as a place of safety and equality? Where our sexuality was valued and respected? I remember what it felt like to participate in a dialogue between the NCC and UFMCC one early November. We were chatting casually beforehand, and I mentioned that once again, as often happened, I was away for my anniversary with my lover Paula (our fourteenth, I think). I remember the looks I got, the internal absorbing of this information, the unspoken questions such as "*They* have anniversaries?" My casual comment, which would have been innocuous if said by a heterosexual, seemed intrusive and jarring to them. Suddenly I felt like I owed them an explanation or even an apology.

I remember the occasion when my oldest niece came by herself for the first time to visit Paula and me. I told my brother that he had to tell her I am a lesbian because the chances were that if she came to church or was around our godchildren for any length of time, she would hear the word. And I wanted her to know, from her dad, that *he* knew and that there were certain vocabulary and information words that she would need to know, which would help her feel more included. I think he did do that, but perhaps he used the word *gay*, not *lesbian*, and I'm not sure that what he said really registered with this ten-year-old. At one point my niece and goddaughter Rechal and I were at lunch when Rechal decided to make some statements about *lesbians*. "What's a *lesbian*?" said my niece.

"Well," I said, "it's like your dad explained to you [hoping he had], sometimes men are with women, sometimes men are with men, and sometimes women are with women."

She pondered this a moment. Perhaps she wasn't quite sure I meant what she *thought* I meant by the preposition (which functions a lot like a verb in those phrases!) *with*. Then she said, "So, how did you and Aunt

Paula meet?" Bingo. I knew she had gotten it. We had had to *meet* somewhere just like her mom and dad had *met*. How did *they* (homosexuals) do that, anyway?

All things being equal, gay folk could just speak freely with heterosexuals about how we met, how we date, fall in love, fall out of love, decide to move in together, make commitments, share children and in-laws, decide actually to have children. These are really not profound mysteries. Mostly, they are not exotic tales.

Almost always when I do counseling for holy union ceremonies for gay couples, when I ask them how they met, they giggle. I've done quite a number of heterosexual weddings as well, and no straight couple has ever giggled when I asked them how they met. Maybe it is because for the lesbian or gay couple, meeting each other often coincides with one or both of them coming out. Or it brings up the anxiety all of us feel when we either venture into the gay world or discover each other in a heterosexual environment ("Is she or isn't she? I think she is, she never mentions a boyfriend, she plays on that softball team; he says he has a roommate, is it his lover or just a roommate; whom can I ask?")

Equality could mean that no one would assume that a particular child is going to be heterosexual. That children would be aware early on that whatever their orientation (whether they think of it as a discovery or a choice), their choice of partner or partners is not going to determine whether or not they have a right to live, breathe, feel, speak openly, live with whom they choose, work in a profession they have prepared for, keep their children with them, have a right to survivor benefits, be on their spouse's insurance policy, or be buried with their loved ones. Equality would mean that I am included at some basic assumptive level in the consciousness of a culture, its politics and spirituality. That I am not permanently an "other," outside of the normal considerations, always an intrusive *exception*, which is what makes us appear to be flaunting our sexuality. I think the opposite of flaunting is disappearing—*the secret wish that we would simply go away and die.*

But we are not going away. Not voluntarily and not at all. We are a necessary and essential part of creation and of every people and every culture. Sometimes honored, sometimes vilified, we are very often those who travel first to the enigmatic borders of cultures and millennia. We are often the "scouts" who see the future approaching and who beckon or warn.

Our planet needs a Sabbath in this time of millennial shifts. We need that time-out in which to reflect, to repent, to ask the deepest questions about what we want the next millennium to offer our children and grandchildren.

What if in our new charter of human existence we come to believe that all people have a right to a Sabbath, and a right to be who they are spiritually and sexually? And that all life forms deserve to be respected? What a powerful millennial vision! Fortunately or unfortunately, depending on your point of view, this is still a *queer* millennial vision. *But hold on, our time is coming.*

Appendix

The Roll Call of Eunuchs

In order of their appearance in the Bible:

HEBREW SCRIPTURES

1. GENESIS 37:36, 39:1 — "... Potiphar, one of Pharaoh's officials, the captain of the guard." This may be the same person mentioned in Gen. 41:45 and 46:20, who is described as an Egyptian priest. He was an "official" of the royal court who was also a priest, and might well have been a *eunuch*. Potiphar's wife tries to seduce Joseph (chapter 38), and the story makes a big deal of Joseph's repeated rejection of her. Does Potiphar's wife find herself attracted to *eunuchs* or those who might reject her? Does Joseph reject her only because he fears his master or because he is not interested?

2. GENESIS 41:8 — The Pharaoh consults, in this verse, with "all the magicians of Egypt and all its wise men." Were these "shamans" who were also *eunuchs*?

3. 1 KINGS 18:3 — Obadiah is described as being "in charge of the palace" (the "palace master" is another term used, which in Daniel also translated "prince of the *eunuchs*"). A parenthetical statement says, in the same verse, that "... Obadiah took a hundred prophets, hid them fifty to a cave, and provided them with bread and water." He is yet another *eunuch* who saves the prophets of God.

4. 1 KINGS 22:9 — In this brief reference, the king of Israel summons a *eunuch*/officer (later referred to as a messenger) to locate a particular prophet.

5. 2 KINGS 9:38 — Two or three *eunuchs* throw the wicked Queen Jezebel out of the window to her death! They act as agents of God and the prophet Elijah.

6. 2 KINGS 20:28 (repeated in *Isaiah 39:7*) — Isaiah prophesies to Hezekiah that Hezekiah's sons will be taken away to Babylon to become *eunuchs* of the king (of Assyria) as if this would be a shameful thing. Would it be a double embarrassment if it were not only a social/political disgrace, but also associated with being emasculated? (Either because of castration or homophobia?) Selfishly, Hezekiah ignores Isaiah, and apparently doesn't give a damn about the fate of his sons!

7. 2 KINGS 18:17 — "The king of Assyria sent the Tartan, the Rabsaris, and the Rabshaken with a great army fron Lachish to King Hezekiah at Jerusalem." "Rabsaris" is probably a title, not a name, and it includes as its root the word for *eunuch*, "sari(s)."

8. EZRA 4:5 and 9; 9:1 — These are references to royal court officials, who function in these cases as lawyers and envoys, in the "go-between" role characteristic of *eunuchs*.

9. NEHEMIAH 1:1–7:5 — Nehemiah, the great leader in Israel's return from exile, was a "palace servant," some say a eunuch, "cup bearer to the king of Persia." He sampled wine and poured it like a butler.

10. ESTHER 1:10 and 11 — Seven *eunuchs* are sent to bring Queen Vashti to the king. They are among the few *eunuchs* actually named in the Bible: Mehuman, Biztha, Harbona, Bigtha, Abagtha, Zethar, and Carkas. What a parade that must have been!

11. ESTHER 1:13 and 14 — This passage names the seven sages ("Shamans," or "wise men," or "privy counselors," also referred to in *Ezra 7:14*) of Persia and Media, who are also named: Carshena, Shethar, Admatha, Tarshish, Meres, Marsena, and Mecumen. They had "access to the king and sat first in the kingdom." Why seven *eunuchs* and seven sages? Are these magical numbers for this special caste of people? Are their names intoned in a certain formulaic way for a reason?

12. ESTHER 2:3 — Mention is made there of Hegai, the king's *eunuch*, who is in charge of the women and their cosmetic treatments! (Ancient Near East version of a hairdresser/cosmetologist!). Eventually, Esther is put in his care (*Esther 2:8*). Hegai then advises her on how, as a new member of the harem, to win the king's favor (2:15).

13. ESTHER 2:14 — Esther does really well, is "promoted," and moves up the ranks of the harem, where she comes into contact with Shaashaz, the king's *eunuch* who was in charge of the concubines.

14. ESTHER 2:21–23 — This is the brief but sad story of two *eunuchs*, Bigthan and Teresh, who conspire to assassinate King Ahasuerus. But Mordecai and Esther foil their evil plot and are hanged (additional reference in *Esther 6:2*).

15. ESTHER 4:4 — This refers to Esther's "maids and *eunuchs*," who are not specifically named.

16. ESTHER 4:5–11 — This is the story of Hathach, one of the king's *eunuchs*, who serves as a messenger, a go-between for Esther and Mordecai. He's sort of like a palace spy.

17. ESTHER 6:4 — *Eunuchs* accompany Haman to the fateful feast in which he is exposed as an enemy of the king.

18. ESTHER 7:9 — *Eunuch* Harbona (mentioned earlier in the list in *Esther 1:10*) cleverly makes the suggestion (pure "poetic justice") that Haman be hung on the very gallows he had prepared for Mordecai. Oh my, don't mess with that queen (Harbona, not Esther)!

19. ESTHER 9:3 — The officials, including "royal" officials, all become anxious to please the Jews because of Mordecai's great power and influence.

20. JEREMIAH 29:2 — This verse refers to the queen mother and the court officials (saris, *eunuchs*) who are recipients of a letter Jeremiah writes to all the exiles.

21. JEREMIAH 36:11–20 — This is the story of how the royal officials, several of whom are named, upon hearing Baruch's scroll of Jeremiah's prophetic writings, sense the possibility of danger and advise Baruch and Jeremiah to go into hiding, thus saving their lives. This is what *eunuchs* typically do in the Bible!

22. JEREMIAH 38:7–13 — The story of Edeb-melech the Ethiopian, a *eunuch* in the king's house, is told here. Edeb-melech saves Jeremiah's life by pulling him out of the cistern, where he was imprisoned, awaiting certain death by hunger. Later, Edeb-melech receives an oracle from God, through Jeremiah, giving him assurances about his safety (*Jeremiah 39:15–18*).

23. JEREMIAH 41:16 — *Eunuchs* are included in the list of categories of people who were captive but were freed by Johanan's forces: "soldiers, women, children, and *eunuchs*." They sound like, "men, women, children, and others (referring to their servant status or sexuality status?)

24. JEREMIAH 53:25 — Are the "seven men of the king's council" the same kinds of sages/wise men referred to in *Esther* 1:13–14? Is the "officer" a "royal official," a *eunuch*?

25. DANIEL 1:1–21 — In the Oxford Annotated NRSV, this passage is labeled as "Daniel and his friends." Daniel 1:3 introduces Ashpenaz, called the "palace master" in the NRSV, or "the Prince of the *Eunuchs*" in the King James Version of the Bible. This kindly, older *eunuch* helps Daniel in a number of critical ways. In Daniel 1:11 the NRSV says the Ashpenaz offered Daniel his favor and compassion. The King James Version says Ashpenaz was "fond" of Daniel. Daniel and his Jewish friends are chosen by Ashpenaz to be trained as "royal pages," which might actually mean they are "eunuchs in training." Daniel and his friends excel in their training and are "ten times" better than the magicians and enchanters for Babylon (Daniel 1:20). Daniel excels at his "shamanistic" dreams and visions, which he, as a good Jew, interprets not magically, but as a gift from God.

The Bible describes the qualifications for the position of royal page to be ". . . boys of royal or noble descent: they had to be without any physical defect, of good appearance, versed in every branch of wisdom, well-informed, discerning, suitable for service at the royal court" Jerusalem Bible (Daniel 1:3). This is a good description of the qualification of eunuchs, I believe. The "handsome young boy" piece of this feels like "gay male sensibility" to me. People's appearance is commented on so seldom in the Bible that when it is, it makes me wonder if the writer was gay.

26. DANIEL 2:1–11 — This is the story of King Nebuchadnezzar's dreams, and of his woes with "magicians, enchanters, sorcerers, and Chaldeans" (Daniel 2:2). The Oxford Annotated NRSV says, "Chaldeans here means not an *ethnic* group, but a *caste* of wise men." (p. 1128 OT) It is interesting that a caste or class of people can be confused with an "ethnic" group. Was that because these wise ones, *eunuchs* were not just a professional class, but their role seemed more related to their identity? Did their identity select them for a particular role or profession?

27. DANIEL 2:12 —Nebuchadnezzar orders all the "wise men" (*eunuchs*) to be destroyed, because they have failed to interpret his dream.

28. DANIEL 2:14–25 —Arioch, a royal official (a *eunuch?*), also the chief executioner, helps Daniel out by giving him inside information. Daniel is very popular with these guys!

29. DANIEL 2:46–49 —Daniel interprets the king's dream and is rewarded handsomely, including being made "chief prefect over all the wise men of Babylon." The "Merlin" of Babylon!

NEW TESTAMENT

1. MATTHEW 2:1–8 —The wise men, called "magi," who were royal court astrologers, Zoroastrian priests, and *eunuchs!*

2. MATTHEW 19:10–12 —Jesus offers a threefold typology of *eunuchs* in response to the disciples' questions about heterosexual divorce.

3. Jesus is a de facto *eunuch* in that the Bible and Christian tradition imply or state that he never married or had children.

4. ACTS 8:9–24 —This is the story of Simon the Magician (the magi, a *eunuch?*) who attempts to buy the "magic" of Jesus' disciples.

5. ACTS 8:26–40 —This story is about the apostle Philip's encounter with an Ethiopian *eunuch,* who is baptized a Christian by Philip. It follows right after the story of Simon the Magician. Are these a tale of two *eunuchs,* one a charlatan, one righteous?

Notes

INTRODUCTION: TRIBAL TALES

1. Metropolitan Community Church is a denomination founded in 1968 by Rev. Troy Perry with a special outreach to lesbians, gay men, and bisexuals but open to all people. For the story of MCC, read Rev. Troy Perry, *The Lord Is My Shepherd and He Knows I'm Gay* (Los Angeles: UFMCC Press, 1994) and Perry, *Don't Be Afraid Anymore* (New York: St. Martin's Press, 1990). See also Frank S. Mead, *The Handbook of Denominations*, new 9th ed., revised by Samuel Hill (Nashville, TN: Abingdon Press, 1990), p. 167.

2. Judy Grahn, *Another Mother Tongue* (Boston: Beacon Press, 1984), p. 6.

3. See Michael Cartwright, "Ideology and Interpretation of the Bible in the African-American Tradition," *Modern Theology* (April 1993).

4. The National Council of Churches, headquartered at 475 Riverside Drive, New York, was founded in 1950 and is the successor to the defunct Federal Council of Churches. In its heyday, it founded Church World Service, had a social activist reputation, and was a fairly progressive vanguard of the mainline churches in America, helping to fund, for example, Martin Luther King, Jr.'s march on Washington in 1963.

5. Martin Buber, *I and Thou* (New York: Scribners, 1970), p. 108.

6. Originally the word was not *martyrs* but *heretics*, according to Rev. Jim Mitulski, pastor of MCC San Francisco.

7. Justo Gonzales, *Out of Every Tribe and Nation: Christian Theology at the Ethnic Roundtable* (Nashville, TN: Abingdon Press, 1992).

8. Gonzales, *Out of Every Tribe*, p. 26.

9. Gonzales, *Out of Every Tribe*, p. 33.

10. See Susan Thistlewaite, *Sex, Race, and God: Christian Feminism in Black and White* (New York: Crossroad, 1991).

11. Perry, *The Lord Is My Shepherd*, p. 201.

12. The same story is told in "An Improbable Pair," *Lotus of Another Color* (Boston: Alyson Publications, 1993), pp. 175–189.

13. Transcription of Chris Cowap's remarks to the NCC governing board, November 9, 1983, in Hartford.

14. The Lima Liturgy was proposed by the WCC Commission on Faith and Order and was composed at a conference in Lima, Peru, prior to the 1991 General Assembly. It is the first ecumenical communion liturgy composed and celebrated by such a diverse international Christian body.

Chapter 1: Healing Our Tribal Wounds

1. Emily Dickinson, "I Never Saw a Moor," *The Poems of Emily Dickinson*, Thomas H. Johnson, etc. (Cambridge, MA: Belknap Press of Harvard University Press, 1955).

2. Angela Davis, "Rape, Racism, and the Myth of the Black Rapist," in *Women, Race, and Class* (New York: Random House, 1981), pp. 172–201.

3. *Presbyterians and Human Sexuality* (Louisville, KY: Office of the General Assembly, Louisville, KY, 1991), p. 2.

Chapter 2: Boldly Exercising Our Tribal Gifts

1. M. Scott Peck, *People of the Lie* (New York: Simon and Schuster, 1983).

2. Harry Hay, "A Separate People Whose Time Has Come," in Mark Thompson, ed., *Gay Spirit* (New York: St. Martin's Press, 1987), pp. 279–291.

3. Freda Smith, "Dear Dora/Dangerous Derek Diesel Dyke," used with permission of the author.

4. Carter Heywood, *Touching Our Strength: The Erotic as Power and the Love of God* (San Francisco: Harper & Row, 1989).

5. Nelle Morton, *The Journey Is Home* (Boston: Beacon Press, 1985), chap. 1, 23.

6. Lucia Chappelle, "Silent Night, Raging Night," in *DeColores MCC Hymnal* (Los Angeles: 1983), p. 6.

7. Mark Thompson, "Children of Paradise: A Brief History of Queens," in Thompson, *Gay Spirit*, p. 52.

8. Hay, "A Separate People," p. 285.

9. Hay, "A Separate People," p. 280.

10. Edmund Bergler, *Homosexuality: Disease or Way of Life?* (New York: Hill & Wang, 1956).

11. Rosemary Radford Ruether, *Sexism and God Talk* (Boston: Beacon Press, 1983), pp. 82, 170–172.

Chapter 3: Texts of Terror

1. Robert Goss, *Jesus Acted Up* (San Francisco: HarperSanFrancisco, 1993).

2. Phyllis Trible, *Texts of Terror* (Philadelphia: Fortress Press, 1984). Phyllis Trible first used this phrase to denote Bible passages that described or justified violence toward women.

3. The "texts of terror" for gay and lesbian Christians are Genesis 19, Leviticus 18:22 and 20:13, Romans 1:26–27, Corinthians 6:9, and 1 Timothy 1:10. See the MCC pamphlet by Rev. Donald Eastman, "Homosexuality and the Bible: Not a Sin, Not a

Sickness," available from Church Services, 5300 Santa Monica Boulevard, #304, Los Angeles, CA 90029. (Also included as "Appendix A" in Perry, *Don't Be Afraid Anymore*, pp. 338–346.)

4. John Shelby Spong, *Rescuing the Bible from Fundamentalism* (San Francisco: HarperSanFrancisco, 1991).

5. Virginia Mollenkott, *Sensuous Spirituality* (New York: Crossroads, 1992).

6. Mollenkott, *Sensuous Spirituality*, p. 167.

7. Mollenkott, *Sensuous Spirituality*, p. 169.

8. Elisabeth Schussler-Fiorenza, "Introduction," *In Memory of Her: A Feminist Theological Reconstruction of Christian Origins* (New York: Crossroads, 1983), p. xvi.

9. John Boswell, *Christianity, Social Tolerance, and Homosexuality: Gay People in Western Europe from the Beginning of the Christian Era to the Fourteenth Century* (Chicago: University of Chicago Press, 1980) and *Same-Sex Unions in PreModern Europe* (New York: Villard Books, 1994).

10. Schussler-Fiorenza, *In Memory of Her*, p. 37.

11. D. Sherwin Bailey, *Homosexuality and Western Christian Tradition*, (New York: Longmans, Green & Co., 1955).

12. Richard Hays, "Awaiting the Redemption of Your Bodies," *Sojourner Magazine* (July 1991): 20:17–21.

13. Michael Cartwright, "Ideology and Interpretation of the in the African-American Tradition," *Modern Theology* (April 1993): 142.

14. James Cone, *The Spirituals and the Blues* (New York: Seabury Press, 1972).

15. Sirach 22:3, New Oxford Annotated Bible, Apoc., p. 115.

16. See Perry, "Appendix A: Helpful Reading," in *Don't Be Afraid Anymore*, pp. 344–345.

17. Bailey, *Homosexuality and Western Christian Tradition*, chap. 1, pp. 21–25.

18. New Oxford Annotated Bible, NRSV.

19. *Anchor Bible Dictionary*, vol. 6, pp. 99–103.

20. *Anchor Bible Dictionary*, vol. 6, p. 100.

21. New Oxford Annotated Bible, OT.

22. *Anchor Bible Dictionary*, vol. 5, pp. 816–830.

23. *Anchor Bible Dictionary*, vol. 5, p. 821.

24. *Anchor Bible Dictionary*, vol. 5, p. 1146.

25. *Anchor Bible Dictionary*, vol. 5, pp. 1145–1146.

26. By the way, the *Anchor Bible Dictionary* is mistaken in this citation of the verse in Leviticus pertaining to homosexuality—it is 20:13, not 29:13. *I didn't even have to look it up!*

27. *New Oxford Annotated Bible*, p. 210, NT.

28. *New Oxford Annotated Bible*, p. 235, NT.

29. *New Oxford Annotated Bible*, p. 240, NT.

30. *The Expanded Vines Expository Dictionary of New Testament Words* (Minneapolis, MN: Bethany House, 1984), p. 349.

CHAPTER 4: OUTING THE BIBLE

1. Perry, *Don't Be Afraid Anymore*.

2. Phyllis Trible, *God and the Rhetoric of Human Sexuality* (Philadelphia: Fortress Press, 1978).

3. Gonzales, *Out of Every Tribe*, p. 25.

4. *Anchor Bible Dictionary*, vol. 3, p. 91.

5. I first heard this concept in a sermon preached by Barbara Haynes at MCC Los Angeles on Mother's Day, 1992. Later I read similar thoughts in Virginia Mollenkott's *Sensuous Spirituality*.

6. Rev. Andy Braunston of MCC in East London wrote to me in 1992 of his corroboration of the theory that gays and eunuchs are linked in the ancient world: "When you were in London you gave a workshop for the three London churches and spoke of your interpretation of the word *eunuch*. You mentioned that there was some scholarly debate on this. Over Christmas I came across a little pamphlet, *Hippolytus: A Text for Students*. In this translation the following is said in the section "Of Crafts and Professions": 'A prostitute, a profligate, a eunuch or anyone else who does things of which it is a shame to speak, let them be rejected.'

The footnote explains that *eunuch* means male homosexual and, more importantly, quotes a French work by Botte (p. 37, note 7) [as] its authority for this. Even though Hippolytus is antigay it might be important that he uses the term *eunuch* in a way we would now understand to mean gay. This might help you with your work.

The texts Braunston consulted are G. J. Cumming, *Hippolytus: A Text for Students* (Bramcote, Nottingham, U.K.: Grove Books Ltd., NG9 3DS 1987), and B. Botte, "A Propos de la tradition apostolique," *Recherches de théologie ancienne et médiévale* 33 (1966).

7. *Anchor Bible Dictionary*, vol. 2, p. 670.

8. *Anchor Bible Dictionary*, vol. 5, p. 87.

9. *New Oxford Annotated Bible*, p. 595, OT.

10. *New Oxford Annotated Bible*, p. 1020, OT.

11. *New Oxford Annotated Bible*, p. 28, NT.

12. Herbert Lockyer, *All the Men of the Bible* (Grand Rapids, MI: Zondervan Publishing House), p. 94.

13. Lockyer, *All the Men*, p. 94.

14. *Anchor Bible Dictionary*, vol. 2, p. 667.

15. *New Oxford Annotated Bible*, p. 3, NT.

16. Mollenkott, "Appendix B," in *Sensuous Spirituality*, pp. 195–197.

17. William E. Phipp, *Was Jesus Married?: The Distortion of Sexuality in the Christian Tradition* (San Francisco: Harper & Row, 1970).

18. *Anchor Bible Dictionary*, vol. 5, p. 422.

19. J. D. Hasting, *Greater Men and Women of the Bible* (New York: Scribners & Sons, 1913–16), p. 320.

20. Hasting, *Greater Men and Women*, pp. 323–324.

21. John McKenzie, *Dictionary of the Bible* (Milwaukee, WI: Bruce Publishing, 1965), p. 501.

22. *Who's Who in the Bible*, Ronald Brownrigg, ed., (New York: Bonanza Books, 1971), p. 257.

23. Vernard Eller, *The Name of the Beloved Disciple* (Grand Rapids, MI: W. B. Eerdman's Publishing, 1987).

24. Eller, *Beloved Disciple*, pp. 53–73.

25. Alexander White quoted in Lockyer, *All the Men*, p. 216.

26. *Anchor Bible Dictionary*, vol. 6, p. 573.

27. Tom Horner, *Jonathan Loved David: Homosexuality in Biblical Times* (Philadelphia: Westminster Press, 1978).

28. Horner, *Jonathan Loved David*, pp. 26–46.

29. New Oxford Annotated Bible, p. 366, OT.

30. New Oxford Annotated Bible, p. 368, OT.

31. Horner, *Jonathan Loved David*, pp. 40–46.

32. Mona West, "Ruth," in Watson Mills and Richard Wilson, eds., *Mercer Commentary on the Bible* (Mercer University Press, 1994).

33. Horner, *Jonathan Loved David*, p. 40.

34. Mary Hunt, *A Fierce Tenderness* and *A Feminist Theology of Friendship* (New York: Crossroads, 1991).

35. "Boston marriages" is a term from the Victorian era, used for women who lived together in lifelong committed friendships that were, it was assumed, devoid of sex. Maybe, maybe not! I remember hearing about "Miss So-and-So," who on her Boston tombstone had inscribed: "I haven't *missed* as much as you think!"

36. *Anchor Bible Dictionary*, vol. 4, p. 423.

37. *Anchor Bible Dictionary*, vol. 4, p. 423.

38. Horner, *Jonathan Loved David*, p. 122.

39. *Anchor Bible Dictionary*, vol. 6, pp. 66–68.

40. *New Oxford Annotated Bible*, p. 131, NT.

41. Mary Rose DiAngelo, "Women Partners in the New Testament," *Journal of Feminine Studies in Religion* 6 (Spring 1990): 66–86.

42. Spong, *Rescuing the Bible from Fundamentalism*.

43. Grahn, *Another Mother Tongue*, pp. 6–8.

44. *Anchor Bible Dictionary*, vol. 4, p. 470.

45. See a fascinating article by Robin M. Jensen in the *Bible Review*, Vol XI, Number 2, April 1995, pp. 20–28. This article documents the earliest known images of Lazarus and Jesus raising Lazarus in which Jesus uses a magic wand to raise Lazarus from the dead! Jensen says "The wand as a magical attribute raises the possibility (perhaps at a popular level anyway) that the early church understood Jesus as a magician . . ." Jensen doesn't directly connect magician/shaman to gayness, except in his own footnote about Lazarus in the Secret Gospel of Mark. In this footnote (p. 45), he notes that "Morton Smith developed a hypothesis, based on the Secret Gospel (of Mark) that Jesus' nocturnal baptism of Lazarus (recounted in the Gospel) was an invitation into an esoteric mystery cult that may have included some kind of 'physical' (sexual) union." The Secret Gospel, pp. 89–114.

Chapter 5: Outing the Sodomite

1. Hays, "Awaiting the Redemption of Our Bodies."

2. Tom Horner compares these stories in the chapter, "The Men of Sodom and Gibeah," in *Jonathan Loved David*, pp. 47–58.

3. The latest update on the Sharon Bottoms case is as follows: On Friday, April 21, 1995, in a controversial 4-to-3 decision, the Virginia State Supreme Court removed three-year-old Tyler from the custody of his mother, Sharon Bottoms, and her lesbian life-partner, April Wade. Sharon Bottoms's lawyers plan to present a petition for a re-hearing to the Court within thirty days. If just one of the four justices in the majority agree that a mistake has been made, a new hearing will be scheduled.

4. *Los Angeles Times*, Letters to the Editor, 22 September, 1993.

5. *Los Angeles Times*, Metro section 25 February, 1994

6. *Los Angeles Times*, Metro section 25 February, 1994.

7. Harold Kushner, *When Bad Things Happen to Good People* (New York: Shocken Books, 1981).

8. M. Scott Peck, *The Road Less Traveled* (New York: Simon & Schuster, 1978).

9. Stephen Hall, *Mapping the New Millennium* (New York: Vintage Books, 1992).

10. Hall, *Mapping*, p. 95.

11. Hall, *Mapping*, p. 101.

12. Hall, *Mapping*, p. 103.

13. See "Introduction," pp. 1–4.

14. See Tex Sample, *Hard-Living People and Mainstream Christians*, (Nashville, TN: Abingdon Press, 1993) for his definition and description of the sociology and spirituality of "hard-living people."

15. I was fascinated and, I must admit, somewhat horrified to read in an issue of the *Christian Century* that a U.S. federal judge had ordered a federal prison to allow a self-proclaimed Satanist to perform Satanic rituals in prison. In our country, satanists will get their religious civil liberties *before* homosexuals, apparently. See *Christian Century* 3, no. 33 (November 16, 1944): 1072.

Chapter 6: Equal to Angels

1. Jean Foye, "Reluctant Prophet," from her collection of unpublished poems that she left to the author.

2. Foye, "But Not Forgotten," from her collection of unpublished poems.

Chapter 7: A Queer Theology of Sexuality

1. Farley Mowatt, *People of the Deer* (Toronto, Ontario, Canada: Seal Books, 1951) pp. 96–109.

2. James Nelson, *Embodiment: An Approach to Sexuality and Christian Theology* (Augsburg Press, 1978).

3. *Anchor Bible Dictionary*, vol. 5, p. 854.

4. I have Nathan Meckley to thank for teaching me this word!

5. From an unpublished speech I gave to the National Council of Churches of Christ in the U.S.A., May 1987.

6. *Presbyterians and Human Sexuality* (Louisville, KY: Office of the General Assembly, 1991).